Making democracy in Spain

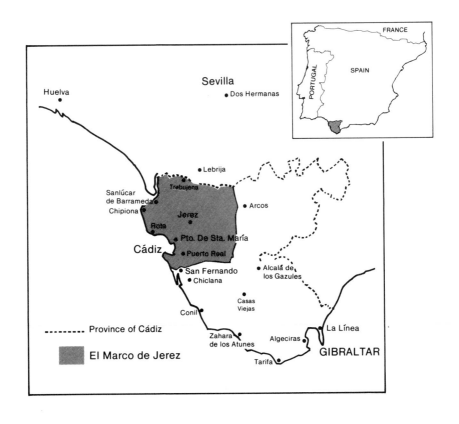

Huelva

Sevilla
● Dos Hermanas

FRANCE

PORTUGAL

SPAIN

● Lebrija

Sanlúcar
de Barrameda
Chipiona
Trebujena
Jerez
Rota
● Arcos
Pto. De Sta. María
Puerto Real
Cádiz
● San Fernando
● Chiclana
● Alcalá de
los Gazules

Casas
Viejas

Conil

●---------● Province of Cádiz

El Marco de Jerez

Zahara
de los Atunes
Algeciras ●
Tarifa ●

La Línea

GIBRALTAR

Making democracy in Spain

Grass-roots struggle in the south, 1955–1975

JOE FOWERAKER
University of Essex

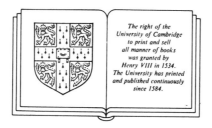

The right of the
University of Cambridge
to print and sell
all manner of books
was granted by
Henry VIII in 1534.
The University has printed
and published continuously
since 1584.

CAMBRIDGE UNIVERSITY PRESS

Cambridge
New York   New Rochelle   Melbourne   Sydney

Published by the Press Syndicate of the University of Cambridge
The Pitt Building, Trumpington Street, Cambridge CB2 1RP
32 East 57th Street, New York, NY 10022, USA
10 Stamford Road, Oakleigh, Melbourne 3166, Australia

First published 1989

Printed in the United States of America

Library of Congress Cataloging-in-Publication Data
Foweraker, Joe.
Making democracy in Spain : grass-roots struggle in the south,
1955–1975 / Joseph Foweraker.
p.   cm.
ISBN 0-521-35406-4
1. Spain – Politics and government – 1939–1975.   2. Trade-unions –
Spain – Political activity – History – 20th century.   3. Political
participation – Spain – History – 20th century.   4. Representative
government and representation – Spain – History – 20th century.
I. Title.
DP270.F65 1989
946.082 – dc 19   88-39691
                                                          CIP

British Library Cataloguing-in-Publication applied for

To Zena Foweraker,
my mother and friend:
Thank you for caring

Contents

Preface

THERE IS NO MORE important topic in political science than democracy and no global issue more pressing than the struggle for democracy. Only a small minority of the world's population presently enjoys the individual rights and civil liberties characteristic of liberal democratic regimes. The great majority of people still live under more arbitrary and dangerous forms of government. More than anything else it is the struggle for democracy which will most directly determine their life chances and those of their children.

This book is about the struggle for democracy in Spain. Its main premise is that democracy can only be achieved and can never be conferred. In short, whoever wants democracy must fight for it. But democracy is only rarely the original goal of democratic struggle. For the greater part of most such struggles the demands are more limited and direct. Yet it is in pressing for the resolution of immediate problems, in seeking just solutions, that people become democratic actors and so achieve their citizenship. The guiding principle of my research, therefore, is that it makes little sense to talk of 'making democracy' without talking of the people who make it.

All social science tells a story. Some of its stories are more compelling and coherent than others, but they are still stories. This is a story not about the famous and fortunate but about the courage and sacrifice of ordinary people. These people found faith in themselves and faith in the future; or they were bloody-minded enough to make democratic demands when the dictatorship forbade them. And in telling this story I want to return this small piece of democratic history to the people who made it. I do not think this is a naïve notion, although I do not deny its romance. On the contrary, the story will require the careful presentation and exegesis of a broad range of empirical materials in order to demonstrate and analyse the political and strategic initiatives which emerged piecemeal from the grass roots of a constricted civil society. In other words it is not enough to talk of faith. I have to talk of the organizational styles and strategic discoveries of these ordinary people's extraordinary struggle.

The making of democracy in Spain was a complex and specific political process (which I begin to define and outline in the introduction to the story). To research it I have had to cross many boundaries, both personal and disciplinary. To talk only of the disciplines, I have used the tools of industrial relations, oral history and ethnography; so in this book you will find elements of economic history, sociology and anthropology. But it is above all a work of political science and in its concern with democracy sits squarely within the grand tradition of the discipline (and not so much Locke or Montesquieu as Rousseau). But this does not make it easily classifiable according to the prevailing paradigms or 'orthodoxies'. On the contrary, my story offers a clear if mainly implicit challenge to the ways in which political choices and strategic calculations are framed within 'rational choice' models of political behaviour; and in analysing democratic achievement, provides an alternative but largely complementary approach to the recent spate of research into 'democratic transitions'. For these reasons amongst others, this may be a controversial book.

My preoccupation with the people who were the protagonists of the struggle at the roots of civil society has had direct consequences for the process of research, for the construction of the argument and even, to a degree, for the use of language. The research began with many months of interviews in Spain, and it is the empirical categories and analytical insights achieved in interview which have done most to structure the argument of the book. In other words, it is the story which was in search of a theory, and not the theory which was in search of a story; and the theory which reaches its fullest statement in the final chapters, and which underpins the analysis, was extracted step by step from the raw materials of research. Without the people who interviewed with me there would be no book, and I wish to thank them both for their collaboration and for their forbearance (their names appear at the end of the bibliography): using a kind of inverse Socratic method, I sought active debate during the interviews, displaying my ignorance in order to achieve a measure of understanding.

In the introduction I spend some time discussing how the story attempts to make the generic and passive notion of 'people' concrete and active; and in the telling of the story itself I begin with the people who made it, and I stick with them throughout. As the book unfolds I explore the social and economic context of their struggle, the concrete syndical and political activities in which they became engaged, and the legal and institutional terrain on which the struggle had to be waged. And even as the analysis proceeds to discuss political organization and political strategy (and so becomes progressively more abstract towards the end of Part III and in Part IV), I try never to lose sight of the people on the ground. Only after I was well into this task did I realize just how ambitious it was. Its success you will judge for yourselves.

I try mostly to tell the story in plain and wholesome English, but I allow myself a small degree of licence with the language in order to get closer to the people. So I talk of syndical activities (and not 'union' or 'labour' activities); of militating in an organization (rather than 'being active' in it or 'being a member' of it); and of companions (as a transliteration of the Spanish *compañero*). Most importantly, I refer throughout to the workers' commissions (the Comisiones Obreras, or CC.OO. in Spanish) simply as the 'commissions', following the usage of those who militated in them. As the story itself makes very clear, this is not intended to deny the changing character of the commissions themselves, which began as local and impermanent organizations, continued as a regionally and nationally coordinated movement, and finally became a structured trade union in the traditional Western European mould.

The result of all this is a story which is necessarily complex in its construction but which aims to be simple in its telling. By telling it I have tried to interpret the political process of making democracy in Spain (as I understand it) and so make it real for those who read it. Social science tells its stories, and so makes reality. But it does not 'make it up'. Social science is not fiction: it only 'makes reality' to the degree that it makes it make sense.

Like every story which sets itself the task of discovery, and not simply of restatement, this book has been a long time in the making. During this time I have received welcome support from a number of institutions. The Research Endowment Fund of the Department of Government at the University of Essex paid for the pilot study I carried out in Spain in 1981; while the long period of field work in 1982–3 was financed by a Social Science Research Fellowship from the Nuffield Foundation (supplemented by a research contract with the Centro de Estudios Constitucionales in Madrid). Most of the writing was done in the winter of 1985–6, during my Fellowship with the West European Program of the Woodrow Wilson International Center for Scholars in Washington, D.C.; and the first draft was completed at the Center for U.S.–Mexican Studies of the University of California, San Diego, with the help of a Personal Research Grant from the Economic and Social Research Council. The latter grant was given to support the comparative investigation of democratic initiatives in Spain, Mexico and Brazil (but that, as they say, is another story).

During the process of research I have presented the results to academic audiences, principally in the Department of Government, University of Essex (Spring 1982); the Department of Political Science, University of Florida at Gainesville (January 1984); the Joint Sessions of the European Consortium for Political Research (Barcelona, March 1985); the Woodrow Wilson International Center for Scholars (Conference of September 1985 and Colloquium of June 1986); the Department of History, Johns Hopkins University (January 1986); the Center for U.S.–Mexican Studies, University of California, San Diego (October 1986); the Center for Iberian and Latin American Studies of the same university (Conference of March 1987); the Department of Politics of the University of California at Irvine (May 1987); and the Center for Latin American Studies of Stanford University (May 1987). I am grateful for these opportunities for criticism and debate.

Friends and colleagues have offered constant encouragement and support, and I am fully aware that I could not have done the job without them. My thanks to Mike Taylor (former Chairman of the Department of Government, University of Essex), Ivor Crewe (present Chairman of the department), Mike Haltzel (Director of the West European Program of the Woodrow Wilson International Center for Scholars), Wayne Cornelius (Director of the Center for U.S.–Mexican Studies of the University of California, San Diego) and to all those who have helped with their loyal criticism and advice, especially Ana Alonso, Raymond Carr, Bob Clark, Meg Crahan, Ann Craig, Gustavo d'Angelo, Robert Fishman, Glennon Harrison, Neil Harvey, Billie Jean Isbell, Bob Jessop, David Laitin, Juan Martínez-Alier, Miguel Martínez, Faustino Miguélez, Dick Morse, Gerry Munck, Daniel Nugent, Victor Pérez Díaz, David Ringrose, Jordi Roca, Jorge Santamaría and Laurence Whitehead. Any errors or infelicities are all my own work.

Please note that parts of the argument of Chapter 13 have previously been published in an essay titled 'The Role of Labor Organizations in the Transition to Democracy in Spain', in Robert P. Clark and Michael H. Haltzel (eds.), *Spain in the 1980s: The Democratic Transition and a New International Role* (Ballinger, Cambridge, Mass., 1987); and that most of Chapter 14 appeared as an essay titled 'Corporatist Strategies and the Transition to Democracy in Spain', *Comparative Politics* 20(1), October 1987.

I hope you enjoy reading this book as much as I enjoyed making it. I cannot pretend that it was always easy. But there were many adventures, and I made many new friends. And I went on learning. My thanks to all of you who gave me love and friendship along the way.

Introduction

Personal networks, political strategies and the making of democracy

THIS IS A STORY of the making of democracy in Spain. Its main aim is to explain how this came about. Its main preoccupation is with the people who brought it about. So I will tell you of the countless unsung heroes who fought for more than twenty years for their measure of human dignity and personal freedom. In doing so I will search out the beginnings of the struggle at the grass roots of civil society, before pursuing the political and strategic initiatives which shaped the forms of struggle in the years to come. Simple as this may sound, it is an ambitious task. I wish to return this piece of democratic history to the people who made it and to return the study of democracy in general to a Rousseauian concern with its roots in civil society. It is my belief that the ways in which the Spanish people struggled to assert more control over the political conditions of their own social lives were the ways they came to achieve their own citizenship; and that this achievement prepared the political ground for the formal achievement of democracy itself.

In this perspective, the democratic struggle in Spain arose spontaneously from the needs and aspirations of civil society and was an organic expression of that society. Its political demands and political organizations grew out of the process of struggle itself. The one struggle was therefore many struggles in many places for many motives; but each struggle contributed to the often contingent and always piecemeal process of making democracy. Moreover, this process was not a natural result of the individual discontent and political dissent latent in civil society but rather required continual political organization and political calculation; and so the political activity of civil society had to be underpinned by its personal networks and sustained by their discovery of effective political strategies.

I do not pretend that this is the whole story (although it is certainly the least studied and least understood part of the story). On the contrary, my claim that the making of democracy must first be explained at the grass roots of civil society does not seek to deny so much as to complement those accounts which concentrate exclusively on elite actors and on centrist political forces. Moreover, I readily admit that the political organizations and strategies of the popular opposition to Franco were not able (either alone or in concert with elite actors) to dislodge the regime; and that reformers within the regime consequently came to play an important role in bringing democracy to Spain. In other words, this story is not about the so-called *transition* to democracy in Spain, which covers the few short years of 'elite settlements' and legal-constitutional negotiations immediately before and after the death of the dictator; but rather about the democratic *transformation* of Spanish society during the twenty long years preceding this transition. Hence, my intention is not to contest or confirm extant accounts of the transition per se but to explain the creation of the political conditions in which the transition took place. Nonetheless, I confess my dissatisfaction with studies of democratic transition (whether in southern Europe or Latin America) which limit democratic achievement to changes of regime at government level, or to the legal-constitutional norms governing the operation of the democratic regime.

The emphasis on transformation and not transition is especially important in the case of Spain, where civil war and the terror which was its aftermath had crushed civil society almost completely. In fact, the violent disputes between left and right, which had afflicted Spain (and so many other countries of Europe) during the thirties, reemerged in the new regime as a bitter division between people and State. No form of free association was permitted, and any sign of independent social or political activity in the Spain of the 1940s was ruthlessly suppressed. Moreover, no help was forthcoming from the outside, and, unlike in Western Germany or Italy, democracy was not restored by the military fiat of the victorious Allies. Yet, despite the isolation and the repression, people made sufficient contact and found sufficient political space to begin to organize; and partly because of the isolation and repression they founded sui generis political organizations and discovered original strategies for extending the boundaries of civil society. But most remarkable is that over time, the new (and nearly always illegal) organizations achieved sufficient political penetration and impetus to alter the balance of social forces in Spanish society, and to put democracy back on the historical agenda. In short, there is no doubt that this struggle did contribute significantly to the successful effort to establish democratic rule; and the story of the struggle therefore has a political interest and potential application far beyond the boundaries of Spain itself. But how did people make the contacts or find the space to carry the struggle forward?

In my view there is no way to answer this question without beginning at the beginning, which is at the grass roots of civil society. Democratic possibilities in authoritarian contexts necessarily have to be discovered (sometimes in the most unlikely places) or invented (sometimes from the most unlikely materials), and the only way to capture this process is to observe specific moments of discovery and invention. This means getting right down to the ground, where 'people' appear as concrete individuals or at least as different social actors with special characteristics. Putting the people back in democracy is therefore a methodological as well as a philosophical choice. But the choice is fraught with difficulty (as much for political scientists in general as for myself). Looking at people *as if* they were individuals [*sic*] makes it impossible to romanticize the making of democracy by invoking the 'people' as some sort of global category (in academically 'demagogic' fashion); but it is equally impossible to look at *all the people* in this way (which is why political scientists like psephologists are content to count them, leaving their characteristics to ethnographers, oral historians and novelists). My response has been to introduce criteria of selection (empirical, analytical and methodological); and each of these criteria has implications for the way the story is told.

First, it is important to recognize that the democratic struggle within Spanish civil society was waged not by all the people equally but by a relatively small group of activists, who were prepared to make their dislike of the dictatorship their life's work. They were not necessarily democratic actors in the sense of cleaving to liberal values, but were unquiet in their hearts, restless in their heads and in revolt against past and present injustice. They grew in numbers as the struggle progressed, but in every locality throughout Spain they were always the small minority of natural leaders who appeared 'when they were needed'. Second, these activists were effective only insofar as they found each other, and as they came together in close and complex relationships, they formed stable personal networks which strengthened incipient political organizations and increased the range of strategic viability. These networks were a key element of the popular opposition to Franco, and analysing the part they played (and the individual choices which entered their composition) also goes some way to operationalizing the struggle of the 'people'. Finally, this is both a *national* study and a *case* study, with the advantage that the entire process of the emergence of a regional leadership in opposition to Franco can be examined in unprecedented depth and detail. Although the case is geographically and socially specific, there is no doubt that in regard to the organizational and strategic aspects of the struggle, it is perfectly well able to serve as a *microcosm* of Spanish civil society overall.

The case in question is that of El Marco de Jerez, the sherry-producing region of Andalucía, which lies between Sevilla and Cádiz in the south of Spain. It is a region with the double presence of a rural and an urban working class, a strong commercial sector, and a successful and united bourgeois oligarchy; and it is a region where the popular leadership which emerged in opposition to Franco conducted one of the most consistent and strategically sophisticated struggles in the whole of Spain. Nonetheless, El Marco is a relatively small region, and I do not wish to suggest that it has anything like the importance of major population centres like Madrid and Barcelona. This would be plainly absurd. But it has the distinct advantage of being manageable and of allowing the kind of investigation which captures the challenges and the contingencies (see later in the introduction) of democratic struggle. At the same time, the detail I can deliver in talking of El Marco creates a better sense of the difficulties of political organization in necessarily clandestine circumstances, and a better understanding of the political process expressed through personal networks and strategic discoveries.

All these choices (namely, the empirical focus on the natural leaders, the analytical attention to personal networks, the methodological priority to the case study) reflect my preference for simply telling the story. But the story of El Marco would be incomplete, even idiosyncratic, without the contextual significance provided by the political economy of Francoism, and the different regional, class and popular struggles carried on elsewhere in Spain over the period from the 1950s to the 1970s. I do not address all of these (and it would not be useful to do so), but throughout my argument a national account accompanies the local account provided by the case study, with the specific aim of creating a comprehensive (but far from empirically complete) analysis of the struggle within civil society. Even when painting the broader picture, my aim is to re-create the view from the bottom up (or from civil society to the State, if you will), and maintain a consistency between case and nation through concentrating on the analytical themes of organization and strategy. In this way I proceed to tell the story while focusing during its telling on the key issues and categories which will later be systematized into a more conceptual approach to making democracy.

CLASS DIVISIONS AND POPULAR-DEMOCRATIC STRUGGLE

It is apparent in both national account and case study that the popular-democratic struggles of this period were also class struggles; and there is no doubt in my mind that it was the labour movement which sowed the seeds of the democratic struggle, or that this struggle continued to have a clear 'class relevance'. Indeed, one reason for choosing to study El Marco de Jerez was the striking clarity of its class divisions, which sharpened the empirical analysis of the connections between class and popular-democratic struggle. Much of this story, therefore, has to do simultaneously with class actors and democratic struggle; and a central concern is to explain why these actors played such a leading role in the struggle. The most obvious, but not the only answer, is the ontological one. Class actors such as the workers' commissions and the Communist Party of Spain succeeded in being there, which was never an easy thing under a regime which banned all opposition activity; and their success was owing in some measure to their intrinsic (but very different) characteristics.

The workers' commissions were a sui generis form of working-class organization, quite unlike any extant model of such organization in Europe or anywhere else. Originally composed of small groups of self-elected activists, they emerged in response to the immediate and concrete needs of the work force; and for many years maintained an evanescent and almost will-o'-the-wisp existence. They would appear as from nowhere to negotiate a demand or launch a strike, and then disband to avoid reprisals. They were ideologically plural and organizationally fluid, and operated at the grass roots in close correspondence to the patterns of personal networking. As the years passed they developed directly democratic practices in their popular assemblies and achieved greater degrees of coordination at provincial and regional levels; but the defining quality of the movement they led remained unchanged. It was above all *organic*, not 'rational, willed or doctrinaire'.

The Communist Party of Spain, on the other hand, was all of these, and owed its survival to its proven capacity for clandestine organization, before anything else. The Party itself was not very democratic (a point I shall return to) but, on the contrary, was often as nasty and as authoritarian as the regime it was committed to combating. But it did provide a structure for organization and coordination which proved effective in fighting the dictatorship; and, even more important, at many times and in many places it represented the *only political option* for those wishing to oppose Franco. Not all those within the Party, and perhaps not even the majority of them, were 'communist', therefore; and many belonged because of the happy coincidence between the operational exigencies of clandestine politics (and especially the work of recruitment and propaganda), and the tight patterns of personal networks built on the confidence and trust created through struggle. At the same time the pragmatism, even the opportunism of which the Party was often accused, paid democratic dividends, because the Party was politically effective precisely insofar as it learned its strategic lessons from the labour movement. One result of this, which is central to the story, is the interesting paradox of a Communist Party making a critical contribution to the achievement of liberal democracy.

One important caveat is in order. I do not claim that the workers' commissions and the Communist Party were alone in the labour movement (although they were certainly hegemonic within it), nor that the labour movement was alone in the opposition, nor that the opposition was alone in making democracy in Spain. To comment only on the opposition, this undeniably came to contain a wide range of political actors, including students, 'nationalists' in the populous regions of Catalonia and the Basque Country, and even Christian Democrats and socialists in some local contexts. But I will argue that the workers' commissions and the Communist Party spearheaded the democratic struggle, and they were successful in this partly because of their intrinsic characteristics, and partly because of the relationship which evolved between them. The contingencies of this relationship, which changed with each shift in local context and overall conjuncture, is one of the most fascinating aspects of the struggle (and one that I shall examine in detail). For now, it must be enough to assert that between them Party and commissions not only offered *places* in the struggle for those opposed to Franco, but also opened up *spaces* in civil society where other actors could begin to organize and build a broader-based civic movement. In other words, they were not only the first to enter the historical scene in opposition to the regime, but were also the standard bearers of the struggle, around which other opposition organizations could begin to rally.

But the characteristics of these "standard bearers" were not a sufficient historical guarantee for their leading role in the democratic struggle. More important were the origin and social location of the demands they put and the legal-institutional terrain on which they struggled. To talk first of the demands, it is of primary importance that the first signs of struggle in Spain's crushed and constricted civil society were generated around the *wage relation*. In fact, the workplace was where the first spaces for democratic initiatives were created. It was not that the workplace itself fostered different political attitudes or affirmed a different political resolve (except perhaps for visceral rejection of a violent, banal and exploitative regime); but that the workers' commissions first emerged to put the kind of economic or "bread and butter" demands, regarding wages and conditions of work, which could not be successfully negotiated through the regime's official apparatus, the Vertical Syndicate (see Part II). In short, the demands were economic rather than political and in the early years often sought nothing more than the proper application of Francoist legality. But it was these merely economic demands which engendered the first autonomous syndical practices and organizations, in the form of the commissions; and it was these same syndical practices which came to catalyse the democratic process. In short, the commitment of those who first struggled against Franco was not to an 'imagined' liberal democratic polity, which motivated political action because it was 'desirable'; but rather to syndical demands and practices, which, when translated into political goals, or when coming to require certain political conditions, effectively forged key elements of the democratic project.

I do not suggest that democracy is a direct result of capitalist development, industrial development or any other kind of development. Historically, democracy is a much more difficult result, which depends (among other things) on the social and cultural specificities of political organizations, strategies and projects. In other words, economic growth and political practice are different and separate from each other. There is no denying the dynamic process of industrial expansion experienced by Spain over the period, nor the massive social impact of the economic changes this brought about; and it is true that this expansion coincided with the rising trajectory of the workers' commissions. But the commissions emerged before the expansion began and were first important in traditional sectors of economic activity such as the mines of Asturias and the vineyards of El Marco de Jerez. So the relationship between them, far from easily explaining democratic process, itself has to be explained.

One plausible element of explanation is that the spontaneous and organic syndical practices of the commissions found a sympathetic response amongst the young and fast-growing generation of workers who, as raw recruits to the industrial environment, were not blinkered by the syndical traditions of the thirties. But this connection demonstrates not only that economic expansion was important, but also that ideology was 'unimportant'.[1] On the one hand, it was unimportant because the new generation of activists did not inherit, and the new forms of syndical activity were not shaped by, the ideological traditions of the thirties, whether anarchist or socialist; on the other, it was unimportant because the political goals which determined the content of the democratic project were not formulated *a priori* within any particular doctrinal discourse at all, but grew spontaneously out of the sui generis syndical activity of the labour movement. Hence, the democratic struggle cannot be understood in terms of any democratic idea, or even in terms of the liberal values it came to endorse. The political process of the making of democracy emerged contingently from the syndical practices of the labour movement, and the democratic project was constructed piecemeal from the possibilities and exigencies of the moment.

Fundamental to my approach is that these possibilities and exigencies were always *strategic* and were therefore discovered and calculated on a specific legal and institutional terrain. The high ground of this terrain was occupied by the Vertical Syndicate, the centrepiece of a global corporatist strategy designed to redefine the totality of relations between civil society and the Francoist State. By definition, this terrain was new, as was the generation of workers the Syndicate attempted to organize and control; and the historical combination of workers unencumbered by the doctrinal or organizational traditions of the thirties, on the one hand, and an unprecedented range of institutional and legal constraints and opportunities, on the other, favoured both new forms of organization and new strategies.

The workers' commissions were one such organization, and while it is certain that they were driven by economic demands, they were also shaped in some degree by the representative structure of the Vertical Syndicate. In fact, the commissions began to establish a more permanent presence once

---

[1] Ideology in the sense of *Weltanschauung* is important to every political process; but the suggestion here is that ideology in the more restricted sense of doctrine, or as a formal expression of a 'utopian' future of any kind, had no important part to play for the greater part of the struggle. However, as argued in Chapter 2, the *Weltanschauung* of the activists of El Marco, referred to in the vernacular of the region as their *forma de ser*, was very important to the personal networks they formed and hence to the incipient political organizations of the opposition in that region.

they began to work within the official syndical apparatus (where there were limited opportunities for representation and even election); but this presence was still illegal, and dangerously so when they had to press their demands through strike action. Herein lay the syndical kernel of what was to become the central political strategy of the commissions (and one they deployed to consistently good effect against the Francoist State), which was the combination of legal and extralegal struggle. The commissions' leaders, who met illegally to launch the strike, also met as the workers' legal representatives within the Syndicate in order to voice their demands; so far from infiltrating the Syndicate in order to subvert it, they did so in order to use its resources (and the political spaces it provided) to extend and reinforce their own organization. This strategy of staying both *inside* and *outside* simultaneously (of combining legal and extralegal struggle) was clearly discovered in the process of pressing economic demands on the specific institutional terrain of the Syndicate; and this demonstrates that the strategic discoveries which most advanced the democratic cause were themselves conditioned by the concerted State strategy for controlling civil society and especially the working class.

By now it is no longer difficult to explain the leading role of class organizations in the popular-democratic struggle. In the first place, it was syndical activity which came to define the political demands and discover the political strategies which structured the democratic project. These demands and strategies may have been formulated and disseminated by the Communist Party, but they were learned from the workers' commissions; and where the Party deviated from the organic strategic range of the commissions, as in its repeated calls for a 'peaceful national strike', it met with conspicuous failure. In the second place, the labour movement was predominant in the struggle for democracy because of Franco's global corporatist strategy for controlling civil society, and because the legal-institutional terrain where the struggle had to be conducted found its fullest institutional expression in the form of the Syndicate. On both counts it appears clear that not only the role of class organizations in the democratic struggle but also the construction of the democratic project itself (and especially the evolution of the strategies which structured it), were outcomes of a highly *contingent* political process.

CONTINGENCIES AND CHOICES IN THE MAKING OF DEMOCRACY

These contingencies in the political process of the making of democracy in Spain pervade all aspects of this process: the coincidence of personal networks with the exigencies of particular forms of syndical and political organization; the relationship between the workers' commissions and the Communist Party; the contribution of repression and the circumstances of clandestine struggle to the conversion of economic demands into political goals; the role of class organizations in the democratic struggle; and the democratic 'effects' and gains of broad-based syndical and popular struggles against the political economy of Francoism. They are therefore germane to the development of my argument, and the empirical analysis is recurrently directed to elicit and elucidate the nature of these contingencies. The success of these efforts readers will judge for themselves; but the analytical results both for the actors and for the story are deserving of emphasis now. On the one hand, it was not the democratic credentials or motivations of either activists or organized political actors which finally made the struggle democratic (although there is no need to assert that democratic values or intentions were irrelevant to the struggle, because they were not). So it does not matter if the 'people' who struggled for democracy did not always see their struggle as democratic. On the other, there is no easy way to extrapolate general lessons for democratic struggle from the Spanish experience. The only way to do so, it seems to me, is first to theorize the contingent process of political organization and strategic discovery as it advances piecemeal in civil society, and this I attempt in my final chapter. Chapter 15 should therefore be read not as a contribution to the debate on democratic *transition* (which it is not), but as an attempt to theorize democratic *transformation*.

The contingent outcomes of this process of transformation contributed to make the struggle for democracy in Spain doubly paradoxical, insofar as a large number of its activists were organized within both the rigidly authoritarian Communist Party and the apparatuses of the repressively authoritarian Francoist State. But neither half of the paradox posed any kind of obstacle to democratic advance. The strategic line and political practice of the Communist Party continued to be conditioned by the syndical activities of the workers' commissions; while the Vertical Syndicate provided not only political spaces but also political incentives to the commissions to organize, and later to create, traditions of direct democracy within the assemblies and of effectively free (if still illegal) collective bargaining. In effect, the paradoxical content of the struggle reveals that this was not a 'war of manoeuvre' (in Gramsci's taxonomy), but rather a 'war of position', which was consistently characterized by the interpenetration and mutual permeation of the contending forces. In particular, the process of infiltration of the Vertical Syndicate occupied exactly the same legal and institutional space as the key element of co-optation within Franco's corporatist strategy; and this will be analysed as but one aspect of the more general ambivalence of democratic struggle.

Underlying and often underpinning the new organizations and new strategies emerging from Spanish civil society were the personal networks which channelled the people's first political choices and sustained their political commitment thereafter. Even the central strategy of combining legal and extralegal struggle would not have been operationally viable, in this context of co-optation and repression, were it not for the personal networks which reproduced the confidence and discipline required to bind together the separate 'operational fields' of the strategy. So not only did the personal networks precede the syndical and political organizations and strategies (even if the growth of these same organizations also helped to extend the networks), but they also contributed to their resilience and reproduction in the difficult circumstances created by a cunning and sometimes ruthless regime. In this sense the participation of the 'people' in the political activities and democratic thrust of Spanish civil society was not ultimately achieved either by syndical or political organization (in commissions or Communist Party), or by political discourse of a doctrinal kind, but by a complex process of personal networking which proved to have a highly flexible organizational and strategic potential, and which gave a new political generation the sinew to stand on its own two feet.

Personal networks remain at the centre of my analysis, then, because they *are* the grass roots of the whole process of the making of democracy in Spain. This was not something I knew before I began the study, and so it stands as one of its main findings. It is also one way of operationalizing the participation of the 'people' in the making of democracy and so allows me to talk of individual activists in a way which supersedes their individuality and affirms their activity. In the social sciences this problem is usually referred to as that of human agency, and, as just suggested, in the final chapter I try to theorize the role of such networks in the individual achievement of political subjectivity and the creation of knowledge. To do so I make free, if not cavalier, use of metaphors from Michel Foucault. But readers should be advised that mine is a very optimistic and democratic reading of Foucault; and if he is mainly concerned with the way that political power is reproduced through the social construction of individuality, I am mainly concerned with how the balance of forces within civil society is changed democratically through a collective achievement of citizenship. This no doubt reflects my wish to return the making of democracy to the 'people' who made it; and if this story has any kind of political and philosophical message it is simply that 'we always have a choice'. Historically, this choice is much more open at some moments than at others, and sometimes is difficult to discern at all; but it can always be created through sacrifice and struggle, which is another way of saying that the exercise of such a choice always requires an accumulation of more particular political and strategic options. It is this choice which makes the story of the making of democracy in Spain so very remarkable; and this same choice which makes the effort to understand the story worthwhile.

PART I

Personal networks, political traditions and state policies

1

Unquiet hearts: the primitive world of the first political men

Almost all the strike leaders were in the patio of Manolo el Pelao's place. They were those natural leaders who always appear when they are needed.

Alvarez de Toledo, *The Strike*

THIS IS A STORY of the way people made a democracy in Spain. It begins with a handful of men in a certain region of southern Spain, and the way they grew up and lived their lives during the years of the Civil War and the terrible times which followed. These are not famous men, and you will not recognize their names. But as the story unfolds you will come to know them as some of the men who fought for democracy in this corner of the country, and who came to be leaders of the organized opposition to the dictatorship of Generalísimo Franco. Many of them are men who began the fight or, more grandly, who were present at the birth of the working-class movement. In the language of the struggle they are known as the 'historic ones' or, speaking with irony of the oppressed, as the 'primitives'. In other words, these are the men who, for reasons of personal history or temperament, first came to feel uneasy in their heart and restless in their spirit. And while most of them never had the kind of learning which comes through books, the simple living of their lives let them know that they did not want the dead hand of the dictatorship upon them.

Just as any one person constructs his or her character piecemeal through individual choices, so the slow shaping of people's subjectivity is intrinsic to the telling of this story. This is not to assert naïvely that such subjectivity is simply equivalent to the political reality of these times. Reality is surely not so much perceived as constructed, and the analysis of any single reality will require many concepts. But both individual character and group perception are immediately important in this story because they explain the first choices without which all further explanation is redundant. These men chose to struggle and found it was possible to do so together. They recognized the restlessness in each other and came together out of respect for

13

it. Through the personal confidence they found in each other they formed
personal networks which over the years came to be capable of acting politically. As such networks spread and found further forms of organization,
they spawned a new syndical practice which in turn came to spearhead the
struggle for democracy. So it is no exaggeration to say that they were the
germs of the newly autonomous associations of Spanish civil society. Hence,
there are good analytical reasons to begin the study of this democratic project
with the people who made it, even were there no sense of the absurdity of
talking about any democracy in the absence of the people to whom it refers.

But let us not go too far too fast. What we have in view are what Miguélez,
referring to the very different context of the Asturian coal mines, called a
'few men of proven honour and great prestige', who, educated in the 'school
of clandestinity', came to establish a 'leadership at the level of personal
confidence' (Miguélez:1976). And even if it is demonstrated that these 'most
restless men' (Soto:1976) succeeded in establishing effective and legitimate
leadership over an entire region, it does not necessarily follow that their
experience is representative of the political process in the national society.
But such 'representation' does not have to be of a statistical or symmetrical
kind in order to be real.[1] Nor is it merely metaphorical. Just as the paleon-
tologist reconstructs the shape of the entire animal through studying a
dinosaur's tooth, so the political practices of these men provide clues to the
making of the democratic project overall. Such a statement will become
more convincing *a fortiori* as the investigation discusses the ways in which
such practices were conditioned similarly in different regions by the same
political restrictions, institutions and strategies; and the ways in which they
became homogenized through progressively closer coordination between
provinces and regions. For the moment the objective is nothing so ambitious.
It is simply to look at these men and consider reasons for their unquiet

---

[1] The seventy interviews I conducted with the regional leadership of the years from the
mid-1950s to the mid-1970s clearly do not constitute a representative statistical sample;
while much of the discussion in Chapters 2 and 3, which focuses on the ideological
and political specificities of this region of the Marco de Jerez, shows any *a priori* notion
of symmetry to be misplaced. Nevertheless, the number of interviews is somewhat
greater than the thirty conducted by Miguélez (some of them group interviews) for his
book on the Asturian miners (Miguélez:1976), or the seventeen carried out by Maravall
for his analysis of the trade union struggle in his book on *Dictatorship and Political
Dissent* (Maravall:1978). Maravall quotes with approval H. S. Becker on the life-history
approach (*Sociological Work*, Aldine, Chicago), which seeks to locate 'those crucial
interactive episodes in which new lines of individual and collective activity are forged',
but admits that while his trade union informants may be 'strategic', they cannot be
considered representative. In my view Maravall's seventeen informants (eight holding
national posts and nine holding provincial posts within Madrid) are incapable of
providing an adequate empirical base for reconstructing the progress of the working-
class movement at State level, which is what he aspires to do.

hearts, always bearing in mind the contention that it was men like these who suffered things like this who did most to make Spain democratic.

So let me begin to introduce them. I am happy to do so, for this is their story, and that of tens of thousands like them. And if they had not told it to me, then I could not tell it to you (and so this author can begin to pay his dues). Their names will soon become familiar and will recur at different moments in the analysis. In writing of them I hope to put the people back in democracy, which is never made merely by the famous and fortunate.

THE FAMILY BACKGROUND

A first glance at the life histories of these men makes it clear that political militancy runs in the family. Emilio Fábregas, a man who will figure largely in this story, had both an uncle and a father-in-law who belonged to the CNT,[2] and he likes to think of himself as having inherited a tradition. Similarly, Paco Chicorro, Juan Caballero and Manolo Romero had fathers who were anarchist leaders, while Manuel Espinar's father was an old anarchist militant of vegetarian-naturist traits, and Miguel Ruíz's grandfather, the secretary of the CNT in Trebujena. Moreover, despite the historical impression of an anarchist hegemony in Andalucía in the years preceding the Civil War, the political colour of the family backgrounds varies considerably. The fathers of both Paco Cabral and Paco Artola were socialists, with positions of responsibility in the Unión General de Trabajadores (UGT) (the former was a regional representative), while Miguel Marroquín's father was communist, and Pepe Mena had uncles in both the CNT and the Communist Youth. Yet other fathers, such as those of José María García, Pepe Rosa, and Rafael Ribeiro were on the Republican left, the latter being the treasurer of the Party of the Republican Left in Medina Sidonia.

The second lesson which leaps to the eye is the high personal cost of such political militancy. Emilio Fábregas' father-in-law was shot, as were Rafael Gómez's father and Juan Caballero's father and elder brother when he was just thirteen years old. Pepe Rosa tells how his fiancée's father was elected deputy mayor and shot some few days after the Civil War broke out; while Paco Cabral's father shot himself in a suicide pact with his own brother, rather than be shot by the 'fascists'. Antonio Ortega's father and uncle were killed in the war, and Manuel Espinar's father had to flee Sanlúcar to avoid

---

[2] Until the Franco era there were two main syndical (or trade union) confederations. One was the Confederación Nacional del Trabajo (CNT), or National Labour Confederation, which was broadly anarchist in orientation; and the other was the Unión General de Trabajadores (UGT), or General Workers' Union, a mainly socialist organization.

being shot. Paco Artola's father was imprisoned during the so-called black two years of Gil Robles,[3] and arrested again later after a knife fight with blacklegs – experiences which left him a broken man. The fathers of José María García and Miguel Marroquín were also arrested, the latter being condemned to death but released after five years with a mortal illness. And Antonio Alvarez recalls the whispered homage paid to the dead in the patio of his family's house after the war: 'Remember, remember so and so, remember, remember...'

Partly as a consequence of their families' paying this price for political conviction, the childhood of these men who made democracy was spent in misery. But social conditions overall were so bad that few enjoyed any vestige of comfort, politics or no politics. Paco de las Flores's father was paralysed at work and in the absence of accident insurance the family lived in poverty; Rafael Ribeiro's father died when he was just five years old, and despairing of finding food for her two sons, his mother fell into the clutches of one of the local bigwigs, who used her terribly; Federico Iglesias's father threw him and his pregnant mother out when his sister married into the local nobility, and Federico remembers waiting from the early hours to go to the Jesuit school which provided his one plate of food each day; and Pepe Jiménez lost his father in 1940 and his mother in 1941, leaving him as one of six orphans. In conditions like these political discrimination appears especially savage: Paco Artola's father failed to find work because of his political beliefs; Juan Caballero's mother had her small-holding confiscated by the Falange, leaving her to manage six children until she died in 1945; and the families of Rafael Gómez, Paco Cabral and many others suffered more than their natural portion because their bread-winners had been murdered. Some were a little luckier. Both the grandfather and father of Eduardo Sánchez had small plots of land they could work to supplement their wages; Fernando Guilloto's family did better for the few years his father worked in the rationing department of the town council (everything was rationed); while José María García and Pepe Mena lived a little better, having a small trader and a skilled worker as fathers. But in general the people went hungry. Seeing the workers around him literally dying on the job, Nicolás Ruíz complained so often that it was all because of 'pan tan caro' (bread so dear) that his nickname 'Pancaro' has stuck with him till

---

[3] The period between the elections of November 1933 until the victory of the Popular Front in February 1936 was known to the Spanish left (and more generally to those who had supported the founding of a secular republic) as *el bienio negro*, or 'the two black years'. In retrospect, it seems to have been a conservative rather than repressive administration, which, by commission or omission, reversed or froze many of the important social reforms advanced in the first years of the decade. In other words, 'rather than a period of resolute reaction it represented a reversion to the negativism of "pure politics" during which the construction of coalitions and frequent ministerial reshuffles revived the jargon of old-fashioned parliamentarianism' (Carr:1966).

this day; and Antonio Alvarez complains of these same postwar years that he was always so hungry that he could not even think.

As we shall see, there was little hope of formal schooling in these families, but the children grew up despite the lack. José Aldana remembers his father and mother quarrelling over whether he could stay at school. The year was 1939. He left. But in 1936, Pepe Rosa, as a boy of some ten years, listened to his father (whom he recalls as an autodidact and restless spirit) as he commented on the press and the imminent end of the Republic; Pepe Mena's uncles took him to political meetings in their place of work and at home invoked collective memories of the Republic; and Rafael Ribeiro swears it was his mother's helpless situation which politicized him and led him to join the UGT as soon as he reached age sixteen. But however many memories remain for the men now who were children then, the greater part of the learning they did in their families came through the visceral experiences of violent bereavement and constant hunger. It is the kind of learning which lies latent, waiting to be activated at a later moment. José María García spent the years of his youth and military service in ignorance of the political world, until one day he overheard a broadcast from Radio Pirenaica (the radio of the Communist Party in exile) issuing a call for the people to go out and organize a Party cell in every village across the land. This so impressed him that he went out the very next Sunday, and it so happened that the first person he dared speak with was Fernando Guilloto; it was only much later that he realized that far from recruiting Fernando, Fernando was in fact recruiting him.

THE EDUCATION

Manolo Romero, Juan Flores, Manuel Verano, Pancaro, Rafael Ribeiro, Luis Jaramillo, Manuel Espinar, Juan Romero and many more never went to school. Where some schooling did occur, it tended to be short, insufficient and very often bizarre. Paco Chicorro stayed just four years, and Paco de las Flores and Manolo Romero Ruíz managed to hang on until they were ten. At the school Antonio Alvarez attended there were no books, just a blackboard (and his teacher had to bring him a book from home to teach him the rudiments of the alphabet). He tried night school, only to find it controlled by the Church. Pepe Rosa's passion for books took him through four years of his baccalaureate, but even he did not manage to complete it. The principal difficulty in the schooling of these children, however, was the complete change that took place in the language and behaviour of the schools in 1936. As José Aldana put it, 'Suddenly, instead of "good day" it was "Ave María" ', and Pepe Jiménez is convinced that the only thing he learned in school was how to sing 'Cara al Sol' – the Falangist anthem. Some of the teachers at Aldana's school even dressed up in blue shirts and pistols (though he also remembers his own teacher crying when it was thought he was to be sent to the front); while Rafael Gómez never attended on Tuesdays, which was the day of Falangist 'training', with singing, saluting the flag and parading down the streets. All a little overwhelming for a boy of eight whose father had been shot by the Falange. Paco Artola meanwhile was attending the best school in El Puerto de Santa María, where the teacher was a distant relation, where the children joined La Flecha (the Falangist schools organization), and where the sons of the gentry played at killing Republicans while the daughters adorned themselves with jewelry made of cartridges. Artola remembers he was just nine when he began to hate the Falangists and Franco, and the same age when he left school.

Notwithstanding the failures of the formal system, many of these children did get an education, and some of them got one of a traditional and 'anarchist' kind. Juan Flores began working the vineyards at sixteen and learned from the talk of the older workers, the anarchists, as they sat around the *fogaril*, or open fire. This was also the case of Pancaro, who learned through the talk and the constant commentary on newspapers and pamphlets; while Juan Romero was posted to watch out for the Civil Guard (Guardia) while his father and uncle spoke of the times of the Republic and made sure he could overhear what was being said. Both Paco de las Flores and, at a later moment, Manuel Verano began their education in similar style, adding that they would also read whatever books and pamphlets came their way. And it was while he was working on a farm northwest of Jerez that Paco heard of the new 'demands', and discovered that he, too, wanted a table to eat from and plates to eat off. At that time he began to get books from the foreman and comment on them for others during the *cigarros*, or short work breaks, in the anarchist way.

As impressive as the tradition is the way many of these children saw to their own education. When Rafael Gómez could no longer stand the humiliation of formal schooling he tried to educate himself through correspondence courses. Pepe Jiménez was still illiterate when first apprenticed to a carpenter, but started to go to night school. Pepe Mena read as much as he could, but could not make much sense of the world until an older shipbuilder befriended him and brought him books on materialism. Emilio Fábregas dedicated his time to reading anarcho-syndicalist literature. In nearly all cases, of course, someone had to give them a start. For Manuel Espinar it was his father, who took on the education of his seven children; for Manolo Romero it was his grandmother, who taught him to read at age seven, after which he read voraciously for eight hours a day every day. Of course, he adds contemplatively, his grandmother was not from Sanlúcar. No one in Sanlúcar knew how to read. . . .

Before 1936, in addition to such education as could be had through talk and books, there were political meetings to attend. At a very young age Manolo attended anarchist meetings, and Rafael Ribeiro and Paco Cabral recall specific meetings which impressed them. Rafael heard an address from

Daniel Ortega, deputy from El Puerto, and the first Communist deputy to be elected in Spain; while Paco attended an open-air debate between Manuel Ballester, the ranking CNT official in Andalucía, and Largo Caballero, then Minister of Labour.[4] After that date the only mass political education available was through the clandestine media of the Spanish Communist Party. Pancaro, Pepe Mena and Paco de las Flores all came to listen to Radio Pirenaica: Paco began in 1960 when an accident forced him to rest for six months (and others who overheard him knocked on his door to recruit him to the Party); while Pepe recalls the sacrifices he had to make in 1955 to buy a radio so that he, too, could tune in. Besides the radio there was also *Mundo Obrero*, the Party newspaper, for those who could read or have someone read for them. It was Manolo Romero who gave Luis Jaramillo his first copy, and his daughter Ana was careful to keep it hidden under the table when reading it to him.

This kind of cooperation between men within the same personal network was never unusual, and indeed became commonplace. Pancaro learned much of what he came to know from comrades who had returned from a period of work in France. And although Pepe Jiménez had originally met Fernando Guilloto in the Falangist youth organization, which he had been persuaded to join by his teacher at night school, when Fernando returned from France himself, he began to talk to him of Marxism during the long evenings they spent just walking in the dark. Moreover, as we shall see in subsequent chapters, many of these men were recruited into opposition organizations once they had spent a suitable stretch of time in close contact with others in the network. Miguel Marroquín, one of the younger militants, was recruited into the Communist Youth organization by Rafael Ribeiro of the 'old guard'; but not before Rafael had taken the time to prepare him and educate him, through encouraging him to read a selection of books which included Dolores Ibarruri's *El Unico Camino*. After that, says Miguel, he could begin to teach himself and make his way in life. And that is the lesson of this kind of learning; that one way or the other, however haphazardly it came to them as children, it equipped them as men to make their own history.

THE WORK AND THE FEAR

Even though, as Alvarez de Toledo says, 'anyone over fourteen is considered a man in Sanlúcar', it is still true that nearly all these men began work as children. Juan Flores began at age six, for twenty-five cents a day and his

---

[4] Francisco Largo Caballero, the immensely experienced leader of the UGT, was Minister of Labour during the first government of the Second Republic, from 1931 to 1933. Manuel Ballester was himself assassinated by the Falange, in Cádiz, during December of 1935 (Kern:1978).

food. At age eight Luis Jaramillo was already working in the fields, sending all his wages to his mother, who suffered from a drunken husband. Manuel Verano was the same age when he started weeding vineyards and treating the pruned vines with iron sulphate, as were Paco de las Flores and Juan Romero when they took on heavy work in the countryside. Paco Artola was just ten when he began working fourteen hours a day in a chemical factory, Fernando Guilloto was just as young when he left school to work as a cook for the Civil Guard, and when Antonio Alvarez began work at the *bodega*[5] Caballero at age eleven, he had to hide from the inspector, being three years short of the legal age. José Aldana and Manolo Romero Ruíz worked throughout their childhood, one for the local small-holders, the other as a swineherd, while even a younger militant like Miguel Marroquín began work at age thirteen in bad conditions for little money. And these circumstances were nothing unusual. On the contrary, Candel (1968), in his study of working-class lives in Barcelona, asserts that not only in this city but throughout Spain it was still entirely usual in the 1960s for children to begin work at any age between seven and fourteen; so that Eduardo Sánchez, as one more example, can note that he began doing 'man's work' at age fifteen, roughly the age that child workers began receiving men's wages.

When it came to work there was no choice, unless it was thieving or contraband. Luis Jaramillo's family were living in misery. Paco de las Flores stayed with his grandfather until he died, and when the Falangists took away his uncle to fight in the war, he had to work harder than ever on the small-holdings of the *mayetos*.[6] Manuel Espinar began work in the same firm as his father as one man's wages were not enough to live on. Fernando Guilloto began to sell contraband bread and lived on the run from the police (he was an unpaid cobbler's apprentice at the time). Paco Artola worked in the chemical factory, a mosaic factory, a pastry shop and as a porter and a chauffeur – often being thrown out of jobs for petty theft and narrowly escaping a spell in prison. But these were the hungry years. His brothers walked unshod, and he robbed to feed the family. And when Eduardo Sánchez began doing his 'man's work' in 1946, the food on the estate where he worked was unfit for animals and on most days of the week there was no bread. So he moved to do piecework on a nearby estate, where Manolo Romero and his brother were also working at the time. By working the equivalent of almost two days in one he made a little extra, and bought his

[5] In the Spanish of Spain, *bodega* can refer to anything from the corner store to a large industrial plant. In this story it refers to the large 'wineries' of El Marco de Jerez, most of which employed hundreds of workers in the production and marketing of sherry.
[6] *Mayetos* is the local name given to the small-holding vineyards in the region of Sanlúcar de Barrameda and Chipiona. The social and economic importance of the *mayetos* is discussed in Chapter 3.

first suit and shoes. A white suit with black and white spats. But when winter came he had to blacken the spats: they were the only shoes he had.

In these circumstances, where all work was bad, any work was good. Both Pancaro and Federico Iglesias started work in an ironworks. Pancaro was sacked and began working in the countryside; Federico moved into construction. Antonio Ortega began work in an ice factory, and Rafael Gómez found himself working in a baker's, a *bodega* and as a bricklayer. Manolo Romero Ruíz tried his hand in a ceramics factory, while Manuel Espinar, having worked as an office boy in a bottling plant, went to work on the American base at Rota – as did many others at this time. Fernando Guilloto's first jobs included work in an orchard and as barboy in a casino; and Pepe Jiménez broke all records by working as a carpenter's apprentice, in a bottle factory, in the town hall, on a building site, with a (portable) bullring that took him to Tangiers, and at different jobs in Sevilla, Cádiz, Jerez and, once again, on the American base at Rota. José Aldana, who at one point was working in the vineyards with Paco de las Flores, took his turn at Rota, before moving on to the *bodega* Terry. This was steady work, but poorly paid and physically exhausting. They tended to employ men from the vineyards who were used to working hard since childhood. And although the work was hard, there were not the same extremes of heat and cold as in the vineyards.

There are one or two exceptions to this hand-to-mouth existence, but not many. Antonio Alvarez continued working in Caballero until he became a foreman at age seventeen and a section head at age twenty-seven. Miguel Marroquín stayed working in graphic arts, and had become head of his workshop at age twenty-four. But for most of the men like Pepe Jiménez, Manuel Espinar and Manolo Romero Ruíz, who volunteered, military service came as an almost welcome break from the struggle of everyday life. Juan Caballero did it late as he was supporting his family; Pepe Rosa wanted to make a career of the navy, but he would have had to ask permission to marry, and as his fiancée was the daughter of a 'Red' it would have been refused; Fernando Guilloto caused what trouble he could so they would put him on night watch where he could listen to Radio Pirenaica undisturbed. And José Aldana got through to his last night of guard-duty in the Canaries before he collapsed with a perforated ulcer and had to undergo surgery on the spot. It was then he decided he wanted a wife.

All these men were to become militants, yet in their accounts of their early work experiences there are but few references to situations of confrontation or conflict. Paco Artola when working in the *bodega* Gonzalez Byass during World War II (producing brandy to put a little fire into the bellies of the Allied soldiers in Europe) was impressed by the lack of militancy. The old socialists he knew, even the friends of his father, wanted nothing to do with him. José Aldana vaguely remembers a work stoppage in the vineyards at the beginning of the 1950s, but he is clear that he had never heard of the 'Syndicate' or the 'commission' at that time. Manolo Romero Ruíz remembers it was not until 1958 or 1959 that he had his first open disagreement with the boss; and Federico Iglesias felt a new 'restlessness' when he became active in the JOC (Juventudes Obreras Católicas),[7] but found no outlet for it as long as the priest always had the last word. As will become clear, there were good reasons for this (false) impression of social peace, and they meant that initially, at least, everyone had to find his or her own individual road to political salvation.

The concierge at the casino where Fernando Guilloto worked spoke to him of politics in Marxist language; but Fernando's version is that simply by studying the parasitic *señoritos*, or 'little lords', who frequented the place he managed to intuit the labour theory of value. Korea was another milestone as it prompted him to ask about communism, and his father spoke of it in the context of the Civil War. And so his interest grew, and with it his combativeness, and he began to lose jobs because he asked for higher wages. He began to mix with anarchists and communists on the building sites, and in 1953, when working at the *bodega* Terry, he took the week's retreat he was offered by a priest who came to deliver a talk every week, and spent the time searching the country library for anything on the working class. In a book on the Soviet Union, albeit a critical one, he discovered that there the working class was in power. With this as an incentive he went on reading, and when the municipal library would not give him the books he wanted, he started on their encyclopaedia. Later in the year Falangists visited the *bodega* to spread their word, and Fernando again feigned interest in order to get near a library. Once there, he stole all their membership cards, his idea being that he would want a record of who they were, come the Revolution.

But Fernando's political advances at this time, and those of his companions, were very private ones, and it was in no way obvious how they would achieve some kind of collective expression. This combination of individual anguish and apparent social peace was symptomatic of the climate of fear which ruled in the world of production, and which itself was a legacy of the terror of the Civil War and postwar years. Manolo Romero remembers that in the first four days of the war the 'Moors' arrived in Sanlúcar, where they met with armed resistance. Although still a boy, Manolo was there building barricades. All those who fought were killed in the fighting, or were shot afterwards, except for a few children amongst whom was Manolo. Sanlúcar became a ghost town. (Four months later they shot some forty men in the bullring of Jerez.) Luis Jaramillo, who was eight at the time, also remembers the shootings and the truckloads of corpses; and that they took his own brother at seven-thirty in the morning, and shot him. Paco

---

[7] The Young Catholic Workers were one of the three independent Catholic worker associations formed during the 1940s. They are discussed in detail in Chapter 6.

Artola's father fled to his aunt's house to avoid a similar fate, but the Falangists sought him out and imprisoned him in El Puerto. Every day for one and a half months they took him breakfast, until one day his mother returned supported by two companions – and he knew that his father, too, had been shot. Juan Modesto in his account of the war (Modesto:1978) recalls Francisco Artola, 'a socialist from the woodworkers union...later assassinated by the Falangists'.

And then there was the war itself, and the years that followed. Juan Flores spent six months at the front, but was then excused further service on the grounds that two of his brothers were also combatants. Rafael Ribeiro served nineteen months before they released him to support his mother. Paco de las Flores lost both his elder brothers in the war; and Benítez Rufo – a new name but another key figure in this story – fought for the Republic throughout the hostilities. But with the end of hostilities and the defeat of the Republic, the terror continued and in some cases intensified. Miguel Ruíz saw both his grandfather and uncle killed during the terror, and Juan Flores asserts that such killing was widespread and indiscriminate; but the sense that these men have of it was that the Falangists were waging their own war on the working class. One of the principal killing grounds was the prison in El Puerto de Santa María, but, for the sake of convenience, many of the shootings took place at the entrance to the cemetery. José Aldana discovered this one morning before day-break when he left for the fields with his father. Walking past the cemetery he felt his *alpargatas*, his rope-soled sandals, wet and sticky with the blood of the latest victims. Later in the day, as they sat contemplating this horror, a man appeared pursued by Falangists with bayonets. The fear had everyone in its grip. But they had seen nothing.

PERSONAL NETWORKS AND POLITICAL CONTACTS

Slowly and haltingly the restless men of the 1940s began to emerge from their isolation, and began to become known to the people who most mattered – each other. When Juan Flores was 'appointed' as representative to the so-called Vertical Syndicate[8] in 1943, he was very much alone and had no choice but to endorse the 'contracts' that were imposed from above; but when Pancaro was called to take part in the Syndicate in 1951, it was at the bidding of Manolo Romero, Emilio Fábregas and Eduardo Sánchez, who had already secured a foothold in the organization. Pancaro continued to be elected to the Syndicate and took part in negotiations over work contracts. As we shall see in Chapter 3, syndical practice has always come easier to these men of Sanlúcar than political organization, and they did not come to join the 'Party' (the Communist Party of Spain) until later in

---

[8] The 'Vertical Syndicate' is the topic of Chapter 5.

the fifties, when they made contact with men from El Puerto like Fernando Guilloto, Paco Artola and Rafael Ribeiro. Moreover, the moment of affiliation to the Party was generally decided not so much by political commitment as by chance personal contacts; although some were content to pursue their syndical struggles to the exclusion of all else. In the town of Trebujena, Miguel Campo is proud to have been of the Party all his life, and was first arrested for the fact in 1951; whereas Paco Cabral, who was president of the 'social section' of the Vertical Syndicate for twenty-five years from 1952 onwards, only joined the Party in 1968.

The construction of the large American base at Rota brought together people from different regions of Spain and abroad, and it was when he was working there that Paco Artola first made contact with militants of the Party and began ferrying propaganda materials from Sevilla to El Puerto, where he was in touch with the group led by Rafael Ribeiro. Until then Paco had worked in a prisoners' solidarity group, and he now began to combine this activity with militancy in the Party. At about this time Juan Caballero and Eduardo Sánchez became active in the syndical movement, and Eduardo was elected to the Vertical Syndicate in 1956 alongside Manolo Romero and Emilio Fábregas; but neither joined the Party until early in the 1960s, when Eduardo was recruited by Manolo Romero, the informal 'leader' of his network. Fernando Guilloto, meanwhile, was working in France but made contact with the Party in Nîmes, and in particular with one Benítez Rufo, who was himself in direct contact with the executive of the Party. Fernando was active in France recruiting emigrant workers and distributing propaganda; and the Party entrusted him with the task of organizing (or reorganizing) the Party in the province of Cádiz. He was given instructions, propaganda materials and money; and within twenty days of returning to El Puerto in April 1960 he had organized a committee – which, as it happened (and as we shall see in Chapter 9), was not the only committee of the Party operating in the town.

It was about 1960 that a lot of people began to make contact. Rafael Gómez, who had already been attending syndical meetings, met up with Rafael Ribeiro and Paco Artola in 1959. Federico Iglesias, only nineteen in 1960, was recruited to the Party by Antonio Cárdenas (but felt he was not entirely trusted and was closely watched as a possible 'submarine'). Antonio Alvarez, although already active in the Syndicate following, as in the case of Paco Artola, a period of work in prisoner solidarity, still had no contact with the Party and remained content for the time with his syndical role. (Acting as workers' representative and facing down the bosses was, as he says, like 'putting on a suit that fitted him'.) Paco de las Flores had remained outside the networks before 1960 because as a gardener he had had little opportunity to establish contacts. In this same year he joined the local committee of the Party in El Puerto as a representative of the rural workers. From 1963, he ran in the syndical elections first at local and then at provincial level in order to provide support to Emilio Fábregas: Paco was elected president of the local 'social section' of the vineyards (with José Aldana as vice-president) and then became vice-president at provincial level at the same time that Emilio continued as president. José Aldana joined the Party in 1961 and became a representative in the Syndicate in 1963; but he stakes his claim to be one of the unsung heroes of the struggle not so much on his militancy as on the seventeen years he spent living in just two rooms with his ten children and his mother-in-law....

From 1962, Pepe Rosa was a militant of the Party as well as a syndical representative for the banking sector, thus fighting, like so many others, on two fronts. Paco Chicorro, who until then had spent most of his time working the small plot of land he owned with his brothers, joined the Party in Sanlúcar in 1962, or rather, as he puts it, he joined up with Juan Romero, Manolo Romero and Rafael Pinilla Romero (also known as 'the carpenter'). Antonio Ortega was also recruited in this year (by Juan Franco) and joined the local committee in the following year. His work really took shape as he began to travel to Puerto Real to see his fiancée, and made contact with both the workers' commissions and the Party in that town. Meanwhile, Juan Romero (Manolo's brother), who had been dedicated full-time to the movement, had to step aside because of his family situation, but, he insists, his personal relations with the network continued strong, and he never left the Party. Manuel Espinar was elected to the Syndicate in the same year, 1962, and subsequently held various posts at local and provincial level. He joined the Party in 1966, brought in by Antonio Alvarez, and so met up with Miguel Marroquín. Pepe Jiménez joined in 1963 but was carefully watched because of his former Falangist affiliations. With him in the same cell were Fernando Guilloto of the local committee, his brother Manolo Jiménez and José María García. José María, who had been a simple militant since 1959, now began to get to know such leaders of the local Party as Paco Artola and Rafael Ribeiro. The fact that he had a car made him the chauffeur of the provincial committee, and he took Pepe de la Rosa and Paco Artola to their key political meetings. So when a place on this committee opened up in 1968 with Rafael Gómez's departure for Barcelona, José María was proposed and voted in. As he says, having accompanied the day-to-day work of the committee for all those years, the formal membership made very little difference to him personally, except that he was now put in charge of finance: never was the transition from personal network to political responsibility illustrated more smoothly.

There are one or two exceptions to the principle of networking, but for the most part these networks become both tighter and more extensive as they find more permanent forms of political organization, and even the stray threads tend to tie in sooner or later. Pepe Mena was one of the restless men who had been protesting in their place of work as early as the 1940s, but he had been in Cádiz and had remained relatively cut off from the growing networks in Sanlúcar, El Puerto, Jerez and Trebujena. He joined a separate cell of the Party in Cádiz in 1959 but then spent most of the sixties out of the country. However, when he returned in 1971 he played a key role in reorganizing the provincial committee, and indeed became its political officer, as well as participating, again at provincial level, in the work of the workers' commissions. Manuel Verano had joined the JOC (Young Catholic Workers) when he was thirteen, and had worked within USO (the Catholic but never confessional union organization)[9] during the 1960s. Not until 1968 did he enter the workers' commissions (which had for their part been doubtful about his Church background), and then joined the Party in the same year. Miguel Ruíz and Manolo Romero Ruíz were other late recruits – but only because they were younger than many of the other militants: Miguel entered the Communist Youth in 1968 and Manolo was recruited to the Party by Antonio Palacios, to whom he was introduced by a friend in one of his local bars. And in this same year Federico Iglesias, who had never been fully accepted into his network, went through the so-called communist baptism of imprisonment and torture, an event, he is convinced, which gave him more 'class' [*sic*] in the eyes of his peers.

The full significance of the roles these men played in the workers' commissions and in the Communist Party, and the importance of the posts they occupied in the Vertical Syndicate (the official syndicate of the Franco regime) can only be appreciated as the story unfolds in subsequent chapters. For the moment it is sufficient to note that as their syndical or (clandestine) political careers advanced, so they commanded more political contacts, and, at the same time, extended and strengthened the networks to which they belonged. Paco de las Flores became national president of the vineyard workers in the Vertical Syndicate, and, at a later date, Manuel Verano became provincial president of the same trade. Fernando Guilloto and Antonio Ortega became local presidents of their trades, transport and graphic arts respectively, in the Syndicate, and Antonio also became head of the Communist Youth and member of the provincial committee of the Party. Finally, men like Emilio Fábregas and Antonio Alvarez came to fulfill such key roles in the process, and to command so much influence, that they had a considerable individual impact on political outcomes. In this connection, two further comments on the nature of these networks are in order, as markers for later analysis: first, when the formal organizations of the commissions and the Party were badly smitten by the repression of the late 1960s and 1970, it appears that it was personal loyalty to the network which kept the political work going. Neither Eduardo Sánchez nor, ironically, Federico Iglesias had been detained following the mass arrests of 1970, and Federico had had the further good fortune to arrive late at a meeting

---

[9] The Unión Sindical Obrera (Workers' Syndical Union) grew out of the Catholic worker associations of the 1940s, as is explained in Chapter 6.

in Madrid where the police had arrested all the national coordinators of the workers' commissions. But the situation put them both under such strain that no political commitment could have kept them in (and, indeed, both of them finally left). Second, when cracks in the formal organizations appeared under the weight of mutual recriminations for the arrests, then they began to split along the lines of the personal networks established during the preceding years.

THE MILITANCY OF THE UNQUIET HEART

These are the names of most of the men who came to lead the struggle for democracy in the corner of the country known as El Marco de Jerez. Their private lives, their individual anguish and aspirations, are their concern alone. But in coming together, they did much to make a democratic project, and that is a matter of history. So these few biographical fragments can serve to suggest the live and often very personal mosaic which made up the political leadership of the region. These men felt the injustices and the lack of freedom personally, and tried to respond politically. In doing so they became militants who were proud of their militancy. It defined them, qualified them as leaders and gave them a measure of strength. For all that, they were mere men: they had to learn to live with fear and could never be completely sure of what they were doing. For guidance they looked to each other, and to a man who for many of them spoke with almost divine authority, and indeed whose *nombre de guerra*, or code name, was often 'Jesús'.

José Benítez Rufo was born in 1913 and came from France to Dos Hermanas in the province of Sevilla in 1945 with the mission of organizing the Communist Party in the south of the country. Dos Hermanas was to be the base for his work as *enlace*, or 'linkman', but in the following year his comrades in the town were arrested while he was in Madrid and the address of his safe house in the capital discovered, and he was condemned to twenty years' imprisonment for membership in a proscribed party and for sedition. He served eight years in the central prison of Burgos and was freed in 1953. Shortly after returning to Dos Hermanas to be with his parents he was called back to France by the political bureau of the Party, and within three months had returned to Andalucía to continue his original mission. He travelled widely but concentrated his activities in Málaga and Jerez, and so was ready at the right time to promote the political struggle in El Marco de Jerez.

There will be time to study the role of José Benítez Rufo in this emerging struggle. For the moment I simply want to consider his life: countless years of constant movement, with no possibility of seeing friends or family. His brother Manolo served twelve years in Valencia gaol, but even when he was freed in 1959, José dared not visit him. All letters to his family had to be sent from France, although he himself was always near. Several times he just escaped further arrest, once in Badajoz, once in Jaén, and another time in Málaga. His brother also returned to political work and made his way up the hierarchy of the Party in Sevilla. At a springtime meeting in that city in 1967 he was waiting, with others of the provincial committee, for the arrival of a man called 'Jesús'. As it happened, it was his own brother. They shook hands, but not a word passed between them.

José was now living in Sevilla, but even though they continued to meet regularly on the provincial committee, no one knew the two of them were brothers until Manolo was arrested in 1973 in the wave of arrests which accompanied the '1001' trial in Burgos.[10] Unlike Manolo, José was never caught again, and when amnesty was declared in 1976 he travelled clandestinely to France (where everyone supposed him to be) and returned to a hero's welcome in Sevilla, where thousands had gathered at San Bernardo station in a spontaneous show of affection and support.

There is no moral to this story, except that which is spoken in different ways by these men who helped to make a democracy. Eduardo Sánchez spoke of his growing sense of exploitation as he moved from one rural estate to the next without bettering his pay or conditions of work; José Aldana talked of the repugnance he felt for the events recounted here, and his deep antipathy to the regime responsible for them; Luis Jaramillo, like many of his generation, cannot read or write but felt the oppression in his flesh and bones. This was the way they felt. Restless. Uneasy. This much they could not help. As for the militancy, Manolo Romero Ruíz was recruited by Antonio Palacios, and so became a 'communist'. But he could equally well have joined the USO or some other 'Christian' organization: 'I consider it a natural thing', he said, 'nothing strange... the working class is at the mercy of so many enemies... rebellion a natural thing... trying to make a more just society... we went and fought... a natural thing, fighting against injustice'. What he and the rest of these men had was an unquiet heart, an *inquietud*; and what the Party offered them was a 'place in the struggle'.

---

[10] This was the notorious trial of a number of alleged leaders of the workers' commissions who had been arrested in June 1972. In interview, one of the defendants (Eduardo Saborido) suggested that theirs was called the '1001' trial because the sentences they received added up to 1,001 years; but another version asserts that the number simply reflects the routine labelling of all trials according to the sequence in which they arrive before the court.

2

The burden of hopes and hatreds: ideological traditions in clandestine circumstance

What useless efforts! What sterile sacrifices!...The legacy of so much labour was going to be lost forever! The new generations disowned the old folks, and refused to receive from their tired and feeble limbs the burden of hopes and hatreds.

Blasco Ibáñez, *La Bodega*

THE 1930S IN SPAIN was a time of open class warfare, and the most exploited and radical of the sectors in struggle was the rural working class, which accounted for three of the twenty-three million inhabitants of what was still a predominantly agrarian nation. In an epoch when the country appeared trapped in a cul-de-sac of economic and political backwardness, more than any other sector these 'workers in sandals' (Claudín:1983b) raised the spectre of popular revolution; and it was they who provided the mass of popular support for the credo of Andalucían anarchism. So it is tempting to see the social struggle in El Marco de Jerez as a continuation of this ideological tradition into the very different economic and political context of the forced accumulation and State-led industrialization of the Franco years; and consequently to argue that, whatever its intrinsic interest, it is something of an anachronism in an historical moment which sees the creation of a new industrial working class and a new class of industrial capitalists (see Chapter 4). But such a judgement would be mistaken for at least two reasons. In the first place, it would fail to recognize the very special economic and political characteristics of El Marco where the labour process and the spatial organization of production have combined to create an industrial working class in the countryside; in the second place, it would ignore the fact that the first responses and some of the strongest resistance of the working class to the Francoist regime took place in traditionally militant sectors such as the mines of Asturias and the vineyards of El Marco. So when Ibáñez (1924) looked prophetically to the proletariat of the cities and said, 'They will be the chosen; while the rustic waited in the countryside with the resigned gravity of the ox, the disinherited of the city was waking to follow the only friend of the miserable and the hungry ... Social Rebellion', he may have been right in general but was premature in dismissing the historical role of the very men whose lives he had so passionately portrayed – the vineyard workers of El Marco. They followed their 'only friend' from the 1870s to the 1970s, and so were 'chosen' for a full century of struggle.

The workers of El Marco have always lived in *pueblos*, or townships, and the main square of the town has traditionally served both as a labour market, where workers are contracted, and as a political space for meetings and demonstrations. The *pueblo* is therefore the first place where their living and work relations coalesce. But this coincidence of experiences also occurs in the vineyard, where it is forcibly projected into the labour process by the traditional obligation to live for extended periods at the place of work; such that it was quite usual for large groups of workers to live at the same vineyard for fifteen days at a time over several months, and so to share living quarters in close and almost constant contact with each other. At the end of the working day they would then gather around the *fogaríl*, or big open fire, and read and talk of their lives and the conditions in which they lived them – in the anarchist way. Moreover, in an industry where each hectare of land requires about 150 man-days a year, the workers also went to the fields in large groups, and for certain tasks such as pruning or sulphating would work a field standing as many as fifty in a line. Working in the traditional manner, they would work from sun-up to sundown, and take six or seven short rest periods in that time; and although this changed under Franco, a number of rest periods, the so-called *cigarros*, remained, and provided further opportunities for talking things over. In most cases the foreman was included in their conversations; he was simply a skilled worker like themselves. And in this way the fields became a factory, with the difference that instead of returning home at night the workers also shared the intimacy of their hours of rest. Such an industrial situation in a rural setting is not commonplace in Europe, and such a mass of industrial workers in agriculture is not found in this form anywhere outside of the provinces of Cádiz and Sevilla and Córdoba in the south of Spain. In view of this, it is no surprise to find in El Marco a quintessential expression of proletarian culture and traditions.

Possibly the only other working sector in Spain with such a strong set of traditions, including the tradition of combativeness, is the mines of Asturias, where a relative isolation and special conditions of work have contributed to inspire the spirit of solidarity. Thus, Gerardo Iglesias argues that 'the miner is solid to the core, because it is impossible to survive down a mine without this solidarity' (prologue to Miguélez:1976), and Miguélez himself goes on to suggest that 'such solidarity helps to explain how in mining strikes the miners come together, organize, obey natural leaders and coordinate their actions without much need for proclamations or pamphlets'. Now, the ability to mount a strike in the absence of formal directives was as true of El Marco as it was of Asturias (as seen in Chapter 7); but if the strength of collective traditions amongst the miners can be explained by the specific social conditions in which they work (and to some degree by the very brutality of that work), the traditions in the vineyards were built, very differently, on the skill and sensitivity required by the labour process, and the pride the workers took in their work. On the one hand, this had to do with a professional interest in the very process of production, where, as in so many other agricultural tasks and quite unlike in many industrial processes, it was impossible to divorce intellectual work from manual work. So it was that the foremen, the most skilled workers, tended to be *mayetos* from Sanlúcar who became so fascinated by their work that they were quite capable of extracting a vine and taking it to a meeting in a barber's or cobbler's shop to decide the best way to prune it. On the other, it had to do with the residual influence of an anarchist morality which taught a respect for nature, both plants and animals, and the dignity of work well done. On both these counts the workers of Sanlúcar, Jerez, El Puerto de Santa María and Trebujena developed a necessarily oral but fully intellectual and mainly humanist tradition which distinguished them from the wage labourers of the *sierra* of Cádiz or the other provinces of western Andalucía. Moreover, they themselves were quite conscious of the difference and were always very reluctant to do any work that was not work in the vineyards: they wanted to defend the special quality of their tradition, and of their *forma de ser*. On their side were the relatively unchanging conditions in the vineyards, where it has proved extremely difficult to mechanize production; against them was the Francoist State.

THE HISTORICAL BACKGROUND

The distinct nature of the tradition in the vineyards was evident in the way union membership split in the 1930s between the UGT, which dominated agriculture in the *sierra*, and the CNT, which organized all the workers in the sherry industry with the exception of a few of the *bodega* workers. Relations between the two unions were not always good, and when the UGT blacked a CNT-sponsored strike early in the decade it led to open confrontation between them. Nonetheless, in western Andalucía as elsewhere in Spain, these two unions tended to divide the syndical, and very often the political map between them; with the exception in this case of a significant Communist Party presence in El Puerto de Santa María, and to a lesser extent in Trebujena and Puerto Real. Mention has already been made of the Communist deputy from El Puerto, the physician Daniel Ortega, whose immense personal prestige did much for the Party in that town. At the same time El Puerto had two Communist councillors in the town hall, one of whom, Ramón Mila Cristán, was the engineer who built and maintained the bell-house in the town church. The 'war commission' which condemned him to death was prepared to commute the sentence were he ready to 'recant', but rather than plead for mercy from his captors he died with his lips sealed. Such moments of sacrifice have succoured many traditions of struggle, and this Communist tradition, minor though it was, merits attention because of the clearly superior capacity of the Communist organizations to survive the ravages of the post–Civil War years, and because of their importance to the working-class movement when it reemerged in the decade of the fifties.

The tradition of the vineyards was put to its most severe test by the terror of the Civil War and postwar years. The Falangists killed more than 100 people in Sanlúcar. In tiny Trebujena, too, out of a total population at the time of some 5,000, more than 130 were called out and shot at the local tavern. And the prison in El Puerto de Santa María resembled an extermination camp, with people being shot by the truckload, 40 at a time. The Civil Guard did most of the killing, which continued intensely for three or four years after the war; and in the prison of El Puerto, those who were not shot were most often destined to die of dysentery or tuberculosis. Mainly they killed 'communists'. The Masons, it is said, suffered less badly as they tended to have sufficient savings to buy their way out. However, despite the severity of this white terror, a prisoners' aid society was formed in order to get food and, where possible, medicine into the prison; and anti-fascist cells survived in El Marco even if they had been effectively eliminated elsewhere. It was difficult to talk politics on the *cortijo*, the large landed estate of the plains; but in the vineyards, around the *fogaríl*, they talked of little else.

The tradition had to survive not only the terror but also the hunger of the forties. With wages at eleven pesetas a day and a kilo of bread at twelve, people were dying. The old union organizations, and especially the CNT in El Marco, had been decimated. Nonetheless, some of the old anarchist militants were still alive, and with the encouragement of captured Republican combatants from across the country, who had been pressed into the work regiment which had been assembled in the region, they began to respond to the most immediate problem – which was the hunger. Over the years of the late forties they succeeded in persuading the authorities to distribute food, and even money to buy bread, in the town of Sanlúcar. This was the so-called *socorro*, and, despite being designed to maintain public order, represented the first 'social security' payment ever made anywhere in modern Spain. But this was something of a favour that was got by petition, rather than a demand that was won; and when a working-class movement in Sanlúcar slowly began to emerge again in the 1950s, it did so in the face of fierce opposition from the old anarchists. In part, this was because they had suffered the years of fear and had lost something of their former spirit. This was apparent later in the fifties when the owners tried to split the workers with an offer to increase the number of full contract workers, or *fijos*, in the vineyards. Considering the anarchist traditions of the region, the reply that was given in the various meetings called by the bosses was predictable: 'todos fijos o ninguno'. Either everyone was to have a full contract, or no one. But it was precisely the old CNT leadership from Sanlúcar which broke solidarity, and those who went with them took the contract. In part, too, it was because the old guard was incapable of accepting that the way forward now was to work within the Vertical Syndicate, which they could only see as collaboration with the regime. These questions will be examined in more detail in Chapter 6. What must be emphasized here is that it was the older militants who broke ranks, or refused to do anything; while the first militants of the new movement were all young. And once their attempts to cooperate with the anarchist rump had all been frustrated, this new generation began to make its own political choices.

It would be difficult to overemphasize the importance for this story of the new organizations and new strategies created and advanced by the *new* generation of workers (and later analysis of the democratic project will return repeatedly to this point in Chapter 6 and passim). But if these new and young workers could not find common political ground with the representatives of the old anarchism, just what kind of political tradition was it that they inherited? In the first place, it was a sense of oneness in their exploitation or, in other words, a sense of the tradition of poverty and dignity symbolized by their rope-soled sandals, the *alpargatas* (OSE:1974b). But even this tradition belongs to them not as peasants but as a rural working class as old as the working class of Manchester, or older, a class which in the following years was to be the cradle of new generations of militants working in the factories and on the building sites of Madrid and Barcelona. In short, the tradition is one of struggle, and this tradition is broader and more encompassing than any ideological expression it may assume at any one historical moment. In this sense the tradition was anarchist partly because anarchist ideas arrived first (which is to state the obvious), and partly because they provided a perfect vehicle for direct involvement in this struggle. The anarchism of the vineyard workers of El Marco had very little to do with FAIism[1] or 'universalism', and everything to do with their personal commitment to the struggle. So, as will emerge later in the analysis, when the only political option in opposition was the Communist Party, the workers of El Marco became 'communist'. But, as we shall see, it was not the

---

[1] The FAI (Federación Anarquista Ibérica, Iberian Anarchist Organization) was founded in 1927 and came to be seen as the 'action arm' of the CNT (Kern:1978). Many of the founding representatives from anarchist organizations in Spain and Portugal, and amongst Spanish exiles in France, pursued a 'pure' anarchism, and sanctioned a potential recourse to political violence, in the face of Primo de Rivera's dictatorship and the progressive loss of civil liberties.

Party which taught them their political practice. This they learned for themselves within a movement of their own making, which was the workers' commissions. In many ways the commissions can indeed be seen as inheriting the anarchist traditions, and especially those of direct democracy through the assembly and continual struggle through the strike. It is true that the Communist Party rapidly established a political hegemony over the working-class movement in El Marco de Jerez, but this was a communism quite unlike that of the Party in exile, if only because it had to be adapted to a strong tradition of struggle and a constantly shifting pattern of personal loyalties.

IDEOLOGICAL TRADITIONS AND PERSONAL NETWORKS

At first sight the relatively rapid switch from anarchism to communism which presaged the re-emergence of the working-class movement in El Marco de Jerez presents something of a conundrum. But the tradition of the movement is not essentially an ideological one (even if, so far as it relates to the labour process, it is certainly an intellectual one), nor do the vineyard workers have the kind of theoretical skills that would allow them to analyse ideological propositions. On the contrary, this is what the anthropologists call a segmented society where the network of personal relationships becomes all-important; and what matters to the workers here is not ideology per se but the men who represent it. Not anarchism or communism, but the commitment to the true tradition, which is one of struggle. The key question, then, becomes the personal confidence the workers have in their leaders, and this confidence, or prestige, can only be acquired through struggle. In this perspective, although anarchism is as important as a *forma de ser*, or way of being, as communism is as an organization, neither is significant as ideology.

However, this is not to suggest that the leaders of the movement were men without ideas, or that they themselves had not at one moment or the other been inspired by ideology. Miguélez (1976) has this in mind when addressing the emergence of the workers' commissions in Asturias, and the fact that they were always led by the most combative workers. In his view these were perceptive men who had responded to political or religious ideas by making them relevant to the common concerns of the workers, and so had succeeded in extracting the simple propositions that helped make them 'natural leaders'.[2] No, it is rather to suggest that the political cement of the

---

[2] Unfortunately, in commenting on the causes of the miners' combativeness, Miguélez does not pursue this insight but rather returns to an economistic notion of 'class consciousness', which is never theorized but which nevertheless represents a privileged explanatory device in his argument. My own view is that there can be no 'consciousness'

movement was provided not by ideology but by personal networks woven around the figures of such natural leaders.[3] But the corollary of making personal confidence the key is that such leaders cannot climb too high too fast without risking a loss of trust; without incurring the suspicion that they are pursuing their own good and not that of the people. 'When one spends a long time away from the workers, the people are not content with him ... they stand away, they do not love him'.

The whole question of personal prestige and its possible loss is central to aspects of the later analysis (in Chapters 6, 9 and 12, for instance), especially insofar as it concerns two of the principal protagonists of the story, Emilio Fábregas and Antonio Alvarez. By way of preview it is sufficient to note that this primacy of personality over ideology is not always viewed positively, and indeed has been dubbed, on the one hand, the '*caciquismo*[4] of the left', so defining it as a decadent cultural trait which apes the *caciquismo* of the parasitic sherry oligarchy of El Marco; and, on the other, 'makeshift messianism', which gives to the desperate and dispossessed a minor messiah to adore. In my view, while both judgements may partake in some degree of the truth, they are far from telling the whole story. It cannot be cause for surprise that a harshly oppressed working class which faces a culturally sophisticated oligarchy in a highly classist society should imitate patterns of behaviour characteristic of that oligarchy; nor that many of the oppressed are susceptible to charismatic voices which promise a road to political salvation. But politics is a kind of alchemy, and what is of critical interest here is the way in which such cultural mores are transformed through struggle into the elements of a political project.

In any event, the importance of personal networks, and indeed of the personalities themselves, means it is difficult to make this account 'objective', in the sense of abstracting the argument from the individuals in struggle, if only because the whole tradition of struggle is carried on by such networks and structured around the figures of key personalities, or figures who have come to have a symbolic significance. An example of the latter is Manolo Vela, who was fairly well known as a syndical leader in El Puerto, and who

which corresponds 'objectively' to a class position in the society. Subjectivity, which is anyway more likely to be heterogeneous than homogeneous, is constructed piecemeal from life experience, by the elements of competing ideological discourses and through political practice itself.

[3] The theoretical underpinnings of this statement are explored in Chapter 15.

[4] In Spain, *caciquismo* tends to refer to the complex arrangements of local and regional power relations which underwrote the political system of the Restoration period, which was oligarchic, patrimonial and parliamentary. The *cacique* himself was the local political 'boss', most often an appointed government official or a point man for one of the main parties (or both), who would operate to dispense patronage and offer protection in return for different forms of political support. The system was almost all-encompassing during the last quarter of the nineteenth century but began to break down during the following decades (Romero Maura:1973).

also played a minor role in the local committee of the Party in that town. He was earning a better than average wage in the *bodega* when cancer was diagnosed, and he was dismissed without a penny – and with no possible means of support. In the months that followed his comrades collected for him every week until he died at age forty-two in 1968. Not one of the great leaders, then, but a poignant moment in this tradition which has always to create itself was made by the demonstration which was his funeral, and, as a challenge to the Civil Guard which forbade it, by his tombstone, which read, 'Tu familia y el MUNDO OBRERO no te olvidan'.[5]

Thus, if the tradition was not made primarily ideological it was because there was no political space for it and, moreover, no political need for it. Remember that the people of El Marco and many other regions in Spain chose the Communist Party not only because it was the only political option but also because it provided an effective clandestine organization at a time when this was the first political priority. The working-class movement faced a range of more or less sophisticated repressive techniques and apparatuses (documented in Chapter 10), which left little room inside the country for debating different ideological viewpoints. At the same time there was no need for ideology insofar as it was enough to be *against Francoism*: a live sense of oppression and of the lack of economic rights and civil liberties was more than sufficient to sustain militancy. Finally, it is worth pondering the 'historical advantages' of the development of personal networks to the detriment of ideological coherence (even if the force of these observations will only be felt later in the argument). On the one hand, the lack of a strong ideological tradition proved to be an important negative condition for the emergence of the workers' commissions which, initially at least, were composed of militants of every political persuasion, including Communists, Socialists, Catholics, anarchists, left Falangists, nationalists and even people of no such persuasion at all. On the other, the component of personal trust was crucial to the political strategy of combining legal and extralegal struggle through an infiltration of the Vertical Syndicate, for through this strategy every militant was obliged to fight with two faces (see Chapter 12).

THE CLANDESTINE CIRCUMSTANCES OF
THE STRUGGLE

The early organization of the underground movement was a very makeshift and not very successful affair. In El Puerto secret messages were tapped out on army typewriters provided by comrades from the Republican army who

---

[5] This phrase translates loosely as 'Your family and the world of the workers will not forget you', but the phrase 'MUNDO OBRERO', written in capitals on the tombstone, is also a clear reference to the principal clandestine newspaper of the Spanish Communist Party.

had been drafted into a local work regiment; and then sent on long strips of folded paper carried inside packets of cigarette papers. Copies of *Mundo Obrero*, the underground newspaper of the Communist Party, arrived from Madrid through contacts in the postal service. Luis Jaramillo used to distribute thirty of the fifty copies which got to Sanlúcar, swallowing his fear and walking down the street with the newspapers stuffed in his boots. He could not read himself, of course, but to be caught with even one copy at that time meant a sentence of some twenty years. Indeed, when most of the twenty or so militants in El Puerto were arrested in 1944, they ended up spending anything from eight to eighteen years in Burgos gaol; and their arrests were followed by a local state of siege with telegraph and telephones tapped, and spies in all the bars. There were more arrests in 1948 after a consignment of *Mundo Obrero* printed in Jerez had been captured; but after the change of strategy of the late forties (see Chapter 8), which implied an abandonment of the guerrilla, the skeleton organization which survived was able to help some of the *guerrilleros* escape to Africa on local fishing boats.

The original organization of the Communist Party was structured in classic clandestine fashion around cells of no more than three people, so that, in principle, no militant knew more than two others. But the statutes of the Sixth Party Congress in 1960 spell out that although three is the minimum number for a cell, as the cell grows it must subdivide into groups of no more than five or six persons, all of whom will together then constitute the cell; and this system was operative in El Marco by about 1965, when there were at least one hundred militants of the Party throughout the province of Cádiz, none of whom was supposed to know more than five others. Such cells were often organized within particular industries or guilds (*gremios*): Antonio Ortega, for example, ran such a cell in the building industry and Antonio Alvarez did the same in the *bodegas*. Where the 'works committee' was controlled by the Party (as it was in the *bodega* Terry by José Marroquín or in the *bodega* Osborne by Antonio Cárdenas and Manolo Vela) then they became almost as important as the local committee itself. Originally such cellular structures subsisted within the individual townships, with very little contact between them; so that the first contacts between El Puerto and Sanlúcar, for instance, depended on one or two people in the latter place, and in particular the man they only knew as 'the carpenter'. As the organization extended, so the contacts increased, and despite the dangers the militants tended to aspire to posts in the local and provincial committees. Nevertheless, for many years the heart of the operation remained mainly 'homespun': Pepe Jiménez, who was the treasurer of his cell, kept the money for his different 'accounts' (Party dues, prisoners' aid, propaganda) in different flower vases on the mantelpiece.

For the underground organization to expand new militants had to be recruited, and this represented a fundamental problem of security for the fledgling apparatus. The problem was that there was no sure way of telling if someone was friend or foe (stooge or 'submarine' in the argot), and for this reason if for no other the clandestine work of the Party depended intimately on personal contact. Moreover, even where there was organization, it was as much an organization of individuals of a certain persuasion as of a political party, properly speaking. So Manolo Romero can assert that his cell had no problems of communication with the larger organization, but only because he knew the men of Jerez who were members of the provincial committee. In general, no one knew who was and who was not of the Party, until he was invited to join. Eduardo Sánchez was already working in the Vertical Syndicate when he was approached by Manolo Romero. All he had to do was nod. Not only did no one carry a card, of course (membership being simply a question of acceptance and practice), but most militants used undercover names. So José María García was Agustín, after his father, or Jaime when in the Campo de Gibraltar. And when Miguel Marroquín was first contacted by the Party in Puerto Real in 1962 everyone went by a number, and no names were used at all. The ambiguities of such a situation are obvious, and were neatly captured by Juan Modesto (1978) when speaking of his own clandestine work in the thirties: 'At that time', he says, 'I was both many people and no-one at all'.

This informal and personal style of recruitment is inscribed in the organization from its beginnings in El Puerto in the fifties, when Rafael Ribeiro's group slowly made contact with Rafael Gomez and sometime later with Paco Gutierrez (Paco de las Flores). It was this tiny group of people which came to form the local committee, which then made contact with people in Jerez. Such contacts were not necessarily with 'communists' but were with people of like mind, who read prohibited literature and were in a broad sense against the regime. It was in this way that Fernando Guilloto made contact with José María García. But when the person was less well known, and it was a question of recruitment to the Party, then it took time. José Aldana noticed a person in the cement factory where he was working by his *forma de ser*, and later found that he had spent some five years in the concentration camp in Chipiona. Only after some months did José dare put him in contact with the cell run by Paco de las Flores. Miguel Marroquín was vetted for some four years before joining, despite the fact that he was already in the Communist Youth. And in general the prospective recruit had to be vouched for by two members, as well as closely scrutinized at home, at work and in the Party cell itself. As the years passed, these procedures were progressively relaxed as people began to be recruited on the basis of the prestige they had earned on a 'works committee', on a workers' commission, or in prison (Hermet: 1974). But the slow style of recruitment, which required talk and more talk, was slow to change. And in José Aldana's view, it was as difficult to recruit to the workers' commissions as it was to the Party, principally because people were afraid, and with good reason.

PART II

Syndical practices, social struggles and political protests

5

The Vertical Syndicate: the mainstay of Franco's corporatist strategy

Labour unions! Don't be stupid. Since when have they ever solved anything?
We're all friends here, so let's not fool ourselves. We know only too well how
we appoint the rabble's representatives. They're under our thumbs! Nobody
listens to them, not even the stones. And the two or three that slip by us are out
there in the streets with the others.

Alvarez de Toledo, *The Strike*

IN HIS ATTEMPT to assess the contribution of the so-called Vertical
Syndicate[1] to the progress of Spanish society, Selgas (1974) asserted that
for thirty years it had provided both employers and employees 'adequate
instruments for the promotion and defense of their professional interests in
a climate of collaboration and social harmony'. The roll of honour in the
achievement of such harmony included José Antonio Girón de Velasco, for
initiating social security provisions; Fermín Sanz Orrio, for the Law of
Collective Contracts; Jesús Romeo Gorría, for extending the social security
net; José Solís Ruíz, for promoting greater participation and so 'modern-
izing' the syndicate; and all those who had worked anonymously in the
'social sections' of the different syndicates, and in the workers' councils. In
this view, the evolution of the Vertical Syndicate sat squarely within a
corporate tradition, which was 'reestablished in almost pristine form in the
Spain of Primo de Rivera and Franco', who 'attempted to deal with the
phenomenon of mass-man by erecting corporate structures that provided
for class harmony rather than conflict, structured participation rather than
rootlessness and alienation' (Wiarda:1973). But such 'harmony' was bought
at a high historical price according to the critics of official syndicalism, who
see its hierarchy, unity and, above all, 'verticality' as a formal restoration
of conservative Catholic ideals and paternalistic relations of domination

---

[1] The idea of a Vertical Syndicate, or *Sindicato Vertical*, became universal usage in
Franco's Spain. It referred to the Spanish Syndical Organization, or Organización
Sindical Española (OSE).

(Moya:1975). In this perspective, very differently, all economic actors were brought under a single command, which was the dictator, who was himself only responsible 'before God and before history', and who appointed his syndical delegate to operate the principle of 'verticality' like a 'creative, just and disciplined Army' (PCE:1965b). By this principle the different social classes were no longer superimposed one on the other but rather existed side by side within the Vertical Syndicate; and by so subordinating the working class, this Syndicate was designed to overcome class struggle by stopping this class from struggling. Thus, for Enrique Tierno Galván (quoted in Vilar:1976) the quality of official syndicalism went far to define the character of the political regime which promoted it: 'Verticality means obedience, verticality means the passivity of the people. In a sense, verticality denies the idea of progress'.

This official syndicalism was the regime's reply to the revolutionary 'workerism' of the Second Republic, and it first germinated in the professional organizations of the 'F.E. de las JONS', the Falangist Party,[2] during the Civil War (Selgas:1974); and the Party statutes later made clear that it alone was responsible for imparting discipline, unity and spirit to this syndicalism, which would moreover be staffed uniquely by its militants[3] (PCE:1965b). But although the new syndicalism was clearly subordinate to the Falangists, the syndicates themselves were constituted separately in the Labour Charter of 1938[4] (Arango:1978), which also made any attack on the 'normality of production' a 'crime against the State' (Maravall:1978); and later recognized as 'unitary' organizations, which bound employers and employees together, by the Syndical Unity Act of 1940.[5] Later, again in that same year, the syndicates were given operational shape by the Law of Syndical Organization,[6] which set up twenty-four syndicates to cover all basic areas of production (Amsden:1972) and included in each syndicate a 'social section' and an 'economic section', to serve as the privileged vehicles of collaboration between workers and management, respectively. Such euphemisms were characteristic of the content of the 1940 law, which in its preface conceived of Spain as a 'gigantic Syndicate of producers' with the State as the 'supreme

---

[2] The F.E. de las JONS was formed early in 1934 by an initially uneasy fusion of the Falange Española of José Antonio Primo de Rivera (the son of the dictator), and of the Juntas de Ofensiva Nacional Sindicalista, which had been dreamed up by a lonely printer named Ledesma Ramos at the beginning of the decade. The Falange remained a small, even insignificant, political grouping until its rapid growth behind nationalist lines during the Civil War.

[3] The statutes of the F.E. de las JONS were established by a decree of 31 July 1939, which made it the single party of the new corporate State. It was commonly referred to as 'The Movement'.

[4] The syndicates were provided for in Article 8 of the Labour Charter or Fuero de Trabajo of 9 March 1938.

[5] This was the Ley de Unidad Sindical of 26 February 1940.

[6] This was the Ley de Bases de la Organización Sindical of December 1940.

master of the economy' (Moya:1975); and the fact that the Vertical Syndicate remained in charge of the importation and distribution of essential raw materials during the years of autarky (FSM:1959) is indication enough that such sentiments were taken quite literally.

THE COMPETING PRINCIPLES OF COMMAND AND REPRESENTATION

The two basic organizing principles of the Syndicate were therefore totality, which suggested that class struggle was now impossible (Moya:1975), and verticality, which sought to ensure this impossibility through a command structure centred on appointed officials at national, provincial and local levels whose primary duty was to maintain strict social discipline within the work force (Amsden:1972). In other words, although the Syndicate was the official framework for the representation of organized labour, all the key representatives were in fact appointed by the regime. In this way, the heads of the provincial syndicates were appointed by the provincial delegate, who as head of the provincial coordinating committee was himself appointed by the national committee, the National Syndical Central (Amsden:1972), whose composition in each case was controlled by the National Delegate, who was in turn appointed directly by Franco himself (Wright:1977). Moreover, the National Delegate was, at the same time, secretary-general of the Movement, as the Falangist Party was known, and an *ex officio* member of the cabinet, thus making the Syndicate directly dependent on the executive of the State administration, in which it already participated through its presence in the Cortes (the corporatist parliament), in the provincial parliaments, or *diputaciones*, and in the municipal governments (PCE:1965b). And although in general it failed to introduce any progressive legislation into these political forums, its wage regulations were regularly signed 'for God, Spain and her National-Syndical Revolution' (OSE:1950). Revolutionary it was not, but just as the Syndicate occupied a central place in the institutional ensemble of a State which defined itself as 'national-syndicalist' (Maravall:1978), so the 'political line' (Alvarez:1967; Candel:1968) of appointed posts within its vertical hierarchy played a key role in the implementation of the regime's social and economic policies.

At the same time, however, the regime took the initiative to make the hierarchical structure of the Syndicate more representative, and a decree of July 1944 called elections for the social sections of the different syndicates at plant level (Selgas:1972). In effect, elections were scheduled once every three years for the post of *enlace sindical* or shop steward, each of whom would represent some twenty-five workers (Candel:1968); and in 1947 another law constituted the *jurados de empresa*, or factory committees, which were meant to represent workers equally to management, the Syndicate and the State (Wright:1977). Elections to the *jurados* did not take place until 1953, and even then the elections were indirect, with only the *enlaces* allowed to vote; and this enshrined an organizing principle of the Syndicate's representative structure, namely that the more important a post, the more restricted and less representative its constituency (Amodia:1977). Moreover, the *jurados* were so hedged about with restrictions themselves that they did not open the structure to wider participation but remained at best a consultative body; and once the elected *vocales* of the *jurados* were in place, then the representative role of the shop stewards was also in doubt. Thus, while the *jurado* appeared to invite more participation, neither the firm nor the State was bound by any decision it took (Arango:1978), and it was almost certainly expected to remain a talking-shop. One of the main demands of the Asturian miners, therefore, in their long struggle with the mine owners, was for effective representation (Miguélez:1976): they wanted the bosses to sit down and negotiate seriously and realistically, irrespective of the other demands. But in Asturias, as elsewhere, decision-making power rested with the political line and not in the *jurados*, nor indeed in any other elective post. Yet after several series of elections across the country there were some 240,000 *enlaces* and about 70,000 *jurados* (Soto:1976; Wright:1977) elected within the twenty-four original and finally thirty separate syndicates which made up the system; all of which clearly acted to enhance the Syndicate's power of co-optation.

On 27 February 1957, José Solis Ruíz was appointed secretary-general of the movement, and National Delegate of the Vertical Syndicate. In this same year the Movement finally fell from grace, and the Syndicate became the rump of its former power system, the last refuge for Falangist politicians and bureaucrats (Amsden:1972). But even this refuge did not seem as secure as it once had. The syndical elections scheduled for April had to be postponed for six months because of working-class agitation (*Mundo Obrero*:15.6.1957), and the reforms of 1958 (discussed in detail in Chapter 7) further weakened the Syndicate at factory level (Mujal-León:1983). With the economic take-off which followed the liberalization of the economy in the late fifties certain sectors of the working class were lifted from the breadline and began to develop new demands (as seen in Chapter 6), and this brought a response from the Syndicate in the shape of its first Syndical Congress, which brought together appointed and elected delegates, and, in principle, was intended to increase communication between them (Wright:1977). Although defined as the 'superior representative organ' of the Syndicate, the proceedings of the congress were dominated by its president, the National Delegate, who also presided over its Permanent Commission, which met three times a year as opposed to the biannual meetings of the congress itself, and which had the capacity both to set the agenda and to control for more than half of the *vocales* or delegates. Nonetheless, the congress was convened four times during the sixties and did achieve greater freedom in syndical elections after 1963, and, at its third meeting, the creation of the workers' and employers' councils.

These councils, set up at both provincial and national levels, were made up both of elected representatives, who were the president and vice-president of all the syndical sectors in the province, and of appointed members such as the permanent secretary, the syndical representatives to the Cortes and legal experts (Amsden:1972). The formal separation of labour and capital was maintained, however, and there were thus two councils for each province, one for workers and one for employers, and any executive action would have to be taken by the provincial council, which was created simultaneously, and which included representatives from both camps and was presided over by the provincial delegate. The councils themselves therefore had no executive power, and were as controlled as the congresses: Article 14 of the Order of 5 November 1964 of the National Delegate stated plainly that his appointee, the National Vice-Secretary of Social Order, was responsible for the organization and agenda of the meetings of the National Council of Workers (PCE:1965b); and identical controls were exercised over the provincial councils by the provincial vice-secretaries. In this way, the councils tended to point up the contradictions of 'pluralism in unity' without resolving them (Amodia:1977), and, in effect, elected delegates to the councils were ousted if they did not fit into the desired profile. Nevertheless, the reforms did increase the number of lower-level elective posts, even if elections to the national representative bodies were at a fourth remove from the base, and even if the political line continued unbroken. And with the spread of 'free' elections after 1963 (syndical elections took place in September 1963, October 1966 and again in 1971) the Syndicate had done much to increase its co-optative power.

These reforms of the Syndicate left its basic structure intact, and the moves towards greater participation were largely cosmetic. There may have been a fragmented attempt to adapt to a changing reality, but the regime appeared to lack the political will to push the process of adaptation too far. It is illustrative that in the First Social and Economic Development Plan, the 'Social' was added as an amendment in the Cortes; and in the meantime the Syndicate continued to damage its credibility by denouncing militants to employers and the police, by preparing blacklists and, more generally, by manipulating the margin of manoeuvre open to workers' representatives in the collective bargaining process (Miguélez:1976).[7] But the Organic Law of the State of 1967 not only purged the Labour Charter of many of its

---

[7] Miguélez was writing of Asturias, and it is probably true to say that nowhere else in Spain did the Syndicate act so decidedly against the interests of the workers. This being the case, the miners of Asturias moved from bitter dislike of the Syndicate to frank indifference to it.

outmoded articles, it also announced a major reform of the Syndicate, which, however, was only to be carried out after widespread and lengthy consultations. In the event, these consultations were confined to the provincial councils and the corresponding national bodies, which, as just seen, were scarcely very representative; but the results were nevertheless both positive and progressive, and rather too much of both for the regime. After more prevarication and 'consultation', it therefore called a syndical congress in Tarragona to debate the proposals, and the result was a predictable anticlimax. Indeed, the most salient feature of the bill that the government sent to the Cortes in September 1969 was the proposed creation of a Ministry of Syndical Relations, whereby the National Delegate of the Syndicate would now have ministerial status. When the bill finally became law in 1971 it changed nothing of substance, and, in particular, met none of the five conditions for authentic reform laid down in an International Labour Organization report (ILO: 1969). In fact, despite the liberal window-dressing the operation of the Syndicate continued to rest as heavily as ever on the principle of verticality and the application of the political line. But with the formal separation of the secretary-general of the movement from the Ministry of Syndical Relations the Spanish State could no longer plausibly pretend to be national-syndicalist.

THE ORGANIZATIONAL STRUCTURE AND SCOPE
OF THE SYNDICATE

It is not easy to convey a clear idea of the organization of the Vertical Syndicate in short order. As Amsden (1972) says, 'an organizational diagram which could denote all parts of the Spanish Syndical Organization and indicate the relationships between them would be as large as most road maps'. But some attempt must be made, if only because subsequent analysis demands it. The political line of command was not complicated: as just noted, the National Delegate, who was appointed by Franco, headed the National Syndical Central, which ran the national syndicate, and controlled its own technical services and welfare and education offices; subordinate to the National Delegate were the provincial delegates, who headed the Provincial Syndical Centrals, which ran the provincial syndicates as well as their own technical and welfare offices. So far so good. However, the relationship of elective to appointed posts was less straightforward. The National Syndical Central was composed of the presidents of both employers' and workers' sections of the national syndicates (of which there were twenty-four originally, twenty-seven in 1967 and thirty by the time the regime fell). The presidents were appointed by the National Delegate, who was also president of the Syndical Congress, which was elected (partially) from the employers' and workers' councils, from which the National Council was selected. Below them there were the employers' and workers' councils at provincial level, which were run by the provincial delegate, who was appointed by the National Delegate, and who presided over the provincial council. These councils in turn were composed of the presidents of the provincial syndicates (both employers' and workers'), who were elected by the local syndicates, which were first elected by the 'economic sections' and 'social sections' at plant level in the individual firms and enterprises. So these were the sections that made the syndicates that made the councils that made the centrals that represented the workers who did not build the house that Jack built.

The most important feature of the operation of the syndical elections within this structure was that they were indirect, so that those elected at one level became the electorate for the successive one. This created greater possibilities for control through fraud and intimidation, quite apart from the influence that the provincial delegate was able to exercise through his technical staffs. The first-level representatives were the *enlaces* or shop stewards, and the *vocales* on the factory committees or *jurados* of the individual firm. The shop stewards were meant to represent workers on a day-to-day basis, but the practical limit of their activity was to report to the *jurados*, which was where real representation at plant level took place. The *vocales* were elected directly by the workers every four years, but as a *vocal* might hold a post for up to eight years, these elections might only affect half the members of the *jurado* (Amodia:1977). (In fact, the amount of time a *vocal* served on the *jurado* was finally decided by the political line and the labour courts.) These *vocales* then formed the electorate within the district or town which elected the local syndicates, whose *vocales* would in turn elect the provincial syndicates, and so on and so forth. Thus, these were the syndical elections in which the candidates of the independent workers' commissions came to participate with such success (see Chapters 6 and 12); and, as will be seen, despite the indirect nature of the elections, some of these candidates even succeeded in reaching the very top of the representative ladder.

The structure of representation in the countryside was shaped by the Agricultural Associations (Hermandades Agrícolas), and, as such, was somewhat distinct from the organization of the main body of the Vertical Syndicate. The *hermandades* had been constituted by the Law of Syndical Unity of January 1940, through the fusion of preexisting agricultural labourers' unions with the employers' organizations known as the *cámaras agrarias*, or rural lodges; and they assumed the powers that in the Syndicate proper were exercised by the syndical centrals. But the *hermandades* were subordinate to the centrals at provincial level, and their workers' and employers' sections had the same appointed president, which made them even less representative than the syndicates at provincial level and below (Martínez-Alier:1971). As Moyano (1984) put it, 'the *hermandades* integrated the different interest-group organizations, both specific and general, in order to achieve representation for the rural sector as a whole and channel its participation in the economic and political decision-making centres of the Francoist State'; and while the organization of rural interest-representation was in fact considerably more complicated than indicated here (certainly at provincial level after 1947),[8] it is sufficient to emphasize its vertical integration into the main body of the Syndicate, and the direct control by the provincial delegate.

In a rural region like El Marco de Jerez, labourers might be represented either by the local associations (*hermandades*) or by the local syndicates; and in the particular case of El Marco the vineyard workers belonged to the biggest of these syndicates nationwide, the Rural Workers' Syndicate. At the same time most of the workers in the *bodegas* of Jerez and El Puerto de Santa María, who worked not to produce grapes but to manufacture wine, belonged to a quite separate syndicate, that of wine, beer and alcoholic drinks (Soto:1976); and the building workers, in their turn, had their own syndicate, as did each of the different trades or sectors of industry. Here, they have all been called syndicates, for the sake of consistency if nothing else, but in the almost deliberately arcane language of the early syndical legislation of the regime they were called *gremios*, or guilds, and so they remained until the Syndical Law of 1971, when they finally became unions (*uniones*), presumably to give them a more modern and European lustre. Moyano (1984) points out that certain of these syndicates or guilds, such as that of wine, beer and alcoholic drinks, comprised employers, technicians and workers from agriculture as well as industry and commerce, and were therefore responsible for representing interests that were sometimes irreconcilable and often antagonistic. But in my view the problems of representation stemming from the horizontal stretch of certain syndicates were insignificant compared with those deriving from the vertical integration of these syndicates into the larger organization.

The organization of the Syndicate was massive. An international workers' group of anarchist tendencies estimated in the late 1950s that there were some 10 million workers organized in 12,500 local syndicates and associations (FSM:1959). A North American commentator put this figure at 9 million in 1964, but added the 3.3 million 'employers' organized by the Syndicate (Witney:1965) (which, given the structure of Spanish industry, is not absolutely impossible). As the national labour force at this time totalled some 13 million out of a total population of 31 million, this meant that 92 per cent of it belonged to the Syndicate, with some 450,000 domestic serv-

---

[8] The Provincial Syndical Associations (Hermandades Sindicales Provinciales) had been supressed in 1947 and replaced at provincial level by the Official Syndical Rural Lodges (Cámaras Oficiales Sindicales Agrarias, or COSAs). The COSAs were part of the Vertical Syndicate and encompassed the Local Associations (Hermandades Locales), the Cooperatives and the Rural Territorial Unions (Uniones Territoriales del Campo). These Local Associations did have different sections for employers and workers, in the same way as the local syndicates.

ants and some 500,000 public employees remaining outside it. And at the beginning of the 1970s a Spanish expert said that the Syndicate represented exactly 7,881,643 members, divided between thirty national syndicates or unions, the biggest being that of the rural workers (1,353,304 members), followed by the metalworkers (1,333,031) and the building workers (1,087,754) (Selgas:1974).

In principle, the Syndicate provided a wide range of services to all of these workers, and, in practice, a great part of the social security system was operated on a decentralized basis by the thirty national syndicates (Pike:1974). Hence, the Syndicate ran 125 training centres, with 110,000 students enrolled as of 1970 (44,000 of them on full scholarships); funded 41 rest and education centres, with 60,000 residents annually; arranged vacations for over 160,000 workers each year; paid for 56 parks and sports facilities; supervised 14,300 cooperatives of various kinds with more than 2,300,000 members and maintained 35 sanatoriums and 21 consultancy centres extending medical services to 5 million patients each year. Moreover, as of 1969, the syndicates had built more than 258,000 housing units and administered mutual insurance programmes covering 6,264,000 workers in 159,000 firms, in order to provide pensions, which in 1970 were being enjoyed by 1,211,383 retired persons. As these are clearly official figures they must be treated circumspectly; but it is nonetheless true that the long list of welfare, education and recreation agencies, called generically 'syndical works' in the accounts, absorbed a full 40 per cent of the Syndicate's budget in the 1960s, and greatly expanded the organization's powers of patronage and co-optation. Although it was the workers themselves and the employers who largely paid for these services (by .003 per cent of their wage and by 1.5 per cent of the firm's payroll, respectively) (Amsden:1972), the administration of the patronage they made possible remained the prerogative of the political line. In a situation where the tax base only grew as fast as the economy overall, and where 'the social services with which the Falange hoped to win the loyalty of the working class were starved' (Carr:1982), the Syndicate continued to absorb about 5 per cent of the total State budget (Frères:1969), and its concentrated powers of patronage provided the regime with a powerful instrument for the manipulation of the working class.

6

The workers' commissions: the national picture compared with the movement in El Marco de Jerez

> The essence of the phenomenon is in its roots, that is in the countless commissions in the workplace and the syndicates which struggle to discover, define and demand their rights, even though the men who make up the commissions may not be fully aware of what they are doing.
>
> Fernando Soto, *A Ras de Tierra*

EVERYONE AGREES that the workers' commissions were an entirely new form of organization, which had no exact precedent in the history of the working-class movement in Europe. But the consensus goes no further than this, and there is little agreement about what the workers' commissions were, or about when or how they began. These basic historical questions remain unsettled partly because there has been a failure to recognize what one rare publication called the 'diverse modes of their emergence' (Frères:1969) in different regions of the country, and a corresponding failure to search for what these different styles had in common. This story will take up this search progressively in the different contexts of the commissions' syndical practices of collective bargaining and strikes (Chapter 7), and of their relations with the Communist Party (Chapter 11), with the Vertical Syndicate (Chapter 12), and with their own members and between themselves in this chapter. There is good reason for looking at who they were in order to answer what they were and when they began, because, especially in their beginnings, the commissions were far from being a universal phenomenon but rather emerged in fragmented fashion in a few pockets of militancy across the country, such as a few mines in Asturias, one or two engineering factories in Madrid, three light engineering factories in Sevilla, and the vineyards of El Marco de Jerez; and in each case they were conceived by the imagination and courage of a few restless men who provided local leadership through the links of their personal networks. Indeed, the presence of the commissions remained concentrated in certain regions and sectors even when they had accumulated sufficient impetus to transform the society as a whole. But in this story that moment is still far away, and the commissions themselves exist only in embryo, if at all.

Some see the beginnings of independent working-class organization in the Catholic associations of the 1940s, such as the Catholic Action Workers' Association or HOAC (Hermandad Obrera de Acción Católica), created in 1945, the Young Catholic Workers or JOC (Juventudes Obreras Católicas), formed in 1947, and the Catholic Workers' Vanguards or VOC (Vanguardias Obreras Católicas) of 1949, the most militant of the three (Arango:1978). These were legal associations, which under the terms of the 1953 Concordat with the Vatican were allowed to organize amongst the working class, and moreover to do so independently of the Vertical Syndicate (Mujal-León:1983). They were not granted official recognition as a separate union, but on the other hand they did enjoy the protection of the Church (Amsden:1972); so they were able to attract militants who were 'uneasy' in different ways, but who were understandably reluctant to defy a regime which had so mercilessly crushed the union confederations of the Republic (Frères:1969). In short, they provided essential experience of collective organization, as well as legitimized a certain critique, founded on a Christian mentality which derived a potent mystique of poverty from the yawning social gap between rich and poor. This critique found expression in a variety of publications, the most important of which were *La Voz del Trabajo* (The Voice of Labour) and *Juventud Obrera* (Worker Youth), which had a regular print-run in the 1950s of 35,000 copies, and was also disseminated through a calendar of cultural events and a range of legal services designed to reach and offer practical assistance to those most in need. While never completely free of police interference, these Catholic activists were able to supply organizational skills in the strike actions of the late 1950s and were especially prominent in the northern provinces during the strike waves of 1962 and 1963 (compare Chapter 7) (Amsden:1972);[1] and insofar as many of them underwent a certain secularization, and began to find political questions more pressing than spiritual ones, they came to play an important role in the workers' commissions, which were characterized in their early years by a heterogeneity of political beliefs in general and an unusual cooperation between Catholics and Communists in particular.

But if the Catholic associations became important to the commissions, they were clearly not the same thing, and so do not explain their birth, or even indicate when that might have occurred. This lack is supplied in some accounts by the 'myth' of La Camocha, which is not a myth in the sense that it is untrue (which myths anyway rarely are), but rather that it substitutes for historical explanation. Yet the many subscribers to the myth (including Ibarruri et al.:1964; Miguélez:1976; Maravall:1978; Mujal-

---

[1] Amsden (1972) mentions that the JOC, which was generally thought to be more 'radical' than the HOAC, participated in syndical elections in Bilbao as early as 1963.

León:1983) are all content to assert categorically that the first commission appeared in the mine of La Camocha in Asturias in the year 1956. The syndical elections of this year had provided an opportunity for miners to meet and talk about the piecework which ruled the labour process, and the commission was formed to negotiate specific grievances which got no hearing in the Vertical Syndicate itself. It was then immediately disbanded. By these accounts, then, the Asturian miners were the first workers to discover the commission, with the caveat added by Miguélez (1976) that its formal structure may have emerged earlier elsewhere in Spain, given the resilience of traditional forms of organization in the mines. But the idea that the commissions germinated in La Camocha, from where they spread like a kind of virus throughout the country, has been accepted too uncritically by too many commentators, and cannot provide a proper point of departure for a study of the phenomenon.

A more plausible explanation is that the commissions emerged and expanded in the context of the changes in collective bargaining brought about by the Law of Collective Contracts of 1958 (see Chapter 7), which opened a space for direct negotiations between employers and workers within the structure of the Vertical Syndicate. In this perspective, the commissions either emerged spontaneously from the liberalization of the economy (Selgas:1974), or were called forth by employers who had found the *jurados* to be ineffective and were seeking genuine representatives from amongst the workers (Arango:1978). But while it is certainly the case that the 1958 law gave an added impulse to the commissions, and accelerated their formation from *enlaces, vocales* and other activists who could not get their interests represented in any other way, the more persistent investigators also assert that the law was a response to a series of strikes and struggles, which begs the question of how those struggles were conducted (Frères:1969). In other words, while the 1958 law may explain part of the expansion of the commissions, it comes too late to explain their emergence, and this is *a fortiori* true of yet other accounts which link this to the wave of strikes that spread across the country in 1962 (Amodia:1977), or even in 1963 (Alba:1979).

It is clearly impossible to resolve these historical questions without historical research, and it is precisely the lack of such research which makes these competing explanations so unsatisfactory. In particular, answers to the questions are unlikely to be had without close attention to the grassroots syndical initiatives of the fifties, and the ways in which these initiatives took organizational shape. For this reason, the syndical demands of a new generation of local leaders will provide the point of departure for my own reconstruction of the commissions' emergence across the country, before I proceed to 'test' these more general observations against the evidence from El Marco de Jerez. The general account will refer to the contextual variety of the commissions' appearance, but the comparison with El Marco will seek to discern what these different experiences have in common. Analytically, it is assumed that the commissions could only have surfaced in different places (more or less) simultaneously if they had some strategic kernel in common, and that this can only be discovered by minute investigation of local political process; empirically, it is my audacious claim that El Marco has a special interest as a microcosm of the larger syndical scenario because El Marco was indeed the historical birthplace of the commissions.

The first commissions were formed with the clear objective of putting the demands which had arisen from the coal face, the field or the shop floor, and which had to do largely with wages and conditions of work (Soto:1976). Thus, they might include complaints about hygiene or accidents in the workplace, or dissatisfactions with piece rates, bonuses or overtime; but in any event, once the demand had been negotiated, successfully or unsuccessfully, the commission was immediately disbanded and its members returned to the relative anonymity of the work force (Miguélez:1976). But no commentaries on the commissions, with the honourable exception of Soto (1976), are prepared to admit that in the first instance they were often self-elected groups of workers who had simply decided to speak on behalf of their fellows. Even Miguélez (1976), who insists that the strike leaders in the mines in the early sixties were all natural leaders, still thinks of them as being elected, although he admits that these militants tended to take their own initiatives, and that the commissions did take on a degree of permanence insofar as it was nearly always the same leaders who were elected on successive occasions. Moreover, he mentions that the miners in Asturias had taken advantage of the minimum legal means available for meetings and assemblies in order to sensitize more of their number to the issues, so that when they mounted the 1963 strike (itself the culmination of almost a year of partial struggles) it was propelled forward by a 'network of leaders...who enjoyed the maximum confidence of the workers'.

This ad hoc and often evanescent character of the early commissions, allied to the concrete and limited nature of their immediate demands, meant that for a time they could lead a semi-legal existence or, at the very least, that they were tolerated by the regime as long as it appeared possible to co-opt them, and harness them to the legal provisions of the 1958 Law of Collective Contracts (see Chapter 7). In this sense, Maravall (1978) can suggest that liberalizing elements within the regime saw them as a 'promising development', while even Selgas (1974), an apologist for the Vertical Syndicate, admits that during the early sixties legal and clandestine syndicalism appeared compatible. At the same time, certain employers began to by-pass the Vertical Syndicate in greater numbers, and to negotiate directly with the commissions, as the authentic representatives of the work force; and even this was tolerated while the belief existed that the commissions could infuse new energy into the corporatist structure of the Syndicate. Therefore the commissions were allowed to put down organizational roots in the years following the strike waves of 1962 and 1963, and leading up to the syndical elections of 1966.

Not surprisingly, this brought about changes in their form of organization, which are seen differently within different perspectives. Santiago Carrillo (1967) saw the main change occurring in the way the commissions themselves were constituted: in the early years commissions of militant workers came together spontaneously with the acquiescence of their workmates, whereas later on the members of the commission were indeed elected from an assembly as real representatives of the mass of workers. Maravall (1978), on the other hand, sees the commissions as changing from a 'movement' to an organization, and according to this view, it was in the second phase that the 'existing trade unions opted out'. What is the truth of these observations?

With regard to the increasing organization of the commissions, 'coordination' is the key word. The turning point came in 1964 when the commissions in the light engineering industry in Madrid set up a coordinating committee, which in turn acted as a catalyst for the development of a network of commissions in different branches of the industry throughout the country (Maravall:1978); and in December of the same year in Asturias, the coal miners met to establish their own coordinating committee at regional level, in direct imitation of the Madrid initiative (Miguélez:1976).[2] In this way commissions at plant level became coordinated first by sector in the big cities, then by geographic area outside the big cities, and finally through regional commissions which elected a national, general assembly (Frères:1969). In other words, the regional organizations were the coordinating commissions (Intercomisiones Coordinadores), which included one or two representatives from each sectoral federation. Thus the commissions, which originally had not been at all centralized or hierarchical, were converted, in Selgas's (1974) slightly slanted view, into 'political committees dedicated primarily to the work of agitation and propaganda ... at the district, local, regional and even national levels'.

THE CONTEXTUAL VARIETY OF THE COMMISSIONS' APPEARANCE

The increasing coordination of the commissions' organizations at regional and national levels did not necessarily correspond to an increasing homo-

---

[2] While this is true, the real embryo of the regional organization of the commissions in Asturias came with the Commission of the Dismissed (Comisión de Despedidos), which, as Miguélez (1976) points out, emerged as a direct result of the regime's attempt to repress the struggle in the mines.

geneity in their political composition – at least not for some time. On the contrary, it is important to insist for a moment on the diversity of their experiences in order to avoid a false impression of closely similar political colours and practices. So in Madrid, for example, the close proximity to the power centres of the Vertical Syndicate meant that many of the syndical leaders who first formed the commissions in 1963 were still imbued with Falangist philosophy, and the commissions themselves enjoyed a quasi-legal existence for their first two or three years;[3] while in Barcelona, Catholics and Communists failed to agree after the 1964 citywide assembly, and the Catholic organization continued to pursue a distinct line opposed to that of the commissions, which finally regrouped for the elections of 1966 under the dominant direction of the Communist Party.[4] The Party played a key role in overseeing the emergence of the commissions in Viscaya as well, but in the Basque Country the commissions had a strongly nationalist and even secessionist streak, and stayed aggressively independent of any outside in-fluences; whereas the Party was again important in Andalucía in providing logistical support to the young generation of workers who were active in the commissions in Puerto de Santa María, Jerez de la Frontera, Málaga and Sevilla.[5]

In this world of regional differences, the Basque Country was by far the most distinctive, and this was where the UGT had most success in practising its traditional unionism, which it often did in opposition to the workers' commissions. In May of 1961 the UGT, the CNT and the Basque trade union the STV (Solidaridad de los Trabajadores Vascos) formed the Syndical Alliance, which firmly refused any compromise with the Vertical Syndicate, and so refused to participate in syndical elections in the way the commissions had come to do (see Chapter 12). Indeed, the UGT clearly saw the com-missions as rivals which were contaminated by the presence of the Com-

[3] Even then these commissions tended to concentrate in the metalworking industries which were small enough for people to know each other. By the time of the syndical elections of 1966, 80 per cent of the elected delegates belonged to the commissions, but in the following year the Syndicate refused to 'recognize' about half of them and they were ejected from the organization. In 1967, when the commissions were finally declared illegal yet more delegates were expelled, so creating a deep divide between the Syndicate and the mass of the workers.

[4] In June of 1967 there was an open struggle between the Communist Party and the Frente Obrero de Cataluña (FOC) for control of the crucial metalworking sector, which the Party lost. It then created a new 'national commission of Cataluña', and as many of the towns and villages in fact did not have commissions, their delegates tended to be Party militants pure and simple. This national commission then assumed all kinds of powers and privileges, which was good neither for the Party nor for the movement.

[5] As indicated elsewhere, the ferocity of the Civil War and post–Civil War purges in this part of the country meant that the working-class movement had to start almost 'without intermediary generations' (Frères:1969). The great majority of militants in Andalucía at this time were not yet thirty years old.

munist Party (Frères:1969), and this attitude was acceptable to many Basques who 'have always been more anti-communist than anti-Franco' (Hermet:1974). In these circumstances, the development of the commissions in the region was delayed, where it was not thwarted altogether (Amsden:1972). But it is surely illegitimate to extrapolate general arguments from this particular experience and imply, as Maravall (1978) consistently does, that the UGT and the commissions played equally important parts in the opposition to Franco.[6] Indeed, Juan Linz (1973) argues the contrary case when he comments on the most important reasons for the rise of the commissions, and focuses on the refusal of the exiled leaders of the UGT to use the legal opportunities offered by the syndical elections, and their adherence to a traditional and outmoded unionism.

This is not to suggest that everywhere outside of the Basque Country it was the commissions alone which constituted the whole of the working-class movement.[7] A number of other groups had grown out of the lay apostolic associations, the most important being the Workers' Syndical Union, or USO (Union Sindical Obrera). USO members included both left-wing Catholics from the HOAC and socialists, and although it became more socialist than Catholic as the years passed, it never lost its strong 'anti-Communist bias' (Amsden:1972). As the largest of the alternative organizations to the commissions, it had a presence in most regions of the country, unlike many smaller groups such as ASO (Alianza Sindical Obrera), which itself fused with USO by the end of 1965, or AST (Acción Sindical de

---

[6] Maravall (1978) talks on page 43 of the commissions as a grass-roots movement but goes on to add that 'the traditional labour unions and the UGT in particular, also experienced a sharp growth resulting from the new dynamics in industrial relations'. This is a frankly misleading statement, as the UGT did not begin to play a significant part in these relations until well into the 1970s. He also says that the UGT joined the new working-class movement which had spread rapidly throughout the country, and especially in the Basque engineering industry, and 'supported the factory committees against the official trade union by trying to turn them into an open challenge to the State-led sindicatos'. He brings no facts to support this assertion, but as part of the legerdemain which is designed to present the UGT and the commissions as having equal political weight, he continually makes a tendentious distinction between the 'elected workers' committees' (by which he must mean the *jurados*) and the 'organized commissions'. Later analysis will demonstrate that it is impossible to separate the two, so intertwined did they become within the democratic project, but the distinction is made to underplay the importance of the Communist Party (especially in the coordination of the movement) and to inflate the really very minor role of the UGT.

[7] Reference here is confined to some of the syndical groups, and no mention is made of the many neighbourhood associations which began to emerge in various ways from about 1967.

The Youth Commissions, which were approved by a general assembly of the commissions in Madrid in the same year, became very politicized in very different directions during the harsh repression of the late sixties and the state of siege of 1969.

Trabajo), whose left Catholic activists finally joined with the commissions. Thus, some but not all of the Catholic groups were consciously opposed to communism, and more particularly the Communist Party, while still entertaining vague notions of socialism; and even some of the Catholic militants who themselves joined the commissions remained in them to counter the influence of the Party, sometimes proving a divisive element because of their moral condemnation of political manoeuvres (Frères:1969). For all that, and despite the constraints imposed on the communication of differing views by the conditions of clandestinity, nearly all the leaders of the commissions during their early years were either Communist or left Catholic, such were the strange bedfellows made by the struggle for democracy.

IDEOLOGICAL DIVERSITY AND
STRATEGIC DIRECTION

Nonetheless, with the increasing coordination of the commissions, tensions arose between those militants, including anarchists, socialists and even left Falangists, on the one hand, who had been attracted to the movement by its success in negotiating higher wages and by its unitarian, syndicalist thrust; and those Communist and Catholic activists on the other, who were the animating force behind the construction of its political organization. Eventually these strains led to the loss of the USO in 1967 (and lesser groups a year or two later), which left the syndical field open to the increasing influence of the Communist Party. To some degree the splits were directly due to differing political affiliations or convictions, but at the same time they reflected the more general difficulty of finding the impossible compromise[8] between the immediately representative, highly flexible and directly accountable commissions of the beginning years, and the bureaucratic and operational requirements of a relatively sophisticated and increasingly stable and centralized organization. And, as will become clear, this general difficulty had a particular stamp in El Marco de Jerez, where the new syndical practices had to adapt the direct democracy of its broadly anarchist traditions to the tight clandestine control and coordination of the Communist Party (or vice versa).

---

[8] In general, as Soto (1976) notes, 'the working class movement was a mixture of spontaneity with a greater or lesser degree of systematization and conscious action', and the compromise in question was clearly more difficult in regions with 'spontaneous' and anti-bureaucratic traditions of struggle. Such a tradition was present both in El Marco de Jerez (see later in this chapter) and in the Asturian mines, where previous syndical initiatives at regional level, namely the *Sindicato Minero* of 1911 and the *Sindicato Unico* of 1934, had depended both on total unity and on mass participation.

By the mid-1960s the commissions were expanding rapidly and, although the other opposition labour groups had far from disappeared, it was the syndical practice of the commissions which was fast becoming hegemonic within the labour movement (Mujal-León:1983; see also Chapter 7). Their new political status was reflected in the national documents they published in 1966, where they clearly assumed the leadership of this movement, and in the results of the syndical elections of September that year, when an 80 per cent turn-out assured them an overwhelming victory. At the time, the liberalization measures announced by the government, such as the modification of Article 222 of the Penal Code, were interpreted by some as signs of the regime's weakness, and many believed that the commissions were about to take over from the Vertical Syndicate. They had campaigned openly for the elections (Amsden:1972), and in Asturias, for example, had taken the decision to set up permanent commissions at plant, local and provincial levels to prepare for them (Miguélez:1976); and in the wake of victory, and following the political line of the Communist Party, the commissions 'came out' and launched their audacious demand for legalization. As Marcelino Camacho put it (quoted in Vilar:1976), 'only mass action can assure success in our daily struggle ... and it is impossible to think of a mass movement which is clandestine'.

It is at this moment that the assembly became central to the syndical practice of the commissions. In Asturias, once the regional assembly of June 1966 had decided on the creation of a commission in every workplace, they were now freely elected in assemblies that were held at the end of the day's work; and the work of the commissions was now both intense and open, with the Provincial Mining Commission representing commissions throughout the region before employers and State authorities, signing agreements, and attending assemblies in the workplaces (Miguélez:1976). Elsewhere, as 1967 approached, the convocation of the assembly had nearly everywhere replaced the spontaneous assumption of representative roles by the natural leaders, and the assembly became the key instrument of participation and decision making in the movement. Mass participation was now the watchword, and this participation was to be achieved not through party programmes of any kind but through a unitarian syndical practice that was above ideological diversity. In 1967 the commissions held their first general assembly at national level, with many of the delegates using the resources available to them through their posts in the Vertical Syndicate to make the journey to Madrid (Soto:1976). In short, as Soto (1976) puts it, 'it is the assembly which gives life and continuity to the commission by converting it into the delegation of the work force as a whole'. In other words, the open assembly, as a characteristic means of legitimizing the commission and advancing the aims of the democratic movement overall, came *after* the commission, and this conversion of the commission coincided with the conjunctural possibilities of a specific stage in the struggle. And although this conclusion runs contrary to the attractive myth that the assembly was democratically constitutive of the commission, it is more faithful to the real development of the working-class movement, which began with small groups of self-elected and natural leaders.

OPEN STRUGGLE AND POLITICAL REPRESSION

It was historically inevitable that such an instrument of direct democracy as the assembly should have developed late in the contest with a highly authoritarian and repressive regime, but even at this stage none of the activities conducted within the assemblies were legal, however open a challenge they now presented to this regime. The commissions had followed their victory in the September 1966 syndical elections with a campaign to boycott the December referendum on the Organic Law of the State and to mount a nationwide demonstration in the January of the following year. But far from presaging the disintegration of the regime, their electoral victory and the mobilizations which followed provoked a massive wave of repression throughout the country, and hundreds of the commissions' leaders were arrested (Mujal-León:1983).[9] Moreover, their very success in the syndical elections had revealed the identity of these men and left them further exposed to political reprisals (Amsden:1972). And these continued unabated following the Supreme Court ruling later that year that the commissions were dependent on the Communist Party and were therefore an illegal political association.[10] In short, the commissions paid a high price for Communist Party insistence that they operate openly, and it is reckoned that between thirty and fifty thousand *enlaces* and *vocales* were dismissed from their jobs over the years 1966 to 1975, and many of them arrested. Hence, although the repression did not destroy the movement, but on the contrary transformed the commissions into the single national symbol of labour opposition to the regime, the debate still continues as to whether 'coming out' was a political error or an inspired strategic decision (Mujal-León:1983).

There is no doubt that the repression succeeded in decimating many of

---

[9] In an article first written for the Opus Dei review called *Mundo*, but which was then suppressed, and later translated and published in *International Socialism* (no. 33, Summer 1968), it was said that 'the most curious feature of their workers' movement is that they appear to have been born headless as it were. From the beginning the commissions have involved a collective organization in which, when it comes to voting or pronouncing an opinion, each person counts'. This is another example of the rather romanticized myth of the birth and growth of the commissions which still has considerable currency; but there was more than some justification for it in the late sixties when the commissions, though not born 'headless', had certainly been 'beheaded' by the repression.

[10] This measure was taken *faute de mieux*. As the regime clearly could not dismantle the *jurados* or outlaw collective bargaining, it declared the commissions illegal.

the provincial and regional organizations, and this success was reinforced by the state of siege imposed across the country in 1969. And although combativeness in the fields and on the shop floor did not diminish, the movement as a whole entered into crisis as it was forced back into clandestinity. Once again the syndical practice of the commissions in each workplace was carried on by the 'three or four men trusted by everybody... through a very informal organization which often had to do without debates or assemblies' (Miguélez:1976); and the struggle continued, often on the basis of solidarity actions, which now made amnesty one of the central demands of the movement. Nonetheless, the repression was certainly responsible for the crisis in the commissions of Madrid, which led to the withdrawal of USO in June 1967 (Hermet:1974); and this was followed by similar splits in the organization in Asturias (Miguélez:1976) and throughout the country.[11] These splits represented both strategic and ideological divergences between the Communists and the Catholics, who objected both to the supposed subordination of the commissions to the Party, and to the price they were paying for the Party's policy of open struggle. The result was that there was no longer full unity of action in key regions like Madrid and Asturias, whereas in the Basque Country the combined effect of the splits and a further wave of arrests in the autumn of this year left the commissions in complete disarray. Paradoxically, at the same time that USO and other Catholic tendencies were withdrawing from the commissions, more and more priests were entering the struggle, and during these years of hard repression succeeded in making hundreds of meetings possible and secure, which would have been not one nor the other without their help: by the end of the decade 'Catholic Spain' had more priests pursued and imprisoned than any other country in the world (Frères:1969).

The working-class movement certainly lost impetus in the late sixties and early seventies because of the repression unleashed against it. And the repression continued until the end of the dictatorship. In June 1972 several of the key figures in the workers' commissions, such as Soto, Saborido, Acosta, Camacho and Ariza, were arrested in Madrid, where they were planning a national overhaul of the commissions' organization; and the damage dealt to the national leadership by these arrests had its repercussions in regions such as El Marco de Jerez, where the local leaders were also in prison and where the local organization was in need of firm national guidance. But after the so-called 1001 trial of these national leaders in 1973, there was a resurgence of the movement, until in the syndical elections of June 1975 the commissions captured as many as 80 per cent of the posts (Arango:1978). Even Selgas (1974) acknowledged this recrudescence of the struggle, and the commissions were so far recovered by 1974 that they won

---

[11] Once again it is indicative of Maravall's (1978) misleading bias that he could say that 'the other organizations – UGT and USO in particular – were not affected by the internal difficulties of the comisiones'.

recognition from the International Labour Organization as the real representatives of Spanish labour (Ayucar:1976).

The debate within the movement at this time, and throughout the so-called transition to democracy, was whether to constitute the commissions as a traditional trade union, and in a meeting of all the rural commissions in Córdoba (Andalucía) in 1976 it was left clear that they, at least, wanted to continue as a movement. In the subsequent (and still illegal) national congress of the commissions in Barcelona, the decision went the other way, partly for fear of losing members to the UGT, which was already tolerated by the regime and was organizing fast with financial and logistical support from the Socialist International (see Chapter 13). But in El Marco de Jerez the commissions' leaders were true both to their traditions and to their practice in wanting to maintain the movement, and although they accepted the national directives, they would have preferred a unitary and plural syndicalism of the kind constantly advocated by Marcelino Camacho. To their minds, this accorded better both with the thrust of their syndical practice (studied in Chapter 7), and with the organizational style which had characterized the emergence of the commissions in the region.

THE EMERGENCE OF THE COMMISSIONS IN EL MARCO DE JEREZ

Contrary to the pervasive myth of La Camocha, the historical evidence suggests that the commissions first appeared in El Marco de Jerez. In El Marco they may have passed unnoticed at first, in a way they could not in the enclosed work environment of the mines of Asturias, and the different traditions of struggle in the two regions may have produced distinct organizational styles; but nonetheless the two experiences had much in common. In both places the commissions appeared after long periods of brutal repression, and had to confront a system of repression which had its own theory and its own special apparatuses. In these circumstances the commissions had to advance demands that derived not from the rights of the workers (which were anyway not recognized by the regime), but rather from their real and immediate needs; and the corollary of this was that only workers who themselves felt these needs could put such demands. So the leaders of the movement were workers who had won the confidence of their workmates in the conversations carried on while changing clothes in the factory or travelling to work in the countryside, and who were able to raise the issues closest to their hearts. And as such workers were recognized, and as they recognized each other, there emerged networks of natural leaders, none of whom had aspired to leadership, much less imagined a political struggle. Their demands were not at first political, but they finally provoked direct confrontation with the dictatorship; and in the struggle which ensued, *needs* and *networks* were the keys to the strength of the commissions.

The commissions in El Marco de Jerez began with a handful of men meeting during the course of their work in the vineyards; and if there was not time enough during their work breaks, then they would meet in the local bar in the evening, or in the woods and fields by night. These first restless men all came from Sanlúcar and included Emilio Fábregas, Paco Chicorro, Juan 'El Pintor' Rodríguez and Juan and Manolo Romero Pasos. They say that the struggle began in November 1953, with the first spontaneous strike in the vineyards. There was no organization as such. They just walked off the fields at the same time and returned to the *pueblo*. No one really knew who gave the word. Eduardo Sánchez supported this and other strikes without knowing how they started; and once he had proved his mettle he was brought into the network of leaders. After this first spontaneous stoppage the syndical authorities wanted to meet with the leaders. 'Let the representatives step forward'. But there were no such representatives, and so they happened to pull out Emilio Fábregas's cousin, by force. Emilio followed him into the office, and, as he knew something about the wage regulations, he began to talk. In that first meeting he won his point, and others began to listen. The authorities, in turn, tried to defuse the situation by persuading some of the old anarchist militants to serve as representatives of the workers, which under threats from the Civil Guard they were prepared to do. But this 'old guard' of an outmoded unionism was not able to impose its own line on the younger generation, because in cooperating with the syndical authorities they had lost all credibility. From this moment it was the network of new leaders who carried conviction. There is no doubt in the mind of Antonio Alvarez, for example, that the movement in El Marco began when Emilio Fábregas decided to open his mouth.

The demands these new men made were very concrete and mainly had to do either with wages or with conditions of work. They are very clear that if they had talked of a political struggle, no one would have followed them; but this was anyway the last thing on their minds. The incipient commissions were designed to negotiate economic demands, not political ones, and it was this thrust which gave the movement impetus enough to lift off. One such demand was to change the so-called *socorro* or aid, which had started as food rations for the hungry in wintertime, to a more equitable system of money payments for the unemployed which were made all year round; and some say that this inspired the coalescence of the first commission in Sanlúcar in the year 1955 or 1956. Emilio Fábregas, on the other hand, believes the first commission to have been formed over wage demands: their idea, in his view, was very conservative insofar as they simply asked for the Francoist laws to be applied correctly; but their success in this gave a further impulse to organize around new demands, and in particular that they should have four rest periods, or *cigarros*, during the working day (as they had had during the Republic), and that these should be included in their eight paid hours. Yet others suggest that the first commissions were in fact strike commissions, which were first formed at the beginning of the 1950s to direct a strike and then immediately disbanded. In this version, the leaders drew on the experiences of the spotty and unsuccessful strike actions of the forties to form commissions which could decide strategy and ensure solidarity.

Whatever motivated the commissions, and all these motives probably played a part, they were at first nothing more than the meetings held in an old *bodega* or in the workers' dormitory in the vineyards, where from Monday to Saturday the workers slept on the floor with the pigs and the chickens, as they had always done. But it is said that whereas in other regions of the country where strikes had begun to take place the commissions were disbanded (if they were not first arrested), in Sanlúcar they were permanent from the beginning, insofar as they always reappeared with the same members. So, at least from the time of the third strike commission of 1955, the commission met more regularly in order to negotiate wages, organize strikes and 'control' the *vocales* inside the Vertical Syndicate; and by 1957 they had established a sufficiently stable organization at the level of the *pueblo* for some, still surreptitious, assemblies to be held. Nonetheless, in this year there could not have been more than a dozen regular leaders of the movement in all of El Marco, and these included Manolo Romero and his brother, Emilio Fábregas, Paco de las Flores, Manuel Romero Ruíz, Miguel Campo and Antonio Palacios. They had no outside guidance for what they were doing, and still less any theory which could inform their practice. Yet by mounting strikes in the way they did they had effectively absorbed the lessons inculcated by the Communist Party on Radio Pirenaica long before the Communists of El Puerto themselves. Thus, in these first years even the leaders were without political affiliations, and they joined together in making a workers' commission 'in their fashion' (*a nuestro aire*),[12] united only by their opposition to the dictatorship.

Nevertheless, from the very beginning nearly all these leaders were shop stewards or *vocales* within the Vertical Syndicate. Quite without paradox, they sought each other out and began to organize within the Syndicate, at a time when elsewhere in the country, especially in the countryside, employers were stacking the Syndicate with representatives loyal to themselves. Indeed, it was through the Syndicate that the leaders contacted and informed the workers, and through their work in the Syndicate that they won legitimacy. And in organizing slates for the syndical elections they effectively *made* the commissions. Such a conscious strategy was operative from about 1956, and in 1958 the commissions were already able to win a large number

---

[12] It is illustrative that the important part Emilio Fábregas played was to some extent accidental. Many of the first meetings of the commission in Sanlúcar took place outside of the town in Monte Olivetti, which was near his home. So he came along out of curiosity, and as soon as he began to speak out he was given the job of chief negotiator.

of syndical posts; and even though the question of the *socorro* was not negotiated through the Syndicate, the yearly wage contracts were – one indication of the early and effective presence of the commissions within it. In this way the commissions got an immediate political cover for their activities, and their meetings could be held under the auspices of the Syndicate, at a time when meetings in any other location were fraught with danger.[13] Indeed, the notion that free assemblies took place in this period is not only ignorant but naïve: later on small meetings were held, often under cover of darkness, in the countryside, but with never more than twenty or so persons present. But in the Syndicate the leaders, in representing the workers officially, could come to belong to a commission without even voicing the word; and if their representation was ineffective, they could then move outside to organize the strike.

The first people to go on strike for better wages were the vineyard workers of Sanlúcar, and over the first years of the struggle Sanlúcar was always ahead of the other *pueblos* which finally joined the movement. At this time news of an impending strike would be heard in the vineyards, where hundreds of workers from different *pueblos* were concentrated; but there was no coordination between the *pueblos* themselves, and strike action tended to be poorly organized and patchy. Yet as early as 1954 the commission in Sanlúcar was keen to contact other *pueblos* and begin to build a broader network of leaders. In this year Manolo Romero was chosen from the small group which included Paco Chicorro, Pancaro and Manolo Seco to make contact with Trebujena, and although some of their number resisted the initiative on the grounds that the workers of Trebujena were 'scabs', Manolo won the argument and was subsequently vindicated by the militant solidarity of Trebujena in all subsequent strikes. Indeed, some of the most bitter confrontations in the following years took place between Trebujena and Lebrija, a town some few kilometres to the north but outside the confines of El Marco, which on several occasions supplied blacklegs to replace the striking workers of Trebujena. At about the same time Manolo Romero and Pancaro had met, with less success, with representatives from San Fernando and Jerez, who included Catholics from the HOAC and even some Falangists, with the idea of concerting the struggle of the vineyard workers on the one hand and the metalworkers of the Bahía de Cádiz on the other; but this initiative proved premature.

Gradually, however, as the commissions in each *pueblo* took on a more stable configuration, the contacts between them became more effective and

---

[13] Thus, for example, the enrollment for a June 1963 course on 'Work Security and Hygiene' run by the Syndicate includes Emilio Fábregas García, José Raposo Rodríguez, Juan Romero Pasos, Manuel Romero Pasos, Nicolás Ruíz Gómez ('Pancaro') and Eduardo Sánchez Fernández, who were all there, organizing the commissions (OSE:1963a).

the networks of leaders began to spread. Juan Flores remembers travelling to make contacts with such leaders in Sanlúcar, El Puerto and Trebujena in 1956 at the time of the renewal of the wage contract in the vineyards; and although these contacts were above all personal, they were not the less binding for that, and a semi-permanent organization began to emerge across the region as a whole. Manolo Romero and Antonio Palacios distinguished themselves in these early efforts at regional coordination, and El Puerto had a more or less permanent commission by 1958 or 1959, Chipiona by 1963, and Jerez by 1965 or so. Although many of these contacts, as already indicated, were made *through* the Vertical Syndicate, the objective was to form an autonomous syndical movement not just in the vineyards but also in agriculture in general and in local industry; and so, progressively, not only Sanlúcar, Trebujena and El Puerto, but also San Fernando and Jerez were brought into the net, until by 1962 or 1963 the commissions were mainly coordinated throughout El Marco de Jerez. Some say that the final impulse in this direction came in response to the vineyard owners' attempt to split the work force by introducing greater numbers of *fijos*, or workers on fixed contracts, from 1961 and 1962; others say that this coordination required the logistical leverage of the Communist Party, which was only ready to provide it at this time. But whatever the truth of these assertions, the final impression is that even now the commissions continued to grow in an ad hoc fashion, without any overall plan of coordination, and still almost entirely dependent on the contacts between such individuals as Paco Cabral, Miguel Campo and the Melillos brothers in Trebujena; the Romero brothers in Sanlúcar; and Francisco Valles and Pepe Rosa in Jerez.

As these contacts continued between the different *pueblos*, efforts were made to recruit more militants to the movement, whatever their political persuasion; and the Catholic associations, which had a not insignificant presence in Sanlúcar, El Puerto, Jerez and Cádiz, contributed a good number.[14] Hence, the ranks of the movement were swelled by recruits from the HOAC, the JOC, USO, and in El Puerto even the UGT; and when later in the sixties USO withdrew from the commissions nationally, their militants stayed solid in El Marco. But there is no doubt that it was the Communist

---

[14] It certainly helped the cause that the Bishop of Cádiz, Antonio Anoveros, was sympathetic to the aims of the commissions and offered them moral if not material support. He exerted pressure to have Federico Iglesias and Antonio Alvarez released from gaol in 1968, and embraced them as comrades when once they were free. Pepe Jiménez recalls that he contacted the bishop when he went to Cádiz to teach the shipyard workers how to build and operate a stencil machine, and after the 'purge' of early 1970 the bishop visited the prisoners in gaol on their saints' days, and argued their case as political prisoners to the prison authorities. Franco would dearly have liked to have him removed, but as, under the Concordat of 1953, he was a direct appointee of the Pope, this was no easy proposition. Later, Anoveros was assigned to a bishopric in the Basque Country.

Party which contributed most to the progressive coordination of the commissions, even if it did not take the initiative in this regard. Pepe Jiménez and Paco Artola both recall a meeting between network leaders and Benítez Rufo in the Venta El Corneta, San Fernando, where Francisco Valles and especially Pepe Rosa from Jerez suggested mounting simultaneous struggles in different places through the structure of the Vertical Syndicate. Rufo himself was clearly reluctant to bring the commissions out into the open too soon, but in a regional preview of national strategy, the Party began to push for more strikes and more open protests; and this resulted in both organizational and personal strains between Party and commissions (see Chapter 11). In particular, Emilio Fábregas, who was by now the undisputed leader of the syndical struggle, was criticized by Party members for his overcautious attitude and repeated reluctance to launch strikes. He was seen as trying to hold back the movement and hobble the initiatives of such men as Paco de las Flores and Manolo Romero, who was the chief political strategist of the movement. But despite such strains, which brought Manolo and Emilio into the second of several increasingly bitter confrontations in 1966,[15] the high though far from complete degree of correspondence between Party membership and syndical militancy ensured a progressively more stable if locally uneven organization for the commissions over the period of the sixties.

In 1960 a small network of leaders emerged inside the wine and alcohol syndicate of the *bodega* Caballero, and this was the nucleus of what was to become the most powerful of all the urban syndicates or *gremios* of El Marco. The network was headed by Antonio Alvarez, and the informal commission which came to dominate this sector was run by a team of his lieutenants including José Manuel Revuelta, Pepe Serrano, José Arroyo, José Marroquín Gómez, José Marroquín Travieso and Santiago Torres. Under Alvarez's leadership this commission was so successful in winning wage rises and improvements in working conditions that not only did it set an example for the commissions in the other sectors to follow it also made Alvarez the chief protagonist of the struggle inside the *pueblos*. Thus, when the commissions took off as a mass movement locally, which, if anything, anticipated their coming out nationally, their regional organization revolved around the axis which ran from the vineyards under the leadership of Emilio Fábregas, Paco de las Flores and Manolo Romero, to the *bodegas* under the leadership of Antonio Alvarez. In effect, the rise of Alvarez accompanied

[15] It is said that Emilio was in the Party, if only for a short time (which he himself denies), but then left, to avoid jeopardizing his official posts in the Vertical Syndicate. But it is the suspicion that he dissembled which most worries the militants of that time; and they refer to the draft statutes of the workers' commissions which Rufo brought back to El Marco from a meeting with Marcelino Camacho in Madrid and entrusted to Emilio, who then not only misplaced them but replaced them with a document which was similar but not the same.

the increasingly open struggle advocated by the Communist Party, one of whose objectives was to bring the natural syndical leaders into its own organization; and the coming out of the commissions nationally was reinforced locally by an extension of the strategic axis of the struggle from the countryside to the towns. This growth in the global organization of the movement was reflected in the assemblies of the workers' commissions of Andalucía which took place in 1967 and 1968, and in the first regional meeting of the rural commissions in 1968; but the impetus of the local movement found its fullest expression in the sixty-three-day strike launched in December 1969, which was conducted and coordinated by the commissions alone across the whole of the region and most of the province. In this instance both the strike itself and its conduct were decided in assemblies which were repeated in all the syndicates of Sanlúcar and El Puerto (*Mundo Obrero*:23.1.1970), and this extraordinary example of direct democracy at work made El Marco a flag bearer of the movement throughout the south of Spain.

Throughout this time the men of the commissions ran in the Vertical elections, and in the first instance they did so simply to make their demands heard. Antonio Alvarez first put together a slate for these elections in 1962, and despite the opposition of the older representatives who had already been co-opted by the system, his list of candidates was successful enough to cement the birth of the *bodegas*' commission; whereas Federico Iglesias was successful in persuading the construction workers' syndicate to accept his informal commission as an authentic negotiating body in 1964, two years before his success in the syndical elections of 1966. Once Alvarez had won the first round, his commission began to contact networks of leaders amongst the building and metal workers in order to organize a concerted assault on the Vertical Syndicate and get their men elected in place of the so-called verticalists. These commissions continued to win legitimacy in the way they had learned to do from the beginning, by solving the immediate and concrete problems of the workers they represented; with the difference that they now sought to organize whole sectors for wage negotiations as well as to capture the lower echelons of the Syndicate for their own purposes. To do this, Alvarez insists, they worked with all political tendencies and tried to stay as close as possible to the workers they represented. Thus, by the time of the syndical elections of 1966 when the workers' commissions nationally were all set to come out into the open, the commissions locally were ready to take over the presidency of the social sections of all the most important syndicates or *gremios*, with Federico Iglesias as president of the building workers, Miguel Marroquín of graphic arts, Antonio Alvarez himself at the head of wine and alcohol, and fishing and light engineering also directed by the commissions. It was the same story in Trebujena, where the commissions won all the posts in the social sections of the Syndicate with an absolute majority; while Emilio Fábregas in Sanlúcar rose first to be president of the provincial workers' council and finally became the only rural worker in the whole of Spain ever to preside over the National Council. Once these posts were under the control of the commissions, they then had an operational base and an institutional cover for their own activities, which for the moment looked unstoppable. Why, the president of each social section had an office, with its own key! They had arrived!

The repression unleashed in 1970 (recounted in detail in Chapters 9 and 10) hit the commissions very hard indeed. Most of the syndical posts they had won were now lost again. Many of their leaders were in prison, and there was no national guidance to compensate for their absence, especially after the infamous 1001 trial. Antonio Alvarez, the unquestioned local leader, was also in prison, and on his release was ordered by the Communist Party to concentrate his efforts on resurrecting the Party organization, not that of the commissions. Notwithstanding the orders, as soon as he was freed in 1972 he rented houses to serve as offices of the commissions in Sanlúcar, Trebujena, Jerez and El Puerto, and begged furniture from local stores and banks to fill them. And while continuing to work in the *bodega* by day, he worked for the commissions by night. Slowly the organization of the commissions was consolidated once more; with the difference that now the negotiations with employers on the one hand, and the meetings with the local and police authorities on the other, regularly took place outside of the structure of the Vertical Syndicate. Indeed, by 1974 the commissions had achieved real liberty of expression and association, even in Jerez, the most 'bourgeois' town of El Marco; and were very much in control of the labour process and wage negotiations in the vineyards. But their directly democratic organizational style remained the same, with the assembly dominating their syndical practice and making them immediately accountable for the conduct of both negotiations and strikes. So when in 1975 the debates surfaced over the convocation of a Constituent Congress for converting the movement into a union, the commissions of El Marco were firmly against it. In their view, unity was achieved through practice, not through doctrine or rules, and there was little point in attempting to establish a unitary union before being sure of that unity. In effect, it was in the context of the congress that the splits began.[16]

---

[16] These splits, discussed in Chapter 13, did not finally damage the performance or presence of the commissions in El Marco or elsewhere in the province of Cádiz. In 1976 there were some 3,000 members of the commissions in Jerez, 2,500 in Sanlúcar and 1,200 in Trebujena, out of a total of about 20,000 members for the province as a whole in 1977 (membership was increasing very rapidly over these years). In February 1977 the Workers' Commissions of Andalucía were constituted, and, in May 1978, out of a total of 373,417 rural workers in Andalucía, 89,586, or 24 per cent, were members of the commissions; while 13.3 per cent, or 20,576 out of a total work force of 154,365, were members in the province of Cádiz alone. The commissions maintained offices in thirty-four of the forty-two municipalities of the province.

7

Wage contracts, labour conflicts and political protests: the syndical practices of the labour movement

> They were two worlds only waiting for a sign from history to destroy each other.
>
> Alvarez de Toledo, *The Strike*

DURING THE TIMES of the Republic labour and capital engaged in direct collective bargaining under the supervision of the State, and every worker carried a copy of his contract in his pocket. This contract contained the clauses which established both the wage rate and the conditions of work, and so composed the so-called *bases* which had been agreed between the employers' commission and the 'workers' commission' (*comisión obrera*) in the presence of the delegate of public order. These commissions sat together to negotiate on a mixed committee (*jurado mixto*), which had considerable power to promote agreement, but which was susceptible to political pressure. In El Marco de Jerez, for example, the working day in the vineyards had always been from sunrise to sunset, but by the end of the Popular Front government the actual working day had fallen to a mere four and a half hours. This situation was rapidly reversed with the successful insurrection of Franco, but in the years which followed, both the Falange, or the Movement which shaped the *jurados* within the Vertical Syndicate, and the working-class movement which spawned the workers' commissions, sought to legitimate their respective syndical practices by invoking the representative forms of the Republic.[1]

From the Civil War until 1958 wages were set by the regulations or *reglamentaciones* of the Ministry of Labour, while the conditions of work in each factory and field were fixed by the 'work rules' (*reglamentos del régimen interior*) (Amsden:1972; Amodia:1977; Wright:1977), which were vetted by the relevant department of the same ministry. On the evidence

---

[1] As the courts which 'tried' Communists and Republicans during the Civil War and afterwards were called *comisiones de guerra*, the term *comisión* was not one which could be easily integrated into the discourse of the Falangist 'Movement'.

from the province of Cádiz during the forties, such regulations were remarkable for their complexity and their rigidity; while in the early years
they also carried clauses governing labour–work ratios and apprenticeship
schemes, which reflected the 'national socialism' of the Falange. Thus the
regulation setting wages in the vineyards in 1947 specified no fewer than
eighteen separate production tasks, each with distinct rates of remuneration;
while the wives of agricultural labourers could work at 60 per cent of the
male rate, although their wages had to be paid to their husbands. But the
bottom line in all these regulations raised the working day to eight hours
or more for lower wages than had obtained during the Republic, as well as
suppressing the customary rest periods, or *cigarros*, of the vineyard workers.
Nonetheless, they continued to be better paid than the majority of rural
labourers, and the regulations always used the wage scale of Sanlúcar as
the bench-mark for rates in vineyards elsewhere; while a straw mattress to
sleep on and cold water to wash in meant that they had maintained their
relatively privileged working conditions too. What was absolutely forbidden
was the negotiation of any independent agreement with the employers or,
in this case, the vineyard owners, who would simply call a meeting inside
the Vertical Syndicate to announce the wage level for the year.

It was not unknown, however, for management to reach informal agreements with groups of workers in this period, and from the middle of the
decade of the fifties a wage drift was discernible in some sectors, which
began to widen the gap between official and real wages (Maravall:1978).
The government had decreed elections for the *jurados de empresa* as early
as 1947, but they were not operational until 1953 and even then were
relatively isolated from the main body of workers, as indeed they were
intended to be. So employers had to seek a way around this
(un)representative body and find more flexibility than the regulations allowed them; and the government, too, had reason to be preoccupied with
the increasingly widespread agitation caused by hunger and deprivation.
The Vertical Syndicate had called the Third National Congress of Workers
in 1955 to address this question, and despite considerable manipulation of
the proceedings, this congress had approved a three-point programme for
a minimum wage on a sliding scale for an eight-hour day; equal pay for
equal work; and social security for the unemployed (*Mundo Obrero*:15.7.1955; FSM:1959; Ibarruri et al.:1964). But the oligarchy of El
Marco de Jerez remained unmoved by the desperate social conditions of
their workers, and their independent bargaining activities were all in the
direction of reducing the official wage rather than raising it. Hence in 1953,
even though the regulation for the vineyards decreed a ten-peseta increase,
they decided unilaterally to pay only five, and the vineyard workers had to
stop work for twenty days to get the full increase (even the provincial
delegate had to agree that they were right, and so could stop work without
actually 'going on strike'); and in the following year the owners tried to

recuperate part of this 'loss' by reducing wages by five pesetas in November, when the working day in the vineyards dropped from eight to seven hours as it did every year for the four winter months, even though the regulation made no such provision. Once again, it required a short, sharp and spontaneous strike[2] to maintain the full wage, which was assailed by a similar maneouvre two or three years later, only to meet with a similar response; and insofar as these strikes catalysed the incipient organization of the vineyard workers, then the greed of the oligarchy certainly contributed to the emergence of the commissions.

With the decree of the Law of Collective Contracts in 1958, however, wage rates were no longer tabulated by the Ministry of Labour but were negotiated between management and labour within the framework of the Vertical Syndicate, in a move most commentators agree was intended to raise the productivity of industry and rationalize the labour process (Arango:1978; Maravall:1978; Mujal-León:1983). The collective contracts which resulted subsumed both the regulations and the work rules,[3] but emphasis was still on agreement within the Vertical Syndicate rather than on the bargaining process itself, and to some extent, as Amodia (1977) suggests, 'the Syndicate was bargaining and reaching an agreement with itself'. In effect, bargaining could take place either on the *jurado*, so highlighting the role of the *vocales* inside the workplace, or between employers' and workers' representatives (the social and economic sections) in the local, provincial or national headquarters of the Syndicate (see Chapter 5); and the resulting contracts could in principle apply to all factories in a particular sector, a group of factories, any one factory, or groups of workers within a factory (Wright:1977), as long as the factory or factories in question had at least fifty employees (Mujal-León:1983).[4] In the course of such negotiations at factory level the chair of the *jurado* would be taken over by an official of the Syndicate nominated by the provincial delegate, and syndical consultants and a secretary were also present and expected to take part; while at local or provincial level the arrangements were the same, but with

---

[2] Emilio Fábregas tells the story of the fellow worker who called across to him, having learned of the five peseta (or *duro*) decrease during the rest period (or *cigarro*), 'What are you going to do about it, cousin?'. And Emilio replied, 'Well, I'm not working' ('Bueno. Así no vengo'). And so the commissions were born in El Marco de Jerez (which is as magical a myth as that of La Camocha in Asturias).

[3] In 1961 new norms were decreed which obliged certain firms to promulgate their own 'work rules'; but in most cases this was a routine exercise with no impact on the real bargaining process.

[4] Negotiations could be requested either by the social or economic sections of the Syndicate for regional contracts, or by the *jurado* or management for the factory, or even by shop stewards in the smaller firms, and the request, with its accompanying report, had to be put in the first instance to the provincial delegate. Once at the negotiating table, discussions could include not only wages but also official employment and social security policies.

the representatives from both sides being indirectly elected in the usual way. Thus, the law simply transferred the first instance of arbitration from the Ministry of Labour to the Syndicate, so letting the workers bargain 'without letting go of them' (Candel:1968).

Hence, despite the new law, and contrary to the conclusions of Mujal-León (1979;1983), negotiations continued to take place within the structure of the Syndicate, and if employers and workers wished to negotiate directly one with the other they still had to do so illegally. So Maravall (1978) seems to overestimate the scope of the institutional changes when he argues that they came as a result of tensions which could not be contained within the corporatist structure of the Syndicate. The Syndicate underwent surgery after the damage sustained from the rising rhythm of working-class struggles in the fifties (see later in this chapter), and even if this allowed a higher rate of absorption of opposition shop stewards into its apparatus, it did not make it a more valid form of representation for the workers overall (Amsden:1972). But what is beyond doubt is the impact the changes had on the process of collective bargaining, especially in the larger firms (Candel:1968), and the stimulus they gave to syndical practices designed to put some muscle into the workers' demands. In effect, negotiations either led to agreement and were then approved, which was possible in the more modern enterprises where employers and commissions had reached some modus operandi, once the commissions had adopted the strategy of working within the official institutions for the purposes of collective bargaining (Amsden:1972; and see Chapter 12); or talks broke down and wage levels were decided by compulsory arbitration, through the Ministry of Labour. Where employers were of a less modern or more intransigent type, as they most certainly were in El Marco de Jerez, then, as the years passed, the breakdown of negotiations was increasingly followed by strike action, before the application of the 'compulsory norms' (*normas de obligado cumplimiento*), or NOCs, by the Ministry.

The change-over from the regulations to collective contracts could only come gradually, and the percentage of workers without such contracts remained high even as late as 1969, when the figure was 47.2 per cent for agriculture, 35.1 per cent for services and 10 per cent for industry (Amsden:1972), leaving more than half the total labour force outside of the bargaining process. Nonetheless, the adjustment did make a difference from the beginning, with 179 agreements covering 427,636 jobs in 1959 rising to 4,772 agreements by the end of the first five years (Maravall:1982); and Maravall goes on to refer to the 'unintended consequences' of the procedural changes such as the explosion in collective bargaining after 1962 and the consolidation of legal and illegal shop floor organization and representation, which increased the gap between the workers and the corporatist bureaucracy especially in the steel, light engineering, chemical and building industries of Barcelona, the Basque Country and Madrid. But this process was not nearly so complete or homogeneous as he supposes, and still less was it the 'determinant of industrial conflict and dissent' (Maravall:1982, p. 27), a judgement which stands reality on its head. More worthy of emphasis is the general move from regional to plant based contracts,[5] which tended to minimize the intervention of the Vertical Syndicate, and this was more apparent in big industry: in an early study of the process Linz and de Miguel (1966) found that employers in the modern firms of Madrid and Barcelona were more prepared to come to terms with authentic collective bargaining, while those in the less industrialized areas remained more closely wedded to the Syndicate. But the preference for plant-based contracts also implied a more general tendency for such talks to fail (Amsden:1972), thus inviting the imposition of the compulsory norms.

By the year 1963 such norms decided the wages of some 63,051 workers, but just two years later this figure had jumped to 438,228 (Maravall:1982); and the ratio of NOCs to collective agreements increased from 2.6 per cent to 20 per cent over the period of the sixties. Amsden's (1972) explanation for this is that workers pressed for the application of the norm simply because they tended to get a better deal this way: NOC awards were higher in real terms over the medium term, and always well above the minimum for the sector concerned. The fact was that a large proportion of the collective contracts had to wait a long time before receiving the mandatory approval of the Ministry of Labour (and although there was provision for back-dating pay awards, this rarely compensated for the rate of inflation); and the NOCs appeared attractive if only because they were renewed more quickly. In this way, the 'provocation' of the NOC emerged as an alternative bargaining strategy open to the workers, which was reinforced by the syndical elections of 1963 and 1966. This strategy was generally adopted in regions and sectors with a history of labour unrest (Wright:1977) or with a militant labour leadership, because it could imply not merely an economic struggle with the employer but also a potentially dangerous political confrontation with the regime. The Ministry of Labour would always be aware, for example, that any settlement in a firm such as SEAT (Barcelona) would be taken as a marker by all workers in the engineering sector (Miguélez:1977). Moreover, although such wage norms were legally binding for two years (Article 12 of the 1958 law), the more militant sectors and regions continually pressed for annual contracts during the sixties (Wright:1977),

[5] The number of contracts and the number of workers covered by contracts on a plant basis was smaller over the period than the number of contracts and the number of workers covered at the provincial level, for example, but the former were increasing faster than the latter (Wright:1977); moreover, there was a higher proportion of plant as opposed to regional contracts in big industry, as already indicated, whereas in the rural labourers' organizations, the Agricultural Associations, there were 1,300 contracts on a regional basis and only 35 on a plant basis over the years 1958 to 1967 (Amsden:1972).

another sign of the increasing strength of labour. By 1972, NOCs accounted for 13.1 per cent of the total number of wage settlements.

BARGAINING AND WAGE CONTRACTS IN EL MARCO DE JEREZ

From the very first year of collective contracts, bargaining in El Marco followed a predictable pattern of negotiation, breakdown, strike and the imposition of the wage norm; and despite the two-year provision, the commissions pressed for negotiations on an annual basis, with the strike following almost as a matter of course. Bargaining was mainly over wage levels, which rose from 70 pesetas for a day's labour in 1961 to 80 pesetas in 1962 and 100 pesetas in 1963, so making the vineyard workers the best-paid agricultural labourers in Spain, and putting their wages way ahead of comparable groups in Huelva or La Rioja and on a par with similar groups in the south of France. But if wages and conditions of work were better in the vineyards than in agriculture in general,[6] and better in these vineyards than any others, it was because of constant struggle. The 1958 law allowed new negotiations to begin three months before the expiry of the existing contract, and each year the workers pressed not only for better wages but for rest periods, compensation for travel time, a reduced working day and wage differentials for the specialists in such tasks as pruning and grafting. In the early years they pressed for agreement in the springtime, when there was a heavy demand for specialized labour for grafting; and the resolution of the provincial delegate in Cádiz in 1963, for example (*Boletín Oficial*:6.4.1963), noted that the economic and social sections had met several times but had failed to agree either on the employment of *fijos*, or on the length of the working day, or on travel arrangements, or on wage levels. But having struck and lost, for the first time, in the spring of 1964 (see later in this chapter), the focus of negotiations shifted to the pruning season later in the year; so that a similar resolution of December 1964 recorded that the two sides had met six times in October without reaching an agreement, and another three times in December (during the strike which remains unmentioned in the resolution), before an agreement was finally reached in January (*Boletín Oficial*:27.2.1965). And so, slowly and haltingly, the struggle advanced.

As well as pushing to provoke the annual imposition of wage norms, in which they were largely successful despite the vineyard owners' repeatedly

---

[6] This had always been the case in El Marco. As Ibañez wrote at the beginning of the century (Ibañez:1924, p. 251), 'En el *Caballista*, los que eran proprietarios de viñas mostrabanse enternecidos por repentina piedad, y hablaban de los gananes de los cortijos ... era lógico que estos se quejasen; no los trabajadores de las viñas, que vivían como unos señores si se les comparaba con los gananes'.

pyrrhic insistence that the contracts run for two years or even three, the vineyard workers also had to mobilize to make their contracts regional. In short, contrary to the tendency for plant-based negotiations to go to compulsory arbitration, they wanted the norms applied simultaneously to the whole of El Marco. The employers for their part were content for Jerez, Sanlúcar and El Puerto to appear in the agreements, but baulked at the inclusion of Trebujena; and moreover Chipiona, traditionally considered part of the large Sanlúcar, was excluded on the grounds that the poorer soil and less productive land could not support the same level of wages. This argument could not be made in the case of Trebujena, however, and the emergent commissions were keen to have it included to avoid the political divisions created between *pueblos* by unequal wage rates. Hence, at one of the first meetings at the headquarters of the Vertical Syndicate in Jerez subsequent to the 1958 law, where all the local syndicates or *gremios* were represented, José Aldana, staking a second claim to his place in history (the first was recorded in Chapter 1), asked why Trebujena was not there. Because they had not requested it, came the reply. But let us look at the minutes of the last meeting, said Emilio Fábregas, who had a better grasp of procedure than most; and when they found the request minuted, the meeting had to be postponed. Even so, it was not until 1965, the year of the first agreement to be negotiated without necessity for a strike, that Trebujena was accepted de facto as part of El Marco; and not until 1969 that it was integrated de jure into its negotiating framework. The agreement reached in 1969 refers to the syndical associations of Jerez, Sanlúcar and El Puerto which represent those engaged in the enterprise of 'Jerez–Xeres–Sherry', as well as to the representatives of those working in vineyards which form part of the Marco de Jerez (*Boletín Oficial*:22.5.1969). This was the first legal recognition of El Marco's claims to a regional contract.

One of the few initiatives on which workers and employers agreed was the switch to hourly rates of pay, which took place in 1963 on the prompting of Emilio Fábregas. The employers were compliant because they saw it as an easy way of suppressing the *misas*, the tradition of not working the two hours on either Saturday afternoon or Monday morning, or both, as compensation for time spent travelling to and from work. Hence, in the agreement of the end of 1964, for instance, temporary workers' rates were already given by the hour, while, at the insistence of the employers, *fijos* (on fixed contract) were still paid by the day; and by the time of the 1969 contract just referred to, rates for temporary workers were increased by 10 per cent for specialized tasks and 25 per cent for mechanized tasks, time spent travelling to and from work was paid, and any worker employed for a minimum of two hundred days in the year automatically went onto a fixed contract. All this had been won by collective bargaining backed by strike action, at a time, it must be added, when the other agricultural workers in the province still had their (minimum) wages set by a regulation, which was now called a Rural Labour Order (*Ordenanza Laboral del Campo*) (*Boletín Oficial*:9.5.1967), or had to agree to contracts at provincial level which specifically excluded the vineyard workers of El Marco (OSE:1969). To their credit, the workers' commissions in the region continued to insist both on these contractual nuts and bolts (to the point where the April 1970 agreement ran through three editions of the *Boletín Oficial de la Provincia de Cádiz*), and on the integrity of El Marco as a productive unit: when the employers tried to exclude workers in the newly planted vineyards from the agreement of November 1974, the commissions launched one of the longest strikes of the entire struggle.

ECONOMIC DEMANDS, EARLY STRIKES AND EMBRYONIC COMMISSIONS

Negotiation and strike action were part of the same struggle, says Miguélez (1976): many workers who were not naturally militant were attracted to the movement by the legal provisions for improving their lot through negotiation, but, once there, were convinced that their longer-term interests lay much beyond the limits defined by such legality; and especially after 1958, says Carr (1982), 'the strike was an essential part of the negotiating mechanism'. This is correct but should not be taken to suggest that strike activity as such only began once the partial mechanisms of limited collective bargaining were in place. Yet this is something of the impression given by Linz (1973), who understood widespread repression and endemic economic insecurity to have precluded labour protest, except for isolated incidents in the mines of Asturias, in heavy engineering in Bilbao, and in the large new enterprises surrounding Madrid. And Maravall (1978) followed his lead by suggesting that working-class militancy under the dictatorship had survived only in the industries of northern and northeast Spain, where conflict reappeared in the ill-organized bursts of strike activity of 1947, 1951, 1953 and 1956.

Yet these strikes were not insignificant. Those in the Basque Country in the late forties announced a rising tide of strike activity in the fifties, beginning with the public transport boycott of 1951 in Barcelona, and the subsequent strikes both there and in Madrid and the Basque Country again;[7] while widespread protests over the cost of living in 1953 and 1955 led to significant increases in the minimum wage (FSM:1959; Vilar:1976). The

[7] Mujal-León (1979) suggests that the 1951 public transport boycott represented the 'first returns' on the Communist Party strategy of infiltrating the Vertical Syndicate. In doing so he accepts uncritically the official Communist Party or 'Carrillista' retrospective reconstruction of this event, which seeks to attribute a political victory to the Party which is not its due. Such 'returns' had to wait for many years, and even when they finally came in, it is doubtful whether the Party could claim all the historical credit. See Chapters 8, 9, 11 and 12.

turning point was reached in 1956 when strikes in Pamplona spread quickly to Asturias and Barcelona, and forced the regime to grant considerable wage increases in both April and November of that year (Mujal-León:1983); and 1957 saw more transport boycotts in both Madrid and Barcelona, and the beginning of the 'continual struggle' in Asturias, with a strike victory which reinstated sacked miners and won further wage increases. These strikes defended predominantly economic demands, and, as such, they continued unabated across the country until slowed to a temporary stop by the wage compression of the 1959 Stabilization Plan.

Similarly, in El Marco de Jerez the first strikes broke out in the late forties and early fifties in Sanlúcar, and spread to the other *pueblos* of the region. They were started by the small network of militants most of whom had already been elected to posts in the Vertical Syndicate, and who decided the timing of the strike between themselves. The word was then passed around the bars by the men and the market-places by the women, in the old 'anarchist style' (see Chapter 2), and pickets were placed on all access routes in the countryside to turn back those who had not heard the word. The pickets carried their food and tools as if ready to work for the day, and would then return to the *pueblo* warning the workers they met on the way: 'There's a strike and we've been told to go home'. At this time (as seen in Chapter 3) some 60 per cent of the workers in the vineyards of Jerez travelled to work on the train that ran between Jerez and Sanlúcar, and the word was passed from waggon to waggon by such leaders as Manolo Romero, Juan Flores and Eduardo Sánchez, with the same leaders from Sanlúcar often travelling to other *pueblos* by bicycle to enlist support for the strike. But the leaders, or at least those inside the Syndicate, were often the only workers who continued to work, because they did not wish to appear to the authorities as anything other than the official representatives of the workers.

In the beginning it was difficult to mount strikes that were solid throughout the region because of the rivalries and divisions between the different *pueblos*. The workers of Sanlúcar, for instance, wanted a straight eight-hour day so they could afterwards work as *mayetos*, while those of Trebujena and Jerez wished to retain the traditional rest periods, or *cigarros*; and the vineyard owners were not unaware of these rivalries when they later tried to exclude Trebujena from the collective contract for the region (see preceding section). Thus, the first big strike of 1953 to demand the ten pesetas prescribed by the regulation against the five offered by the owners, was launched by Sanlúcar alone, while the other *pueblos* continued to work; and once the strike was won (despite a propaganda campaign in the local newspapers designed to convince the workers that five pesetas was the official increase), the foremen of the vineyards had to keep *trebujeños* and *sanluceños* apart to avoid violence. But in the following year, when they struck again to prevent the owners reducing their wages during the winter months, Trebujena was solid with Sanlúcar. Between them these two towns contained the great majority of vineyard workers, and once in harmony they could begin to make demands which were not merely defensive, as in 1953 and 1954, but which sought to improve their wages and conditions of work. So from this moment there were strikes every year, which were always launched in the spring, which often spread in chain reaction, and which could last for anything from ten to twenty to forty days. And it was through these strikes that the movement in El Marco found and formed its leaders.

Manolo Romero, Emilio Fábregas, Pancaro, Juan Romero, Eduardo Sánchez and Paco Chicorro amongst others in Sanlúcar; Miguel Campo, Paco Cabral, Juan Caballero in Trebujena; Paco de las Flores and José Aldana in El Puerto; Juan Flores in Jerez – these are just some of the names which made up the network of syndical leaders in El Marco in these years. They succeeded in mounting strikes without support from the *bodega* workers who manufactured the sherry from the grapes they produced, or from elsewhere, and so in this period remained relatively isolated in their struggle. They were aware that the day Franco dubbed San José Obrero or San José Artesano was Labour Day and tried to honour it on one or two occasions, despite the threats of the Civil Guard; and once on 7 May 1958 they even struck in solidarity with the miners of Asturias. But for the most part they did not even know of the struggles in the city of Cádiz[8] a mere 40 kilometres away, where in the same year Pepe Mena had tried to lead a strike in recognition of the Communist Party's Day of National Reconciliation (see Chapter 8). But notwithstanding their isolation, and the 'vertical' splitting of the regime, and the occasional rivalries both between *pueblos* and between leaders such as Manolo Romero and Emilio Fábregas, they founded a syndical unity which was almost entirely of their own invention.

THE TRAJECTORY OF STRIKE ACTION DURING THE RISE OF THE COMMISSIONS

It is generally agreed that the tide of strike action, which had subsided immediately following the Stabilization Plan of the end of the fifties, began

---

[8] These struggles were as primitive as elsewhere in the province. The first one-day strike in the shipyards came in 1954 on the occasion of the accidental death of some of the workers which their workmates blamed on the absence of safety regulations. Workers were always dying on the job, and on this day they had to break a police cordon to carry the bodies home. Then in 1956 the workers again protested when the President of INI visited the shipyard and ordered a ten day salary bonus for the managers, but only one day's wages for them. And in 1958 they struck in recognition of the Day of National Reconciliation (discussed in Chapter 8). Their more Luddite ideas, like running their machines at high speed until they broke down, never came to anything, but they did manage to sabotage the 'clocking-on' mechanism, which paralysed the plant for at least some part of the working day.

to rise rapidly again during the latter half of 1961, before bursting through the institutional defences of the regime in April and May 1962. These months witnessed a massive wave of strikes across the country (Amsden:1972), led by Asturias[9] (Miguélez:1976), which marked a watershed in the history of the working-class movement; and from this moment on strike actions were an 'almost permanent' (Vilar:1977) and 'normal political phenomenon in Spain' (Miguélez:1976). In 1962 alone there were at least 425 major labour conflicts in the country as a whole (Maravall:1982), involving over half a million workers (Miguélez:1976), and many of these strikes were in solidarity with the miners of Asturias who were spearheading the struggle. The regime's immediate reply was to impose a state of siege in Asturias, under which it made hundreds of arrests and, moreover, tortured many of those arrested. But when José Solis, the National Delegate of the Vertical Syndicate, was sent from Madrid to end the strike he had to negotiate not with the official representatives of his Syndicate but with the workers' commissions. The release of those arrested and the wage increases won by the commissions stimulated strike action elsewhere in the country, as well as legitimating the syndical claims of the commissions themselves; and henceforth it was the commissions which tended to organize the strikes, whatever their immediate motives.[10]

As the working-class movement grew in subsequent years it tended to concentrate in the Basque Country, Asturias, Barcelona and Madrid, which between them accounted for 70 per cent of all labour conflicts in the period 1963 to 1974, which themselves clustered in the steel, engineering, mining and building industries, and especially the first two areas, where 47 per cent of all conflicts took place during the years 1967 to 1975 (Maravall:1982). Although these figures are barely compatible with those of Miguélez (1976), who asserts that in 1968, for example, 40 per cent of all strikes in Spain were in Asturias, and 90 per cent of those were in the mines, they are broadly illustrative of the more general shift in the concentration of com-

---

[9] The strike in Asturias in 1962 was the most important since 1934. There were three main zones in the mines: Caudal with 5,132 workers, Nalón with 13,361 and Aller-Turón with 3,786; and most struggles were waged at the level of the zone (less frequently in Aller-Turón which was less combative), except for the very big strikes which united all three.

[10] The strikes in the mines had mainly been motivated by bad working and living conditions and poor wages, but with the repression triggered by the strike, solidarity issues began to play an important part too. Then from 1962 onwards the strikes were organized principally to defend jobs; but, as with the Concerted Action plan of 1963 and the creation of the INI holding company HUNOSA in 1967, the regime appeared increasingly responsible for the deterioration of the mines, so the fight to defend jobs turned into a continual political confrontation. Despite the struggle, the work force declined from 44,995 in 1957 to 43,971 in 1962, to 40,9012 in 1965, to 35,135 in 1967, to 31,284 in 1970 and 30,983 in 1971. In this latter year there were 25,000 miners amongst the 31,000 employees (Miguélez:1976).

bativeness, noticed by Linz (1973), from the countryside, where it had been in the thirties, to the industrial centres, both new and old.[11] Maravall (1982) adds that the main new area of combativeness was Madrid, and believes, with Linz, that this was due to the creation of a large new proletariat. In this perspective, 'only in the decade of the seventies did working class militancy spread to other areas of the country, through the combined effects of the policies of illegal class organizations[12] and of the occupational changes associated with rapid industrialization' (Maravall:1982). As an example, 12.6 per cent of all conflicts during the years 1970 to 1974 took place in Andalucía, but only, it is further suggested, because the working-class movement had taken off in Sevilla and Granada.

Now, although I do not wish to contest the main lines of this thesis, it is at least possible that the evidence from many regions of the country is not yet in; and the fact that 67 per cent of all conflicts over the years 1968 to 1974 are supposed to have occurred in industrial plants with more than one hundred employees, which at the time represented only 1.3 per cent of the total number of enterprises, may reflect both the concentration of conflicts in large and modern industry *and* a bias in the collection of the evidence. Moreover, such a bias, if it exists, directly mirrors that of the Communist Party, which in its clandestine publications consistently focused attention on the conflicts in the mines of Asturias and the modern industries of Madrid, in that order, largely to the exclusion of other regions and sectors. Thus, while it cannot be denied that the working-class movement was based over many years in some few pockets of militancy, and while these strategic groups of workers certainly catalysed the more generalized pattern of conflict, the relative importance of such organization amongst the rural proletariat – for example, in Catalonia, Valencia and Andalucía – is still an open question. At the very least, it is remarkable that with one or two fleeting exceptions (Parti Comuniste Français:1962; Hermet:1974; Vilar: 1977) there is no reference in the growing literature to the long and widespread struggle in El Marco de Jerez.

Contrary to these accounts of the development of strike action across the country as a whole, in El Marco it was the countryside which led the syndical struggle over the first years, and the strikes always began in Sanlúcar. Moreover, these strikes tended to be long and bitter: the vineyard workers had no option but to press for higher wages, as they had to survive the four or

---

[11] Linz says in his footnote 100 that 'this is largely but not only the result of migration and industrialization; there remain large numbers of underprivileged farm labourers and farmers [but] the difficulty of organizing protests in a rural setting with an efficient State apparatus accounts for the few and generally unsuccessful protests and the low penetration of the Communist Party in the countryside'. In this connection El Marco is one of the exceptions to prove the rule.

[12] This is one of Maravall's euphemisms for the Communist Party of Spain, which he is always loath to mention in a favourable light.

five months of the year when there was no work; but, on the other hand, they had to suffer the economic consequences of strikes which now lasted anything from twenty to sixty days. As the combativeness of the vineyard workers was well known, and as their strike was always the main event of the syndical calendar, it is no surprise that one of the main objectives of the Communist Party was to foment and organize these strikes as part of its overall strategy, and this it certainly attempted to do from the moment Benítez Rufo appeared on the scene (see Chapters 9 and 11). But if the Party and other industrial sectors in El Marco expected the vineyards to come out in support of their objectives, such solidarity was rarely reciprocal; and this remained true even after leaders like Antonio Alvarez had come to the fore. In this context it is easier to understand the opposition of Emilio Fábregas to some if not all of the strikes, because he insisted, and often correctly, that the strikes should serve the interests of the vineyard workers and not some abstract plan of mobilization. Nonetheless, to suggest that the Party simply manipulated the militancy of the vineyard workers would be to protest too much: it is true that many of the militants in the commissions were also in the Party, but the intransigence of the sherry oligarchy meant that the mainly economic demands of the vineyard workers had to be backed by strike action if they were to be won.

The first such strike to be mounted and coordinated across the region of El Marco coincided with the watershed of the national movement in 1962. This strike was organized by the leaders of the commissions who had begun to consolidate their own regional network through the organization of the Vertical Syndicate in which many of them already held posts. Such was their confidence that they advised the Party's clandestine Radio Pirenaica beforehand, so that on the day the strike was launched it was also announced over the radio. At least seven thousand workers came out on that first day, despite the display of force by the Civil Guard, who for about a month previously had stationed its *parejas* (the Civil Guard always patrolled in pairs) at all stops on the railroad station and at all important cross-roads in the countryside. But as the commissions had had time to verify the Guards' locations, and seeing that these did not vary from day to day, they succeeded in placing their pickets within a few metres of the Guards, and there they stayed to mend their bicycle puncture or rest from carrying a heavy sack of slack coal.[13] But if this appears like playful sparring, the strike is remembered in Trebujena and elsewhere as the biggest and most bitter of all the sixties strikes before that of 1969; the employers did everything in their power to break the solidarity of the workers, including the publication of

[13] The mayor of Sanlúcar at this time owned some vines, and complained to the Lieutenant of the Guard that his foreman had been turned back by pickets. But there are no pickets, came the rather testy reply, and if there were any, then they would have been arrested!

articles in the newspapers attesting that the wage agreement had already been signed. But the strike stayed solid, and the demands were won; and then the Party called for and got a second strike in solidarity with the miners of Asturias, which brought out not only Sanlúcar and Trebujena but also El Puerto and even the shipyards of Cádiz. The commission sent out runners to spread the word, and El Marco was paralyzed for forty-eight hours while the massed presence of the 'forces of order' stood and waited.

The second strike at the level of El Marco as a whole occurred in the following year and brought out even greater numbers of workers than in 1962, if for less long. Then in 1964 the vineyard workers struck in the springtime, as usual, and lost. This was partly because the strike was poorly prepared, and launched on the personal initiative of Manolo Romero, who had met informally with leaders from the other *pueblos* in the headquarters of the Syndicate in Jerez. This was partly to force the issue on Emilio Fábregas, who had wanted to postpone the strike until more arguments could be brought to the talks; whereas Manolo wanted it immediately, and to coincide with the first anniversary of the death of Julián Grimau (see Chapter 8). This division in the commission caused the failure; but the more lasting result, apart from a more embittered rivalry between the two leaders, was the shift of the annual strike from springtime's grafting season to wintertime's pruning season in all subsequent years of the sixties. The strikes continued every year, with progressively greater degrees of coordination across the region; but when it came to the strike of 1966 the commissions' chief man in El Puerto, Paco de las Flores, was away on a clandestine mission in France, and the person left in charge was José Aldana. The Syndicate called him in and ordered him to stop the strike; but José explained that he knew nothing about it, and that if he didn't leave soon, then they would start without him. . . .

Once such strike action had begun in El Marco, the vineyard owners took steps to counter it. In the first instance they brought in blacklegs from Extremadura and Huelva in order to break the strikes, but not only did the blacklegs meet with a serried and sometimes violent resistance from the workers, they also lacked the specialized skills required for work on the vines; it was in the wake of this failure that the owners first succeeded in introducing *fijos*, or fixed-contract workers, into the vineyards in 1960 and 1961. In the majority of vineyards such contracts comprised some eighty or ninety workers, who were employed on a permanent basis so that certain essential tasks such as pruning could always be carried out, and so that strikes would be harder to win; and the broad design of dividing the work force of El Marco was immediately understood by the workers themselves, who (as we saw in Chapter 2) had responded in traditional anarchist fashion by asserting 'o todos o ninguno': either everyone was to have such a contract or no one could.

This demand could not be won, and Emilio Fábregas was almost certainly right in saying so; and the *fijos* did succeed in dividing the work force in some degree. There were bitter discussions and disputes between the *fijos* and the rest of the workers, and these confrontations often led to fights and beatings. Finally, the *fijos*, who were seen, rightly or wrongly, as traitors who betrayed the strike leaders to the Civil Guard and therefore as responsible for many of the arrests and tortures, were completely ostracized, and no one would eat, drink or talk with them. Juan Flores's brothers and cousins 'went *fijo*', and he never spoke to them again. So the owners' tactic met with considerable success, even if it was costly to them, too, in financial terms; and this situation only began to change again in the 1970s, when Manolo Romero and Antonio Palacios, amongst others, sought to win the *fijos* over and bring them into the movement. By this time some of the *fijos*' leaders had been elected to the Syndicate, and a few like Francisco Blanco Murillo of Sandeman's were even militant in the commissions, and so able to mediate in disputes between *fijos* and the rest. Thus, towards the end of the dictatorship, instead of working overtime to cover essential tasks when the work force of El Marco went on strike, the *fijos* would 'work to rule', which indicated some change of heart, if not total solidarity.

THE INCREASING NUMBER AND CHANGING NATURE OF LABOUR CONFLICTS

The number of labour conflicts increased from 2,062 in the period 1963–6, to 3,063 in 1967–70, to 4,623 in 1971–4 and to 3,156 in 1975 (Texanos:1978); and the number of working hours lost through strikes rose from 1.5 million in 1966 to 8.7 million in 1970 to 14.5 million in 1975 (Maravall:1982), by which time Spain was one of the European leaders in this regard. Moreover, not only did the number of conflicts multiply but so did the movement's demands, and with them the nature of the conflicts themselves. The first demands always had to do with wages and conditions of work, but these broadly economic demands were transformed both by the growing maturity of the movement itself and by the political repression which tended to shift the centre of the struggle away from conflicts with employers and towards confrontation with the State (Vilar:1977). As a result workers began to perceive a political need for real representation in collective bargaining, for the right to strike and for amnesty for those disciplined by employers, the Syndicate and the courts.[14] Thus, one motive for the huge increase in the number of strikes is that many of them were now called in

---

[14] The discipline exercised by employers is very evident in Miguélez's (1977) study of the SEAT factory in Barcelona, where the work of the commissions was hampered by the rigid and hierarchical control maintained by the management, the political vetting of workers, and the rapid recourse to sackings in the event of a conflict. Notwithstanding these controls SEAT had struck in solidarity with Asturias in 1958 and 1962, and first struck for its own ends in 1967.

solidarity with workmates who had been fined, fired or arrested;[15] and Santiago Carrillo is equally clear that the rise of a more open mass struggle in the late sixties was a reply to the offensive of the employers and the State against legally elected syndical representatives (Carrillo:1967).[16] This switch in the nature of the conflicts was quite dramatic and is captured by Maravall (1978), who notes that between 1963 and 1967 only 4 per cent of conflicts involved demands of a specifically political sort, and especially demands for solidarity; whereas between 1967 and 1974 such conflicts constituted 45.4 per cent of the total. Hence there were not only more strikes but more demonstrations, confrontations and street violence, which increasingly came to fill the pages of the newspapers after 1967 (Carr:1982). In this way the progression of demands from wages to solidarity to syndical rights to political rights finally achieved a qualitative change in the nature of labour conflicts.

This change was also patent in El Marco de Jerez, where over the years of the sixties the struggle came out into the open, and led to direct confrontations with the Armed Police, the Civil Guard and finally Franco's secret police, the Political–Social Brigade. In this period almost any motive served for a political protest, which was usually backed by some form of mobilization or demonstration. Hence, on 1 May 1964, for example, which had been decreed the national holiday of San José Artesano by the regime, there were protests both in the countryside and in the towns. The vineyard owners denied a holiday to their workers, who took one anyway, and when they were not paid for it, promptly struck to demand the day's wage, and got it; whereas in the towns the *bodega* workers were paid a small bonus by their paternalistic employers, so long as they went to church and said mass. But on coming out of church in El Puerto they demonstrated in celebration of Labour Day, and although some workers were arrested, the demonstrators demanded their release, and got it. These small incidents

---

[15] The increase in the number of conflicts in the mines of Asturias was exacerbated by the creation of the INI holding company HUNOSA: the traditional response of solidarity to the death of a miner was to stop work throughout the mine, and this response was now extended to the whole sector. HUNOSA tried hard to break this tradition but failed (Miguélez:1976). In general, however, strikes in solidarity were a new phenomenon, as they were in Sevilla in the late sixties, where 45 per cent of strikes by the engineering and building workers were motivated in this way, with only 25 per cent to protest redundancies and only 20 per cent to press wage demands (Maravall:1978).

[16] Carrillo talked of 350,000 to 400,000 workers and students being involved in these mass protests and demonstrations, which was clearly a polemical exaggeration; but it is nonetheless important to know that El Puerto was not alone. None of this was any surprise to Carrillo, even if it disturbed those he scathingly referred to as 'drawing-room sociologists' (*sociólogos de salón*). But it is sometimes hard to distinguish drawing-room sociologists from 'Paris restaurant revolutionaries'.

illustrate the shifting centre of the struggle over these years, which began to move from the countryside, where the strikes continued in the same pattern as before, to the towns, and especially to El Puerto, where the rising rhythm of mass protest appeared to convert the entire population to the revolutionary cause. And with this shift a new network of leaders came to the fore, whose support was founded not in the vineyards so much as in the *bodegas* and on the building sites. Paco de las Flores was still there as a leader of the vineyard workers, speaking so eloquently to his public that he brought tears to the eyes; and Federico Iglesias emerged as the most important figure among the building workers. But at the head of the whole movement in El Puerto was Antonio Alvarez, who pursued its ideals with the same awful energy which promoted his own image, and whose courage was as legendary as his vanity was consuming. But he was the right man for the moment, with the kind of charisma which led many to recall the first time he spoke: a small knot of syndical representatives at the head-quarters in Jerez were silently watching the late arrival of the Syndicate's legal consultant, when the voice boomed out, 'And who do you think you are to keep twenty and more people waiting for over an hour?'

By 1967 strikes could not be easily divorced from demonstrations in El Puerto and Jerez. In this year Antonio Alvarez seconded by Pepe Jiménez, had called a meeting in the Syndicate to push for a strike in the *bodegas*, but when they arrived they found the building cordoned off by the police. Alvarez was arrested when he smashed the camera of one of the policemen who were taking photographs, and a Tribunal of Public Order, holding court in El Marco for the first time, sent him to prison. This triggered a near general strike of seventy two hours in El Puerto, and a demonstration headed by the presidents of the social sections of the Syndicate marched to the police station to demand his release. Surprisingly they got it, and so on this occasion Alvarez did not manage to make himself the kind of *cause célèbre* he wanted. But the strike by the *bodega* and building workers and the coopers, and the mass demonstration of some six hundred workers in the Plaza Arenal of Jerez, marked the definitive transition to a different type of struggle; and the *bodega* owners themselves must have sensed this when they brought pressure to get Alvarez released. But after the demonstration they still fired those whom they saw as the ringleaders of the protest.

All this had occurred during Holy Week, and on 30 April the leaders met again to organize a meeting on 1 May in the Plaza Peral of El Puerto, which was again surrounded by the police and the Civil Guard. Antonio Alvarez, Pepe Jiménez and Pepe Marroquín were all there, watching the Guard finger their machine guns as they sat in their jeeps. No one looked like backing down. But the mayor sought first to save his own political skin and agreed to the celebration's taking place out of town, on the sandy banks of the estuary. There they sang their revolutionary songs in the presence of the

Civil Guard, who finally retired on the promise that they would not march on the town.[17] And so it was that for the first time during the dictatorship, Labour Day was celebrated 'legally' in at least one small corner of the country.

In this same year of 1967 there were strikes in the *bodegas*, in the building industry and in the glass factories, and *Mundo Obrero* (15.5.1967) reported big demonstrations in Sanlúcar, too, where the great mass of workers was without work; while later in the year there were more strikes and protests in the shipyards of Cádiz and San Fernando (with violent confrontations between strikers and police) and in Jerez, in Sanlúcar and again in El Puerto (*Mundo Obrero*:30.11.1967). But the next big confrontation came with the building strike of 1968, which began after the breakdown of talks over the renewal of the wage contract. There were about a thousand workers in the industry in Jerez and the surrounding towns, but as they were divided between a hundred or more tiny firms they had proved difficult to organize until a rousing speech from Federico Iglesias convinced them to come out. As was usual by now, the workers did not merely down tools but held meetings with the commissions of the other syndicates, which always ended in protest. One day, a meeting moving out from the Plaza Arenal was pursued by the police, who not only arrested the leaders of the building workers like Pedro Ríos and Pepe Navarro, but also detained and beat many militants from the other commissions.[18] But even this could not now break the spirit of struggle, which next found expression in the funeral held for Manolo Vela in June 1968, and the procession of seven thousand people which accompanied his coffin to the cemetery, where the pall-bearers with the red carnations in their lapels laid it down beside the forbidden tombstone with its epitaph for all who had fallen in this struggle: 'Your family and the Working World will not forget you'.

In the following year it was again the building workers who were in the forefront of the struggle in a strike led by Federico Iglesias, who was now the president of their syndicate. But if Federico led the strike, it was Antonio Alvarez, perhaps predictably, who broke the police cordon, and they were both arrested. This provoked yet another demonstration, followed by an occupation of the Church of Saint Jacob near Alvarez's own home. On this occasion it was the Communist Party which did most to organize the demonstration in front of the police station, where by some accounts as many as three thousand people gathered to demand the release of their leaders. A delegation was sent to speak with the mayor, and despite the tension

---

[17] The more graphic details of this story include another attempt, this time by the secret police, to arrest Alvarez, who shook them off as he and his comrades were being beaten by the Civil Guard; while the meeting of 1 May had a real flavour of *romería*, with songs sung, stories told and the young militants learning from the 'historic ones'.

[18] *Mundo Obrero* (15.6.1968) estimated that there were some two thousand workers on strike in Jerez, and noted that this strike coincided with yet another in the vineyards.

created by the ubiquitous presence of the grey ones, as the Armed Police were called, the leaders were again released without incident.

In the view of some of the militants such victories were almost too easily won, as they fed a growing triumphalism which was to bring the movement to grief. Many of these criticisms focused on the figure of Antonio Alvarez, who appeared at times to think of himself as some sort of messiah of El Marco, or at least as a provincial Julián Ariza. In the case of the occupation of his home church, Alvarez reported to the Party in the person of Rufo that the whole of the *pueblo* had been there, and Pepe Rosa backed this up. But Alvarez was in prison at the time and Pepe Rosa in Cádiz, and when an authentic witness like Paco Artola suggested the more realistic figure of some three hundred people, no one wanted to believe him. By such small steps the movement inflated its idea of its own power, without properly calculating the strength of the forces of reaction and repression; and once Rafael Gómez had left for Barcelona in 1968 there was no one to steady the movement and preach caution at certain critical moments. On the other hand, no one questions Alvarez's honesty and courage, and it is at least possible that the conjuncture required a leader to push ahead and lead from the front. After all, at least some strikes had ceased to be 'crimes of sedition' in 1965, and there were arguments for 'striking while the iron was hot'. And the strikes and protests in El Puerto and Jerez, not to mention those that continued in the vineyards, accompanied other historic conflicts in the engineering industry and urban transport sector of Sevilla in 1965 and 1966, in the building industries of Sevilla and Granada in 1970, and in Intelhorse of Málaga and Electromecánica of Córdoba. In other words the struggles were now waged on a broad enough front to condition the political and institutional terrain where such struggle took place, and so made Andalucía one of the first regions of the country to construct unitary organizations of democratic opposition to the regime.

THE CULMINATION OF THE CRESCENDO OF PROTEST

The crescendo of strike activity in 1969, when strikes in the *bodegas* in September coincided with others in the shipyards of Cádiz and San Fernando, culminated in the sixty-three-day strike of the vineyard workers which began on 9 December. Two or three representatives from the workers' commissions in each *pueblo* had met to decide a common set of demands and a common strategy; and even though their wage contract had not expired, the majority were for the strike, with only Emilio Fábregas holding out against the position advanced by Manolo Romero, Paco Cabral, Manolo Romero Ruíz and Antonio Palacios. With this degree of coordination between the different *pueblos* the strike was completely solid from the moment it was launched, and seven thousand vineyard workers immediately stopped work in support of their demands for three hundred pesetas per seven-hour day with payment for travel time: in their view the employers had not respected Articles 68 and 76 of the contract which made provision for such payments for travel over two kilometres, and moreover, they demanded the 'wage of El Marco' for workers from Trebujena who were being paid less than those from Sanlúcar (*Diario de Cádiz*:14.12.69). Early meetings between the social section and the Syndicate had hardly begun when Lebrija and the beet-pickers came out in solidarity, bringing the total number of strikers to twelve or thirteen thousand; and no sooner had representatives from all the syndicates of El Marco drafted requests for further solidarity from other sectors, than Rota, Chipiona and Laboral also stopped work. The commissions then voted their representatives onto a regional commission to meet with the Minister of Labour. As *Mundo Obrero* (23.1.1970) later intoned, 'this is the most exemplary strike ever mounted in the countryside under this dictatorship'.

The strike had begun in the usual way, with the word being passed along the train from Sanlúcar to Jerez, so by the time it arrived the only passengers it carried were the Civil Guard. But the commissions were consolidated by this time, not only locally but nationally, too, and not only did the workers in the local *bodegas* and regional light engineering factories come out in solidarity, but donations for the strikers began to arrive from engineering factories in Sevilla, the Perkins factory in Madrid, the SEAT factory in Barcelona, and from Germany, from Civil War exiles and even from the Church. Within the region collections were taken in the churches and elsewhere for the support of the most needy families, and thousands of people, especially young people, helped to collect and distribute these monies. What's more, although the strike had been launched and coordinated by the commissions, it was the Communist Party which did most to build this broad base of support for the strikers, thus giving this strike a more directly political thrust than those which had gone before.

In El Puerto de Santa María, the commission approached the civil governor of the province to ask permission to collect money for the strikers, but the governor passed the buck to the provincial delegate of the Syndicate; and at a meeting of the commissions from each syndicate on 29 December they anyway decided to work all available overtime and send the extra money to the strikers. In Trebujena, when the leaders of the commission in charge of the strike funds were arrested by the Civil Guard, the whole *pueblo* massed in front of the barracks and, having first cut the telephone wires, threatened an attack with the shotguns they brandished aloft unless their neighbours were freed. In short, the whole region was mobilized for the struggle, with continual meetings and collections, and the *pueblos* painted over with graffiti. In José Aldana's view, however, there was no work to be had in those months anyway: it was raining too hard.

The employers for their part stuck to what they conceived to be the letter of the contract, and would not cede; and as the struggle progressed they tried to bring in blacklegs from Montilla and Huelva, which only served to heighten tensions in the region. Such tensions were also tending to accumulate in the national arena, as the strike in El Marco exactly coincided with a full regional strike in the mines of Asturias,[19] and yet another in the region of Valencia;[20] and in Asturias as much as in El Marco the character of the strike had been transformed by a solidarity fund which had attracted resources both nationally and internationally. In short, it was the coincidence of these strikes which probably reinforced the fear of a general upsurge within civil society which might place the power of the regime in check. So when the reaction came it fell simultaneously on Asturias, Valencia and El Marco; and within El Marco, not initially on Sanlúcar, where most of the strikes started, but on El Puerto, where the recent spate of mass meetings and mobilizations had done most to attract the attention of the Political–Social Brigade. Everywhere the Brigade descended in force, and in El Puerto it effectively locked the town up tight in its effort to intimidate the local population. The people were not easily cowed, however, and even now hundreds of them were ready to march on the police station to protest the beating of a thirteen-year-old boy. The breadth and ferocity of the repression (see Chapter 10) lent authority to the Communist Party's judgement that 'this strike has been a bitter pill for the regime to swallow … and has struck directly at the stability of the government' (*Mundo Obrero*:21.2.1970).

There is no doubt that the not unexpected reaction of the 'forces of order' interrupted the steady growth of the working-class movement throughout the country, but Amsden (1972) was premature in his judgement when he pointed to Valencia, for example, as the first place where the 'repression that was to bring the whole experience to an end was undertaken'. In fact, after a relatively brief lull at the beginning of the seventies, the movement began to regain the initiative, and in 1973 strike actions increased by 82 per cent in relation to the previous year, with a further cumulative increase of 62 per cent in the following year (Maravall:1982). This new impetus is confirmed by the figures on labour conflicts and working days lost cited by Baklanoff (1978); and not only did the number of such conflicts increase,

---

[19] The miners themselves were almost certainly unaware of this, as their solidarity tended to be rather 'exclusive': 'in recent years they have never supported working class actions in other regions' (Miguélez:1976, p. 265). This was a point made frequently in El Marco: they were expected to be solid with Asturias, but would Asturias be solid with them?

[20] The economic organization of Valencia was not at all dissimilar to that of El Marco. The work force was largely agricultural, and the factory workers tended to retain their links with agriculture through regular or occasional work in the orange groves, whether their own or belonging to a friend or family member, which was not unlike the *mayeto* system of Sanlúcar and Trebujena; while in the city of Valencia itself the commissions were strongest in the building and banking industries, just as in Jerez.

but 'new types of action' were also apparent in the 'area general strikes' (*huelgas generales locales*), which brought together the workers from all the industrial sectors of a particular zone or region to press their economic and political demands (Maravall:1982). There were several successful strikes of this type in the Basque Country, Catalonia and Madrid, and they were increasingly current towards the end of the dictatorship.

On the evidence from El Marco, however, where such strikes had begun to coalesce in the later sixties, and where they were 'perfected' in 1969, there is some question as to how far this type of action was 'new'. In this as in other respects, El Marco de Jerez appears to have been ahead of the general pattern of the national movement, notwithstanding the consistent implication in the extant accounts of this movement that such peripheral regions joined the struggle reluctantly and late. So, far from the strikes which had been concentrated in the industrial centres of the country spilling over into 'underdeveloped regions like Andalucía and Galicia' (Vilar:1977), it is clear from this story that at least some of these 'backward' regions took the historical initiative in strike action and opposition organization. In general it is probably the case that the pockets of labour militancy and syndical struggle which finally succeeded in moving civil society as a whole in the direction of democracy were far more widespread than has previously been suspected.

But it is as true of El Marco as elsewhere that the repression had left many of the commissions' leaders locked up in gaol, and the rhythm of the struggle fell off considerably in the early seventies. Almost no one ran in the syndical elections of 1971 and for two or three years there was very little strike activity. Sanlúcar was less affected than El Puerto, if only because the repression had caused fewer casualties there, and its work force was already mobilized again in 1971 to demand an effective form of social security: in an early example of the kind of direct action which would characterize the dying years of the dictatorship some twenty-five hundred unemployed workers cut access roads and built barricades to call attention to their case. By 1973 not only Sanlúcar but all of El Marco was again engaged in mass struggle, and in this year there were extensive strikes in the vineyards and in the building industry, with the commissions of the two sectors working closely together. In the vineyards so many new vines were being planted that there was a heavy demand for pruning, so when the employers' offer was rejected the workers struck in August, just before the pruning season. On this occasion, not only did the *fijos* continue to work as in previous years, but the owners also drafted blacklegs to break the strike; and to prevent their passage the vineyard workers, along with their wives and children, blocked the roadways in another impressive example of direct action. For all that, the strike was lost.

In this same year the workers in the shipyards of San Fernando had refused to repair a ship from Chile, and the shipyards in Cádiz came out in their support. They had to face riot police from Madrid and Córdoba, as well as the covert action of the Political–Social Brigade, and some arrests were made. In 1974 there was an important building strike again, with mobilizations in all of the *pueblos* of El Marco. Again the commissions' leaders were arrested, but the workers massed every day in the Plaza Arenal of Jerez until they were released: Fraga Iribarne had gone on national television to assert categorically that 'the streets are mine' ('la calle es mía'), but apparently his writ did not run as far as El Marco. Meanwhile, in the vineyards the struggle continued. There were strikes in April and May 1974 to win a cost-of-living wage increase which the employers pretended was already included in certain bonuses, and again in December 1974 and in April 1976 (*ABC*:1.4.1976). In each case the range and detail of the workers' demands was impressive. By this time the commissions were working in the open, and in varying degrees were in control of industrial relations. In 1974, Manolo Romero and Antonio Palacios had even been prepared to call and get a short, sharp strike to win the reinstatement of a sacked agricultural extension expert who belonged to the CNT. Thus, in many ways these years represented the high point of the struggle of the commissions in El Marco, the cumulative accomplishment of the long years of clandestine organization.

The general lament in the region in recent years is that the workers have gone 'cold' and, as they are no longer used to striking every year as in the past, they have lost the spirit of struggle. An exception to prove the rule was the strike in the vineyards in 1982, which saw a massive mobilization in the old style, with flying pickets sent out from Sanlúcar and Trebujena, and even the *fijos* staying away from work in the first days. But even so the strike was not entirely solid, and with the two major union organizations, the workers' commissions and the UGT, now in contention, the employers were able to play one off against the other, and the strike was lost. This relative lack of success in recent years perhaps illustrates the different order of difficulties in organizing labour under a democratic regime: under the dictatorship the movement's economic demands came to have clear political implications and objectives they no longer have today. To a great extent, the syndical struggle under Franco was successful precisely because it was a struggle for democracy.

PART III

Political practices, repression and strategic responses

8

The revolutionary paradox: the changing political line of the Spanish Communist Party

The political sphere is, in fact, the privileged domain of the dominating classes, and Communist Revolution must be the negation of politics insofar as politics is superimposed upon society, an autonomous mediation between men and their own social life.

Jorge Semprún, *Communism in Spain in the Franco Era*

FOR MOST OF ITS HISTORY, political opposition to the Franco regime was constructed by highly politicized but clearly minority organizations, such as the Socialist Party (PSOE), the Popular Liberation Front (FLP) and the Communist Party; and with only rare exceptions, such as that of Maravall (1978), it is generally agreed that it was the Communist Party which did most to combat the political control of the dictatorship. But even when its combativeness is recognized the Party is still criticized for its 'intransigent, stalinist, dogmatic and sectarian attitudes' (Vilar:1976), which hurt rather than helped the cause of socialism, and this ambivalent view of the Party is mirrored in the contrasting images of the communist militant as a ruthless subversive in thrall to a foreign power, and as a modest and prudent hero, who is courageous under torture and who bears no hatred (Hermet:1974). But even where sympathy is lacking it is difficult to deny the fact of the Party's survival in political conditions which proved lethal for many potential allies in the struggle. In the early years of the opposition movement the other organizations were nothing more than 'committees without means or reflections of exile' (Alba:1979), which had been progressively corroded by repression and disillusion. The success of the Communist Party is then attributed to the abundant resources, and especially the money and the militants, which created its capacity for clandestine resistance. But these resources were not so great as is sometimes suggested, and the Party's preeminent place in the opposition was created in large degree by the regime itself, which, by crippling competing organizations and by singling out the Party as the privileged object of its opprobrium, contributed to the popular

133

perception of the Party as the only political alternative to the dead weight of the dictatorship.

The clandestine Communist Party was certainly not a large party, although such estimates of its membership as exist give no clear indication of just how small it really was. In April 1964 the Secretariat of the Party in exile claimed 40,000 organized members, but a year later the CIA put the figure at just 5,000, and it is the lower estimate which is quoted with approval by Hermet (1974), Ayucar (1976) and Alba (1979); while the latter suggests 20,000 members at the time of Franco's death, and Morodo et al. (1979) say that even by 1977 membership in the Party did not exceed 35,000. But the methods for arriving at these estimates remain something of a mystery, and in reality they are nothing more than guesswork. No one who was active in the Party carried a card, and there were no central records which collated the Party's organizational capability in different parts of the country. On the evidence of the results of the campaign for thirty million pesetas of 1968 and 1969, it appears that the Party was strongest in Madrid and in the industrial and mining areas of the north, each of which accounted for about a third of the membership, with the remainder spread more widely across the country, except for a strong concentration in the provinces of Sevilla and Cádiz (Hermet:1974). But even if the degree of militancy in the relatively small region of El Marco de Jerez was not typical, much of its style of organization certainly was so; and this suggests that the Party's own figure is more realistic than that of the CIA. Hence, it seems probable that by the end of the sixties the Party could count on some 20,000 to 30,000 militants.[1]

The real issue here, however, is not the Party's absolute size but its political influence, and this was greatly enhanced by the size and sophistication of its propaganda apparatus. In the first place there was Radio Pirenaica, so called because it broadcast from the southwest of France in the immediate post–Civil War years, before being removed to Prague as Radio Independiente España, or Radio Free Spain. Then there was the Party's underground press, which was led by the fortnightly *Mundo Obrero*, with a print run of about fifty thousand copies, not counting the provincial editions published in Andalucía and elsewhere; and which also included *La Voz del Campo* for the farm workers, *Lucha Obrera* for the militants of the unsuccessful Workers' Syndical Opposition (OSO), and the bimonthly *Nuestra Bandera* and the quarterly *Realidad* for the intellectuals of the Party. These publications were likely to have reached a wider audience than the mere membership of the Party, and so to have catalysed recruitment to the Party or

[1] In 1970 the Secretariat of the Party claimed 10,000 members in exile. This figure again seems low considering that in 1967 there were some 150,000 Spanish Republican exiles in France alone, and upward of a million migrant workers in France, Germany, Switzerland and Belgium (Hermet:1974).

its affiliated organizations such as the Unified Socialist Party of Catalonia (PSUC) and, from the sixties, the Communist Youth. But even if membership did not rise as a result of the propaganda effort, 'what is supremely important', says Hermet (1974),

> is that this membership, no matter what its numbers, should be so organized as to make possible the Party activities of a nucleus of communists, the training and replacement of its militants, and the emergence of an elite that will discharge organizational, ideological and, if possible, political tasks . . . viewed in this light, local organizations relatively weak in numbers can be quite adequate for this role; perhaps even better than larger but more vulnerable and less coherent groups.[2]

But here is the rub. The argument that local Party cadres had a much more important political impact than their mere numbers would suggest is entirely plausible, but difficult to prove for lack of evidence. This lament is general in the literature. In the first major academic study of the Party, Hermet (1974) insisted that 'it is difficult to obtain any very exact idea of the nature and condition of the underground organization . . . information on the . . . methods of action, means of propaganda and educational activities of the Party is hard to come by and unreliable. Facts about the Party's strength, its methods of recruitment or the social, political and geographical provenance of its members are even scarcer'. A dearth of information about a clandestine organization should come as no surprise, and as the regional command centres of the Party maintained communication with the Secretariat in exile but not, by and large, with each other, then local Party leaders would themselves be unlikely to have an informed picture of the national

---

[2] Interestingly, Hermet was referring precisely to the organization of the Party in El Marco de Jerez. 'An example is the Cádiz provincial committee', he goes on, 'rounded up by the police in 1970. Although it had hardly more than a few hundred members, divided between Cádiz, Rota, Sanlúcar de Barrameda, Jerez and Sevilla, and organized in a variety of groups and cells, the committee was at the top of a complex pyramid of well-defined organizations which was virtually the mirror image of the structure of equivalent committees working in legal conditions. In addition to its Secretary-General, it had a secretary for propaganda, with three assistants, a finance secretary, a liaison officer, and a secretary for relations with local and works cells. They were organized, above all, in the building industry, and in some of the great wine-producing companies such as Caballero, Osborne, and Terry. It also had a branch at Jerez whose job was to circulate the communist press at regional and occasionally national levels. In addition, there were separate organizations of the Communist Youth and Young Workers' Commissions. This whole machinery gave the officers and militants of the Party what almost amounted to a sand-table model with which to play a sort of permanent war-game, maintaining good-will under pressure and selecting those best adapted to the work of directing and inspiring the Party'.
  Hermet took his information from an article in the Spanish newspaper *Ya* of 8.2.1970 entitled 'Desarticulación de una organización clandestina en Cádiz'. The organization and events he refers to are documented more closely in Chapters 9 and 10.

scope of their own organization; and their sense of the regional picture would come through the personal contacts they made within the local political networks, or what Hermet called 'a few isolated activists having contact with like-minded men in other villages'. So, although the most important component of the 'interior' organization of the Party came to be the provincial committee, and although the Communist Party had sufficient organization in thirty of the fifty Spanish provinces, including the eight provinces of Andalucía, to constitute such committees, the history of the Party as it has been written to date has been the history of the Party in exile and not the history of these thirty committees; let alone the history of the relationship between the two. Hence, Mujal-León (1983), in the second significant study of recent years, complains that 'there have been no empirical data available to give us a clearer picture of what the ordinary Communist militant or sympathizer thought about the changes impelled by Party leaders during the Franco era, but certainly talk of civil liberties and emphasis on individual rights found little echo in the lower ranks of the Party'.

The first part of this complaint is substantially correct, and the lack will be supplied in some measure for the militants of El Marco de Jerez in Chapter 9. But to imply that it was only the leaders of the Party in exile who were concerned with the achievement of democratic rights is to mistake the nature of the democratic project pursued by the labour movement with the constant collaboration and occasional orientation of Party cadres; and it is to take a very elitist view of the way this project was conceived and constructed. It was not a project delivered to the 'people' from above, nor was it sent from abroad. On the contrary, the key strategic elements of this political project were learned through the syndical practices of the labour movement itself, even if the Party played a key role in theorizing, systematizing and disseminating these strategic lessons. These points will be debated in greater detail in Chapters 11 and 12. In the meantime, it remains important to distinguish between the Party in exile and the Party inside the country precisely in order to highlight what the imagination and courage of Communist militants in the labour movement could achieve, often *despite* the strategy shifts and what Semprún (1980) called the 'subjectivism' of the Party executive (see later in this chapter). This is not to deny that many of the initiatives taken by the Party's 'national' leadership had important repercussions in the organization inside the country; nor is it to suggest that these repercussions were all negative, or that Party organization was not crucial in resisting the repression of the regime. But the contribution of the Party was composed of organization and discipline; its strategy was reflexive and often learned late; and its leadership lacked the political acumen and political vision to learn from its mistakes. Perhaps it is for these reasons that Semprún (1980) complained that 'historians do not have access to Party archives', and feared lest these archives 'somehow conveniently disappear'.

THE HISTORICAL BACKGROUND TO THE PARTY'S POLITICAL PRESENCE

The Party came into being as a result of splits in the social democratic movement, when the Young Socialists of Madrid formed the Communist Party of Spain in December 1919. Almost two years later a left faction of the Socialist Party also joined the fledgling organization, which at that time counted about 1,200 members. Over the years before the Civil War the anarchist CNT dwarfed the Party, which appeared as the bureaucratic vehicle of an alien revolution, and there was an almost complete divergence of views between the anarchists and the Communist International. In the late twenties a big CNT group from Sevilla joined the Party, but for the most part it lost members through splits and defections, and by the early years of the Republic had been almost eclipsed. But in 1931 it began to publish *Mundo Obrero*, and on the evidence of the Fourth Party Congress in Sevilla in the spring of 1932 its membership had risen again to about 5,000, not counting the members of its affiliated trade union, the Unitary General Confederation of Workers (CGTU), which was strongest in Asturias and Sevilla. In the latter city the Party even managed to rally some anarchist trade unions to its side for the 'revolutionary' strikes it launched at this time.

In the opening sections of his autobiography, Juan Modesto (1978)[3] talks of joining the Party in El Puerto de Santa María in 1931, when it had only four members: Daniel Ortega, Ramón Mila, Juan Gandulla and Alfonso Manzaneque. He was the political secretary at the moment the Republic was proclaimed, and remembers seizing the town hall in the Plaza Peral, where Daniel Ortega addressed the crowd from the balcony. The Party began to flourish, its Workers' Centre (Centro Obrero) had twice as much movement as the Socialists' People's House (Casa del Pueblo), and the print run of three hundred of its weekly paper *The Proletarian* was always sold out by the end of Saturday. A provincial committee was formed in Cádiz and, with the backing of a strong Communist Youth organization, the Party began to lead many strikes and labour struggles. In an uncanny historical dress rehearsal for the drama enacted by Antonio Alvarez in the sixties, Modesto was arrested and held incommunicado, only to be released under pressure of a huge mass protest. At the Party's regional conference he met with José Díaz and Antonio Mije, and helped elect the first of the two and Daniel Ortega as representatives to the Fourth Congress. At this time, he says, El Puerto had several hundred militants.

---

[3] Juan Modesto Guilloto was an organizer and commander of the Fifth Regiment and the first general of the Popular Army in the Civil War. He was active in and around Madrid during the war, and was shot by the Falangists after the capitulation of Casado (Ibarruri:1966).

The turning point in the Party's fortunes came in October 1934 when it led the Asturias revolt, and membership increased from 5,000 or 10,000 at this time to some 50,000 on the eve of the Civil War. The Party was successful in profiting politically from Largo Caballero's[4] late discovery of Marxism, and not only did the CGTU merge with the UGT but also, and more importantly, the Socialist Youth merged with the Communist Youth in April 1936 to form the Unified Socialist Youth, or JSU (Juventud Socialista Unificada). The secretary-general of this organization was Santiago Carrillo, who promptly joined the Communist Party after a visit to the Soviet Union, as did Fernando Claudín after a similar visit in the same year. As is well known, the Party then experienced a period of exponential growth during the Civil War years, with membership rising from 100,000 in July 1936 to 300,000 by June 1937, or 380,000 including the PSUC and the Basque Communist Party. The majority of these members were rural and urban middle class, with most of the working class still organized by the CNT, the UGT and the Socialist Party. With the defeat of the Republic the Party's legal existence came to an end in March 1939, and Carrillo and Claudín kept company with Togliatti in Madrid almost until the last moment.

During the 1940s it proved almost impossible for the Party in exile to maintain contact with militants inside Spain, and although as many as five 'delegations' were sent from the Central Committee to reorganize the Party, all of them were captured and most of their leaders executed (Alvarez:n.d.; Mujal-León:1983). The only political objectives of the Party in these years were survival and the so-called National Union, the Councils of National Union being designed to group a broad gamut of social forces around opposition to Spanish entry into World War II on the side of the Axis (Ibarruri et al.:1964). At the same time, the Grouping of Spanish Guerrillas was formed as the fighting arm of the councils, but it failed to attract any significant support from socialists or anarchists. In the meantime the exile community had been divided over the competition between Dolores Ibarruri and Jesús Hernández for the post of general secretary of the Party, following the death of Jose Díaz in 1942; and in the following years the exiled leaders used underhand tactics, including assassination and betrayal, to impose the Party lines on its cadres within Spain. Quiñonismo (after Heriberto Quiñones) and Monzonismo (after Jesús Monzón) became heresies to be extirpated, and to this end the Party Secretariat ordered the elimination of many of its own activists. Mujal-León (1983) believes that Santiago Carrillo was in some strange way unaffected by this atmosphere of blackmail and untouched by the settling of old personal scores, but this appears improbable. It was, after all, Carrillo who had set up the 'commission of the interior'

---

[4] Largo Caballero was the general secretary of the PSOE, the Spanish Socialist Party.

on his return to France in 1944, precisely in order to assert exile control over the Party inside the country.

In July 1945, the Party joined the National Alliance of Democratic Forces, which had been set up late in the previous year by the Socialists and the CNT. The decision to join the alliance, the acquiescence of the Socialists and, indeed, the brief participation of the Party in the Republican government in exile, which began in January 1946 and ended in August 1947, must all be seen in the light of the euphoria which followed the liberation of Europe. In general, the Party's relations with other parties on the left were not good, and in Party writings (Ibarruri et al.:1964; Ibarruri:1966) it sometimes appears that the anarchists were more hated than Franco himself. In March 1948 the Party's call for a National Front of all forces opposed to Franco went quite unheeded, because by this time the Party was almost completely isolated; and although the Party had shown some growth, especially in Andalucía, the immediate post–World War II years were the hardest for the cadres inside the country (Semprún:1980), which were badly hurt by the successes of the repressive apparatuses in 1948. The isolation and the repression turned the Party into a small and introverted organization, given to periodic purges to discover mostly imagined traitors; not to mention the shameful commissions it set up to investigate the political loyalties of those who had survived the concentration camps. The Party was in disarray, and ready for a change of strategy.

THE FIRST MAJOR STRATEGY SHIFT

As late as 1947 the two principal strategies of the Party were the guerrilla struggle and the clandestine class unions, such as the illegal UGT. The guerrilla was still important at this time, and in June to October 1946, for example, there were 266 guerrilla actions, with 119 of them in Andalucía (Modesto:1946); while even in 1949 *Mundo Obrero* (1.8.1949) was still reporting such actions in Granada, Málaga, Sevilla and Cádiz, in all of which the guerrilla apparently came off best. But despite this optimistic coverage, and the rather wishful exhortations (*Mundo Obrero*:6.10.1949) to the guerrilla fighters to become peasant leaders, the strategy, launched to catalyse armed insurrection against the regime, had not been a success; and with the coming of the Cold War and the consolidation of the regime, the guerrilla struggle entered into irreversible decline. Hence, the decision to dissolve the few remaining and rather scattered groups was not a difficult one; but the simultaneous decision to take the struggle to the people through infiltrating the mass organizations of the regime itself was far less obvious and far more daring, and signalled a significant switch in the Party's political line and a new departure in its fight against the dictatorship.

The commission of the Central Committee charged with writing Party history in the early sixties (Ibarruri et al.:1964) notes that in 1944 the Party had canvassed the idea of clandestine syndicates to compete with the Vertical Syndicate, but without result. So in October 1948 leaders and militants of the Party (and the PSUC) met 'to examine the relations of the Party to the working class and to revise the syndical tactics of the Party'. They concluded that 'the duty of the communists was to work in the heart of the Vertical Syndicates in order to join up with the masses and unite them around working class demands'. And it was this key moment of 'self-criticism', adds Alvarez (1967), reinforced by the Socialist reluctance to join forces, which opened their eyes to the impossibility of making the revolution with just the vanguard. Interestingly, neither account, no more than a later one by Carrillo himself (1978), mentions the fact that in this same October of 1948 the leadership of the Party, including Dolores Ibarruri, Francisco Antón and Santiago Carrillo, sought an audience with Joseph Stalin, who himself decided on the new political line. 'The truth is', asserts Semprún (1980), 'that it was the trenchant and categorical directives of Stalin that were responsible for the Spanish Party's change of strategy',[5] and the new strategy was 'essentially a correct one ... even though it is owed to Stalin, the god of Theory and the Gulag'. Thus, far from the change coming from a careful analysis of the conjuncture and cool self-criticism, it was simply Stalin's say-so which impelled the Party to join the Vertical Syndicates, and so broaden the base of the struggle.

In this way the decision was taken to combine legal and clandestine activities with the newly proclaimed strategy of infiltrating the official syndicates (Hermet:1974), and from the early 1950s the Party was committed to rebuilding its organization inside the country with a strategic programme of struggle from within (Maravall:1982). The previous strategies were definitively abandoned by 1951, with the liquidation of the guerrilla (Semprún:1980). But all was not quite this clear cut, as there was still what is retrospectively called the Party's 'deviation' (Camacho:1980) in organizing its own clandestine union, the Workers' Syndical Opposition, or OSO (Oposición Sindical Obrera); and it was anyway difficult to explain to its own militants that the guerrilla could not win, and that the way forward was through pressing for the kind of concrete demands with which the workers could identify. But slowly the idea took root of infiltrating the Vertical Syndicate in order to gain the kind of support amongst the working class that the Party had always lacked (Mujal-León:1983); while the OSO, which had been active principally in Madrid, saw its leaders arrested and its organization fall into disrepair. The Party's posturing in claiming credit for the strike actions in Barcelona in 1951 was clearly premature; and it did not openly urge its supporters to participate in the Vertical elections in order

---

[5] Semprún's version directly contradicts Carrillo's account in chap. 5 of *Eurocommunism and the State*, although Carrillo had confirmed it in an earlier publication, *Mañana, España* (1974), as had Enrique Lister in *¡Basta!*.

to elect 'genuine representatives of the working class' until its Fifth Congress of 1954. But even Maravall (1982) now admits that Party militants were running in these elections for shop stewards and syndical delegates (*enlaces* and *vocales*) from 1957, and in many places this certainly occurred earlier. In this way the Party gave formal direction to the 'natural' tendency of the workers' commissions to infiltrate the central corporatist institution of the Francoist State.

PARTY STRATEGY AND PERSONAL STRUGGLES IN THE FIFTIES

In 1950 the Party in exile was expelled from France and took up residence in Prague; and a hostile judgement on the Party's progress in the following decade (Ayucar:1976) concluded that the farther removed it was from Spain, the less effective its conduct of the struggle inside the country. In Ayucar's view the Party was so inactive during the fifties that it mounted a systematic campaign of misinformation and half-truths to keep its activities, or rather the lack of them, secret; so that it proved easier to get information on the highly repressive forties than on the later period. But this view conveniently forgets that the fifties saw the progressive definition of the strategy which, for better or worse, was to orientate the work of the Party until the time of the transition to democracy, and which first culminated in the call for National Reconciliation.

Early in the decade Carrillo began to argue for the inclusion of Communists from inside Spain in the Central Committee and the Political Bureau as part of the effort to break down the Party's isolation and to lead other social forces in the fight against the dictatorship, and the Fifth Congress of 1954 adopted a two-stage strategy of a wide anti-Francoist National Front, to be followed, once victory was won, by anti-feudal and anti-monopoly measures (Mujal-León:1983). This strategic analysis was pushed one step further in the Central Committee meeting of June 1956, which first discussed the actual policy of National Reconciliation: in the Party's view, the policy was appropriate to an historical moment when diverse classes and groups from the proletariat to the national bourgeoisie were coming into increasingly direct conflict with the 'monopoly oligarchy'. Both Alba (1979) and Ayucar (1976) point out that this formal initiative responded to the mood of the Twentieth Congress of the CPSU in Moscow and Khrushchev's call for peaceful coexistence, and followed the Italian Communist Party's acceptance of democratic methods; but while the broad strategy may have sought an alliance of all anti-Francoist groups on the basis of increasingly limited struggles with a democratic rather than revolutionary content,[6] and

---

[6] Ayucar (1976) refers to the Party pamphlet of 1956 entitled 'Declaration of the Spanish Communist Party for National Reconciliation, and for a Peaceful and Democratic Solution to the Spanish Problem'.

through the creation of unitarian platforms (Maravall:1978), the initial call for National Reconciliation was accompanied by an exhortation to all militants and sympathizers to prepare for the peaceful national strike which was to overthrow the regime.

The August 1956 plenum of the Central Committee finally approved the new policy, which was specifically designed to combat sectarianism in the opposition to the regime, and another plenum in September of the following year set the first Day of National Reconciliation for 5 May 1958, which was to be marked by a boycott of public transport and short work stoppages throughout the country. But the call elicited almost no response, and the response to a further call for a peaceful general strike on 18 June of the following year was limited to Madrid and a few *pueblos* of Andalucía,[7] and even in the capital was very patchy (Amsden:1972). The reasons for the failure were principally twofold: on the one hand there were the preemptive detentions and intimidation by the forces of order, which were intended to nip the protest in the bud; and on the other the continuing isolation of the Party, which was more than partly the fault of its haughty disdain for the Socialist Party and its frank dislike of the anarchists (Hermet:1974). And while the Communists were quicker than the Socialists in shedding the anticlericalism which had been so integral to the Spanish left (Mujal-León:1979), the commissions were not yet sufficiently organized or coordinated to provide the kind of political meeting ground for Communists and Catholics they came to be in the decade of the sixties. In short, the Party failed to make particular alliances to support National Reconciliation, and its invocation of what were later called the 'forces of work and culture' (Frères:1969) was too general to make an impact. Yet for all that, in 1959, Carrillo and selected members of the Political Bureau travelled to Prague to convince Dolores Ibarruri that the general strike had been a success, and had thus confirmed the policies formulated by Carrillo in 1956. She was convinced to the point of later asserting that 'the mobilization of the masses was extraordinary' (Ibarruri et al.:1964); and while the masses themselves could be forgiven for being less than euphoric, Carrillo's insistence on this 'success' meant that the Party would go on talking of the 'peaceful national strike' for which the 'right moment . . . will come very shortly' (*Mundo Obrero*:1.8.1960) for many years to come. The importance of the policy of National Reconciliation lay therefore not in its immediate impact on Spanish society but in the direction it gave to the Party at the beginning of its journey to Eurocommunism.

The 1950s were also a decade of struggles inside the Party, which had

---

[7] At the time that he was making regular journeys to Sevilla to fetch propaganda materials for the Party in El Puerto, Paco Artola remembers bringing news of the Day of National Reconciliation, which indicates that the initiative was at least known about at the grass roots.

mainly to do with personal rivalries but were not entirely divorced from the changes in the political line of the Party insofar as Carrillo presented himself as the spokesman of change and the architect of the new democratic strategies. These strategic questions entered the debates following the death of Stalin in March 1953, and in July of the same year Antón was ousted from the Political Bureau, leaving Ibarruri, Vicente Uribe and Carrillo in effective charge of the Party. Carrillo then began to extend his bases of support with the entry of activists from Spain into the Central Committee on the occasion of the Fifth Congress and with the revision of the statutes, but he did not yet present any direct challenge to the status quo of the existing leadership. Indeed, Ibarruri (Ibarruri et al.:1964) later talked of the 'monolithic unity of the whole Party' at this time. Then in 1955, when Spain was first admitted to the United Nations, Carrillo unwittingly went out on a limb by declaring himself for the initiative in an article published in *Mundo Obrero*, while the Party line was to argue against Spain's entry on the grounds that it was a betrayal of the 'anti-fascist' cause by the nations of the West. As soon as the article came to her attention, Ibarruri threatened to have Carrillo expelled from the Party for factional activity and indiscipline. Carrillo immediately dispatched Jorge Semprún to Bucharest, where he persuaded Ibarruri to take no action before the meeting of the Political Bureau in April of the following year; but Ibarruri merely bided her time while she mobilized support for a showdown, and to this end invited Fernando Claudín to join the Party's delegation to the Twentieth Congress of the CPSU in February. Thus, by early in 1956, there was no doubt that Carrillo was on the verge of expulsion from the Party. His luck held good, however, and he was saved by the unforeseen circumstances of Khrushchev's condemnation of Stalin, which happened to coincide with the first widespread strikes in Spain since the Civil War. Ibarruri rapidly shifted her support from Uribe to Carrillo, who not only survived the marathon meeting of the Political Bureau in April and May, but also consolidated his position at the plenum of the Central Committee in August. There, after a masterful piece of 'self-criticism' which laid all the blame on Uribe, he co-opted six of his supporters as new members of the Political Bureau and used the revelations about Stalin and the reaction to the 'cult of personality' as a weapon against his real and possible opponents. In particular, anyone who had opposed the policy of rapprochement with Catholics and moderates no longer had a career in the Party.

Carrillo had not really analysed Stalinism or its implications, and was in basic agreement with Khrushchev that it was an aberration within a good system, contrary to the views of Semprún, Claudín and Togliatti that the phenomenon had institutional roots. But Carrillo's concern was not with the issue but with its instrumental use; and he had, as ever, worked pragmatically to buttress his own position and to secure his own election as general secretary of the Party at its Sixth Congress in Prague in January

1960. Moreover, this same Congress was persuaded to forget the failures and ratify the strategy of National Reconciliation, while still endorsing the peaceful general strike as the 'ultimate solution'; while the application of the Party's political line was reinforced through the hierarchical and centralized structure which placed the executive Secretariat at three removes from the Congress, making it answerable first to the Executive Committee, and second to the Central Committee, both of which could be controlled by the inner circle of the leadership. Finally, the Party statutes were modified to allow membership in the organization without formal participation in its cells, which marked another strategic shift designed to create a mass party despite the conditions of clandestinity. While this shift has passed relatively unnoticed in comparison with that occurring at the beginning of the 1950s, it was to have important consequences for Party practice inside the country. The task set by the congress was to create Party committees in all the factories, colleges, villages and urban districts of the land, and so make a Party with tens of thousands of militants; and it was in obedience to this programme that the Communist Youth was founded in the following year, along with a propaganda publication, *Horizonte*, aimed at this new Party constituency.

THE POLITICAL PRESSURES ON THE PARTY LINE IN THE SIXTIES

According to Maravall (1982) the 1960s was the period when the Party enjoyed the greatest influence on the left of the political spectrum, owing to 'the severe crisis of the PSOE, the radical pragmatism of the PCE, the activity of its militants, and also the rewards of its policy of infiltration'. But, as Mujal-León (1983) points out, this same pragmatism left the Party open to criticism from left-wing groups, which saw its politics of National Reconciliation as a capitulation to the Spanish bourgeoisie: the uncertain search for alliances with the middle class, far from contributing to the achievement of democratic liberties, would simply dilute the revolutionary content of the Party's political practice until it disappeared altogether. The potential strains implicit in this contradiction between 'pragmatism' on the one hand and 'purity' on the other were no doubt common to all or many of the organizations of the opposition, but they mattered more to the Party if only because it was the one organization which commanded cadres of political leaders throughout the national territory (Alba:1979); and institutional strains within the Party were likely to find expression in tensions between the leadership in exile and Party cadres working on the ground inside Spain. Moreover, the political developments of the beginning of the sixties tended to throw this relationship between the Party on the 'outside' and the Party on the 'inside' into higher relief than ever before.

First there was the beginning of the mass emigration in search of jobs, which involved hundreds of thousands of Spanish workers over the follow-ing years (see Chapter 4), and which came to provide crucial links between the organization in exile and the practice of leadership cadres in the localities. The Party in exile deployed its militants to recruit and organize the migrant workers in France, Belgium and Germany; but in so doing it was forced into close contact with the changing reality within the country. It provided social venues for the Sunday entertainment of these lonely hordes of shocked workers and ran courses for the more politically motivated of them; but in so doing the Party was exposed to their own social and political preoccu-pations. Soon it occurred that some workers travelled abroad not to work but simply to attend such courses, and in these ways the phenomenon of emigration provided a strong stimulus to the fight against Franco, at the same time that it forced the Party to examine its own political line and led some, at least, to discover that in practice, theory is different. This result was reinforced by the 'generational effect' of the thousands of very young militants who joined the Party in the sixties, and who had a far better sense of the political constraints and opportunities operating within the country than did the leadership installed abroad. Being exposed to the daily dangers of their political militancy led them, and some elements of the leadership as well, to take a less sanguine view of the imminent decomposition and collapse of the regime. Finally, the distinct perspective on the political pro-cess inside Spain, and its implications for the Party line, which lay latent in these developments was crystallized by the *cause célèbre* of the arrest and execution of Julián Grimau García in 1963. No repressive act of the dic-tatorship was more fiercely contested or more widely appealed, and the final rejection of such appeals for clemency from everyone from Khrushchev to members of the hierarchy of the Catholic Church even split Franco's cabinet (Linz:1973); while among the militants inside Spain at the time no event is more widely recalled or more passionately condemned. And Claudín (1983a) has it very clear that the Executive Committee of the Party in exile, and especially General Secretary Santiago Carrillo, were directly responsible for Julián Grimau's death.

STRATEGY, 'SUBJECTIVISM' AND INTERNAL CRITICISM OF THE PARTY LINE

Fernando Claudín had been a member of the Communist Youth since before its merger with the Socialist Youth in the 1930s, and, as a member of the Party's Secretariat and Executive Committee since 1956, was third in the Party hierarchy after Carrillo and Ibarruri. In 1963, following the execution of Grimau, and with the support of two other members of the Executive Committee – Jorge Semprún (whose *nombre de guerra* was Federico Sán-chez) and Juan Gómez – he began to criticize the Party line, asserting that National Reconciliation could never be an instrument of democratic revolution and condemning Carrillo's 'catastrophist' and 'subjectivist' interpretation of the Spanish reality, whereby the fall of Francoism was always 'imminent' and was only awaiting the *coup de grâce* which would be dealt by the long wished for and much worshipped peaceful national strike. In their view not only had Carrillo consistently overestimated the so-called crisis of the regime, he had also become obsessed with the peaceful national strike; whereas, in reality, there was no immediate prospect of a change in the balance of social forces in favour of the opposition, and meanwhile the 'subjectivism' of the leadership's predictions lost the Party credibility and, more seriously, led to the sacrifice of many good Party activists who had loyally pursued mistaken Party policies. Thus, by insisting on the imminence of peaceful change, which could not be frustrated by any reformist faction within the regime, and so trying to please everyone, the Party line was in danger of pleasing no one.

Although the regime was not in immediate crisis, argued Claudín and Semprún, Spanish society was indeed changing and becoming richer and more complex, and this required of the revolutionary vanguard a more differentiated, more carefully elaborated and, above all, more contingent political practice. Analytically, they may have been correct, says Mujal-León (1983) in retrospect, but they did not understand the 'psychology' of the clandestine Party as well as Carrillo, who had the constant responsibility of instilling faith and revolutionary fervour and sacrifice into the Party's militants. The 'subjectivism', he implies, was simply the price that had to be paid for what he calls Carrillo's 'activist vision'. Unwittingly, Mujal-León echoes the revised view of Juan Gómez, who recanted his position in order to save his political skin and later tried to salvage his rather unconvincing self-criticism with an explanation of the year-long confrontation (Gómez:1965), which may have appeared to debate the rate of growth in the number of tractors, the rural exodus and the instruments of State monopoly capital, but which in fact addressed the 'problem of the two paths': in short, Claudín and Semprún had attempted to divert the Party from the path that would lead the masses to democratic revolution. But within a few years these arguments were invalidated by Carrillo's tacit acceptance of the criticisms he had rejected at the time, and by his progressive adoption of many of Claudín's views. Not only were there far fewer references to the imminent demise of the regime, but after 1965 the Party pursued a gradualist strategy and embraced political pluralism, while relations with the USSR and the CPSU were ever more strained. By 1974, Carrillo was able to admit (Carrillo:1974) that Claudín's 'mistake' had been to 'be right too soon'.

At the time, however, Carrillo rejected Claudín's criticism as a 'right-wing liquidationist attempt', and the response of the Executive Committee was to expel Claudín and Semprún first from the Central Committee of the Party and then from the Party itself. On one level this had been yet another factional squabble which had more to do with personal rivalry than principle, insofar as its pedigree went back to the differences of opinion in the JSU of the 1930s between the former Communist Youth members headed by Claudín, and the ex-Socialists led by Carrillo; and even on the level of strategic divergences the challenge had deep roots within the Party, insofar as Claudín's critique was linked to Togliatti's Memorial of Yalta, his political testament, and the thesis of democratic decentralization and coexistence with competing organizations in order to win power (Ayucar:1976). For this reason, Claudín and Semprún were dubbed 'Italians' when they were not called 'right-wing elements', 'neo-capitalists' and 'socialist reformists'. But the expulsion of long-time militants for no greater crime than loyal criticism, and the deliberate distortion of the content of the debate, was not a pretty business, and the Seventh Party Congress in Prague in 1965 was shrouded in secrecy, not only to avoid the arrests which had followed the congresses of 1954 and 1960, but also to hide the dubious nature of these internal disputes. Nonetheless, these events had unforeseen political consequences. Felipe González, the present prime minister of Spain, was studying in Lorraine at the time and so could follow Claudín and Semprún's expulsion more closely than through the censored Spanish press; and he is quite categoric that 'they are responsible for me not being Communist' (*El País*:10.10.1982).

Ayucar (1976) interprets the confrontation in the light of what he calls 'the bible of Carrilloism', which is Carrillo's text *¿Después de Franco, Qué?*, first published in 1965. He points out that the book devotes one solitary and deprecatory paragraph to the 'Chinese' split, which was the reflection inside the Party of the confrontation between Mao and Khrushchev, even though it had led to heavy losses of young militants and the appearance of clandestine syndicates opposed to the Party; whereas considerable space is occupied by his account of the 'Italian' affair, which involved no more than a few students and intellectuals. In Ayucar's view, Carrillo was not too concerned by splits on the left of the Party, because they allowed him to hold to the centre, which is where he wanted to be; but splits on the right of the Party tended to push him farther left, which he was determined to resist. In the case of Claudín and Semprún, they came close to pointing in the direction which Carrillo himself was intending to travel, and so were expelled from the Party as traitors. But if anything this makes Carrillo out to be more Machiavellian than he really was (which in itself is not easy to do), because the broadly 'popular front' political line defended by Carrillo (and advocated by Claudín) had first to be endorsed by Moscow, as it was in a *Pravda* editorial of autumn 1965, which advocated alliances between Communists and 'social democrats'. In this way, the policy shift in Moscow which was designed to promote French Communist Party support for Mitterand in the French presidential elections, allowed the leadership of the Spanish Party to make another pragmatic strategy shift, which in Maravall's (1982) view was one more example of the kind of ideological opportunism[8] so typical of the political history of the Party. In this case he is right, but the Party kept playing the old tricks too. As late as the Eighth Congress of 1972 it was still talking of the national strike as the 'modern form of the popular uprising'; and even when announcing the Junta Democrática in July 1974 it was still hoping for a peaceful national strike, which in obedience to the historical moment was now called a 'national democratic action'.

What slowly emerged from this series of strategy shifts and personal confrontations was a consolidated idea of a 'democratic road to socialism' to be achieved by forging broad-based alliances with the 'forces of work and culture', which together would win the ideological battle against the monopolies and transform society without violence through a process of 'revolutionary reformism'. This idea was expressed in several publications of Carrillo, and in official party documents of the seventies, especially in the report of the Eighth Congress of 1972 and the 1973 Project of the Manifesto-Programme which was adopted by the Second Conference of the Party in 1975. Thus, National Reconciliation, general amnesty and the Pact for Liberty were milestones in the making of a movement which would restore democratic liberties. But the problem with these political formulations was that they were very vague and provided little guidance to concrete political practice within the country. Carrillo was a prolific political propagandist, and it is tempting to take his writings as a reflection of historical process, whereas, in fact, they merely defined the Party line as decided in Paris or Prague. Indeed, it is precisely because he takes Carrillo's political formulae rather too literally that Mujal-León (1983) tends to construct the whole of his own argument from the bizarre perspective of what the Party had to do 'to insure for itself a national presence in the post-Franco era', which allows him to tailor the facts to fit his teleological purposes. For the Party militants within the country the only questions were survival and the fight against Franco; and if the Party apparatus in exile had time and space to contemplate what was required to 'develop and legitimize its national presence' [sic], these militants certainly did not. Similarly, when Carrillo comes to elaborate his notion of Eurocommunism, it is ambiguous on key issues (Eaton:1981),[9] and offers no clear perception of the role of the Party within a liberal democratic system.

---

[8] Not everything was ideological opportunism. Carrillo was completely opposed to the invasion of Czechoslovakia, and almost broke with the CPSU over the issue, and this led to the expulsion of the 'soviets' in 1969, followed by that of Enrique Lister, José Barzana and Celestino Uriarte, the party leader in the Basque Country, in 1970. The Lister affair crystallized the rivalries between the two tendencies of monolithic Communism, on the one hand, and, on the other, the polycentrism which allowed Carrillo to pursue his own national strategy of peaceful pragmatism.
[9] In this text Carrillo talks explicitly of the 'democratic road to socialism', where public and private forms of ownership will coexist, but then limits this coexistence to the 'pre-socialist' phase. He distinguishes Eurocommunism from social democracy on the

DEMOCRATIC CENTRALISM AND
AUTHORITARIAN DISCIPLINE

The modal organization of the Party was pyramidal and was based on the Party cells in the different localities of the country, which in turn provided the members of the local or sectoral committees, from which the regional committees and finally the Central Committee were drawn; in principle, the Central Committee then appointed the secretary-general, the Secretariat and the Executive Committee, which was the standing executive body between plenums of the Central Committee, which was itself subject to the policy decisions of the Party Congress, which was the meeting point for representatives from the provincial and regional committees. The Eighth Congress of 1972[10] added another tier to the pyramid, which was the conference, bigger than the Central Committee but not as big as the congress itself, and which included the political secretaries from the provinces and the leaders of the Basque and Catalan parties; and there were also to be regional conferences, which would elect the regional committees, which together with the conferences would coordinate the organization of the Party within the country. The different committees of the Party within the pyramid each elected its own secretariat, composed of secretaries for political action, propaganda and finance, and as many other members as were considered necessary (Morodo et al.:1979). The committee was thus conceived as the key vertical connection of the whole Party structure, and it was the committee which conferred on this structure its highly centralized character. Hence, the organization of the Party was as hierarchical and as centralized as that of the Vertical Syndicate of the Francoist State; and its committees were as effective as Franco's delegates in applying the 'political line', which is the phrase used by both these organizations to describe the internal operation of their authoritarian rules.

In the augmented plenum of the Central Committee of 1956, Carrillo emerged as the man who had 'de-Stalinized' the Party, and in keeping with the mood of the moment the committee reorganized the Executive Committee in order to reinforce the internal democracy of the Party.[11] This initiative re-

grounds that Eurocommunism will transform capitalism and not merely administer it, but does not indicate what he means by this. There will no longer be a 'hegemony' of the monopolies, but one of the 'working and cultural forces', and the Communists do not expect to be the only or even the dominant political party representing these forces, although they will be in the vanguard. But Carrillo does not specify the programme of these forces, and so gives no idea of the kind of society he has in mind; and although he embraces parliamentary democracy, he says that there may be circumstances where violent revolution is necessary and desirable.

[10] In 1972 the Central Committee had 118 members, the Executive Committee 24 members, and the Secretariat 7 members.

[11] On the Executive Committee at that time were members of the 'old guard' of the thirties, including Dolores Ibarruri, Ignacio Gallego and Gregorio López Raimundo,

sponded to the general principle of democratic centralism, which was designed to safeguard the elective content of the committees and so place
democratic checks on the central authority. But in the very statutes of the 1960
congress, which 'coincidentally' elected Santiago Carrillo to the position of
secretary-general, it was noted that 'in the present clandestine conditions the
application of the principle of democratic centralism cannot be fully guaranteed insofar as it refers to the elective character and accountability of the executive organs of the Party', which clearly meant there was to be centralism but
no democracy. Indeed, looking back on these years of struggle from the van-
tage point of a newly democratic political system, the Party in Sanlúcar in El
Marco de Jerez recalled the 'iron discipline and the orders which in their majority were not debated by those who had to carry them out' (PCE: 1979); and
a generally sympathetic view from France of the Party's activities during the
sixties concluded that 'many of the inadmissible manoeuvres of the Party can
be explained by its incapacity to envisage any form of working-class organization which is not vertical and centralized' (Frères: 1969). Naturally enough,
the shadowy presence of a Party which could appear as bureaucratic and authoritarian as the regime it was committed to combat and defeat caused most
unease amongst the militants inside the country, who often felt coerced by a
seemingly alien political line which sometimes had little to do with the reality
they were living. In particular, they were unnerved by the dissensions and splits
of the sixties, not understanding how the Party could maintain its autocratic
character after its earlier condemnation of the personality cult (Ayucar: 1976).
But any criticism of the Party in exile always met with the objection that the
'real' Party was working on the inside. Well and good, replied Lister before his
expulsion: let all who wish to militate in the Party go to Spain, leaders first.

MANIFEST DESTINY AND LIBERAL DEMOCRACY: THE REVOLUTIONARY PARADOX

At the beginning of 1974, Francisco Romero Marín, one of the two or three
principal leaders of the Party inside the country, was captured after seventeen
years of continuous clandestine activity. This event, and the constitution of
the Junta Democrática in the same year, marked the end of the epoch of
clandestinity, just as the meeting with Stalin in 1948 had marked the end
of the armed struggle. By the late 1960s the objectives of the Party had
become almost identical with those of the democratic opposition to the
regime, insofar as both clearly wanted liberal democracy (Amodia: 1977),
but, as already observed, the reformist leadership of the Party could be said

as well as Eduardo García, who was responsible for the Party's clandestine organization, and Santiago Alvarez, who was responsible for international affairs. García,
who had been Carrillo's second-in-command after 1960, was finally expelled from
the Party in 1969, when his place was taken by Alvarez (Ayucar: 1976).

to have taken the liberalization of the regime in this period too seriously, and its militants inside the country were very exposed when the crackdown came at the end of the decade. However, if the repression and the consequent crisis in the movement made mass participation more difficult, it once again placed the Party at the centre of the struggle to the degree that the ideological pluralism of the workers' commissions became a thing of the past; and the repression thus contributed to create the core of dedicated labour activists around which the Party in exile hoped to build a mass organization.

In 1975, with the moment of the formal and constitutional transition to democracy approaching, and for the first time in many years, the leadership was very unsure of its political line. Indeed, it was not entirely sure of what it now was: a Marxist party with liberal democracy as just an instrument of social transformation; or a progressive party canvassing for votes and a place in the sun. And its legal future was anyway uncertain: the leaders of the Socialist Party already moved freely about the country, while the Communist leaders were still hunted. Over time, these questions of formal identity were resolved by the removal from the statutes of many clauses relating to the operational conditions of clandestinity, and the addition of others which conferred on the Party a more democratic cast. So the statutes decided in the Eighth Congress of 1972 defended the Party as a 'combative union based on marxist-leninist ideology', while the Ninth Congress of 1978 concluded that the Party could be organized 'on the basis that today there is no point in maintaining the restrictive idea that Leninism is the Marxism of our time'; and whereas in 1972 'the foundation of the Party was the base organization which is the cell', by May 1978 this 'base organization is the grouping (*agrupación*), which will organize the politics of the Party within a geographical area' (Morodo et al.:1979). The idea of these changes was to give a new content to democratic centralism by introducing more participation from the base (the grouping) (Eaton:1981), and by rejecting 'as something alien to Marxism, the phenomenon of bureaucratism and Stalinism'. But these formal and statutory changes proved insufficient to change the political character of the Party, even though they were enough to create severe dissensions within it.

It was in the plenum of the Central Committee meeting at the beginning of 1977, when the Party was still illegal, that Carrillo had proposed the grand lines of a transformation from a 'Party for the masses' to a 'Party of the masses', and it was with the specific objective of recruiting members en masse that the cell was suppressed in favour of the grouping. But this was a Party which had operated for forty years in clandestinity with a relatively reduced number of militants, and neither these militants nor the Party organization per se were prepared to absorb a huge influx of new members hoping to 'inherit the earth'. Rank-and-file activists became disenchanted with the national leadership's modelling of the Party, and resented the new groupings which tended to eliminate the power of the sectoral organizations;

while new recruits with more formal education tended to dominate the meetings of the groupings, and in many provincial organizations the shift to these groupings was used to strip power from such die-hard elements. For the Party now felt encumbered by the very militants who had fought hardest, and who were precisely the ones who found it hardest to adapt to the new rules; while they felt cheated by the absence of any dramatic rupture with Francoism, and by the rise to favour in the Party of more educated men who knew nothing of the working-class movement and had not wanted to know during the years of the repression. At the same time, the character of the Party did not change because the leadership did not change; and although it was Carrillo and his clique who promoted the formal changes, they themselves did not feel bound by them to the point of changing the habits of a lifetime. This insidious sclerosis meant that initiatives taken by the congress were no more likely to be put into practice now than before; while the executive continued to reject genuinely open debate and to expect the same kind of discipline it had required in clandestinity, which proved to be a recipe for increasingly acrid divisions.

In short, the Party attempted to adapt itself to the conditions of democratic politics, but failed. It did so for two main sets of reasons. On the one hand, despite formal adjustments in Party ideology and organization, the democratic transformation of Spanish politics was not accompanied by a similar change in the Party itself; on the other, the Party line was impossibly distorted by its respect for the stability of the incipient democratic system.[12] After all, it can be argued that despite or perhaps because of its pragmatism, the overall strategy of the Party was coherent in its broad lines from the announcement of National Reconciliation in 1956 to the formation of the Junta Democrática in 1974. But from this moment the Party committed a series of tactical blunders as it staggered disorientated through the fast-moving conjunctures of the early years of its legality. The sudden switch from being a Republican to being a Monarchist party was more than most of its militants could hope to understand; as was the insistence that a former minister of Franco, Fraga Iribarne, be included in the national wage negotiations which came to be known as the Pacts of Moncloa, so that the whole range of social forces be represented. And when the agreements reached in those negotiations were not respected, the Party did not mobilize for fear of impairing that fragile stability. The results of the June 1977 legislative elections were a disappointment for the Party, insofar as they did not reflect the far-reaching influence which the Party's close networks of

---

[12] The Party's moderation at this time reflected concern not only for the survival of the democratic system but also for its own place within that system; and eased the difficulties of reformist Prime Minister Adolfo Suárez as he worked to legalize the Party without provoking a right-wing and possibly military backlash. Nonetheless, the old-guard militants saw such moderation as an abrogation of Party principles.

activists had had in the clandestine struggle against Franco; but the results of the October 1982 elections were a disaster, which came near to condemning the Party to democratic oblivion.[13]

Jorge Semprún (1980) believes that men devote themselves to politics in order to achieve civil society and its personal freedoms; and that abstract models of society are likely to suffocate such freedoms. The liberating quality of communist revolution, recalling the quotation with which this chapter opened, is, then, the negation of politics 'insofar as politics is superimposed upon society'. The huge paradox of the Spanish experience is not merely that a deeply authoritarian and highly bureaucratized Communist Party should have made a crucial contribution to the achievement of liberal democracy in that country; but also that in committing itself to the liberation of the political process overall it negated not politics, but its own political practice, and effectively condemned itself to a political purgatory.

---

[13] Electoral support for the Party had continued to grow, if only very slowly, until the 1979 elections (the second of the democratic period and some time after the Pacts of Moncloa). In the longer term, however, this pale reflection of a growing confidence in the democratic credentials of the Party clearly failed to compensate for the internal disarray provoked by the attempts at democratic adaptation.

9

A place in the struggle: personal
networks and political practices in
El Marco de Jerez

I come from Pepe, and he asks to be remembered to you.

Anon.

THROUGHOUT THE RISE of the independent working-class movement in Spain the Communist Party was the principal organization of the clandestine opposition. But while it is not difficult to learn of its political line as proclaimed by the propaganda apparatus in exile, trying to reconstruct the Party's political practice on the ground is quite another matter. In part this has to do with the dearth of documentation: time and again Party militants recalled that any incriminating piece of paper could make them liable for as many as twenty years in gaol. In part it is a question of the intrinsic characteristics of clandestine operations, which mean that even the most dedicated of the militants have a picture of the process which is always incomplete and sometimes simply incorrect. In short, if they only see a small part of the process, it is because they were struggling in the dark. So the task of recuperating the key moments and meetings which can provide points of historical reference for local political practices is a delicate and fascinating one, which moreover departs from the central premise that these practices were woven from the tenuous threads of the personal networks which brought the restless men of the opposition together. But just as such networks contributed to make whole cloth of the local Party organization, so personal differences between local leaders could tear it apart. All this and more will emerge in the slow discovery of this part of the story, not with the intent of reproving the men who struggled in difficult and sometimes impossible circumstances, but, on the contrary, in the hope of recovering a piece of their own history, and returning it to them.

In the immediate post–Civil War years the only place that the Party maintained any presence at all was in El Puerto, and even here there were but five people in the one cell, including, exceptionally, one woman. At first their only ambition was to make contact with Communists who had lost touch with the organization, and by this means they managed to form a local committee in 1942. There is some unconfirmed talk that Benítez Rufo first came to the region in these years, prompted by his contact with Juan Modesto during the Civil War itself, and spent some six months in an early and unsuccessful effort to establish links between the Central Committee and the embryonic local organizations; but his arrest, and that of successive central committees (see Chapter 8), proved that such efforts were premature.[1] The local organizations, on the other hand, did succeed in establishing a provincial committee of sixteen members in 1944, which was led by the men of El Puerto but included representatives from Sanlúcar, Chipiona, Cádiz and Algeciras. Rafael Ribeiro was in charge of propaganda until the first wave of arrests (see Chapter 2), which was followed by long prison terms for such men as Valerio Ruíz, who served seventeen years in Burgos gaol. The effects of the repression failed to stop the organization, however, which not only began to extend through parallel networks in Sanlúcar and Jerez but even succeeded in printing *Mundo Obrero* in a bookshop of Jerez for distribution throughout the region.[2] But this proved too much provocation for the time, and 1948 saw a wider and more debilitating round of arrests.

In the early fifties the men of El Puerto were trying to rebuild their organization and reconstitute their local committee, and most of the political time of such men as Rafael Ribeiro was spent in recruiting the future leaders of the new generation, such as Rafael Gómez and Paco Artola. At this time there were perhaps no more than eight or ten people of like mind who listened to Radio Praga (Radio España Independiente), Radio Moscow and the British Broadcasting Corporation, and commented on the broadcasts amongst themselves. In Sanlúcar, Rafael Pinilla Romero, or 'the carpenter' as he was universally known, organized a similar small group, which included Juan Romero and his brother Manolo, Juan Ponce, and Emilio Fábregas. (Manolo had joined on sufferance, having first been rejected by Fábregas for being too 'anarchistic'!) Only very slowly did the small groups in the different *pueblos* begin to discover each other, and so loose were the networks that there is no clear consensus on how these first contacts took place. Rafael Ribeiro and Paco Artola remember 'the carpenter' as being the main link between Sanlúcar and El Puerto, before he finally went to France; but Juan Romero and Fernando Guilloto are convinced that the first contact was actually made with Emilio Fábregas. This discrepancy is explained, as becomes apparent below, by the presence of two separate

[1] It is said that Rufo visited virtually all the *pueblos* of the province except El Puerto, which is where the prison was situated, and which was infamous as a killing ground of Republicans and Communists.
[2] Rafael Ribeiro recalls that the bookshop was owned by Juan Vergara y Sasi, who was an intellectual related to the Osborne family, but who had served the Republican cause in the war, and who was sympathetic to the opposition to the Franco regime.

groups in El Puerto, which for a brief period were operating in ignorance of each other; but despite this confusion it is clear, even at this early date, that Sanlúcar was brought into the broader network by El Puerto, and finally came to have contact with the central organization of the Party only through El Puerto. The main objective of this first contact was to organize the vineyards, and by 1958 all but one of the leaders of the commissions in this sector had indeed joined the Party, subsequently constituting a local committee which included Manolo Romero and his brother Juan, Eduardo Sánchez, Sebastian Ribeiro, Emilio Chulián, Paco Chicorro, Pancaro, and Emilio Fábregas. At this time Fábregas was one of the most aggressive recruiters for the organization, and by some accounts it was he who first made contact with Paco Cabral in Trebujena, which is made plausible by their common role as representatives of the vineyard workers in the Vertical Syndicate. Others suggest that contact with Trebujena came by way of Jerez in the context of coordinating Party organization at the regional level, and was made with Miguel Campo rather than Paco Cabral; and this makes sense insofar as Miguel was one of the first young men of El Marco to join the Party, whereas Paco did not join until 1968. Whatever the truth of this, it was Paco Artola who came to act as the link between the committees of Trebujena and El Puerto (a task which was easy to combine with his trips to Sevilla to collect propaganda materials), with El Puerto continuing to act as the hub of the organization.

At one point in these developments there were two separate groups operating in El Puerto simultaneously. The original group of the self-styled 'primitives' (or *primitivos*), which included Rafael Ribeiro, Paco Artola and Manuel Fernández; and the group formed by Fernando Guilloto on his return from France in the spring of 1960. He had instructions to form a local committee, and the men who met on a beach on 1 May to do so included Antonio Cárdenas, Domingo López, José Luís Gamiz, Francisco Varguero, and Carlos Arébalo Arias, who had done military service with Fernando. The original group had been meeting on most days and were in contact with Sevilla; while the activities of the second group were initially confined to the distribution of *Mundo Obrero*. Fernando then returned to France, where he met with Benítez Rufo, who instructed him on the clandestine and cellular organization of the Party; but by the time Fernando came back to El Puerto in the autumn of 1960, the 'primitives' had been alerted to the presence of the new group by the number of *Mundo Obrero* on the streets. By this time Carlos Arébalo Arias had met with Rafael Ribeiro and Rafael Gómez of the 'primitives', who in turn were increasingly aware of the competition, which had now added such men as Juan Franco and Luis Lacera to its ranks, and had the advantage of being in direct contact with the Executive Committee in France. In one version of these events, the 'primitives' only learned of the new initiative when Fernando Guilloto was arrested for distributing *Mundo Obrero*, but in fact his arrest in February of 1961 came too late to have given the signal.

It was Benítez Rufo, who first arrived in El Puerto in October 1960, who took the initiative in fusing the two groups. The 'primitives' were distrustful of the initiative, fearing a police trap, and, as the day set for the first joint meeting happened to coincide with one of Generalísimo Franco's hunting trips to the region, the streets were full both of regular police and of the Political–Social Brigade.[3] Some say it was Fernando's youth which most worried them, but this must be a retrospective view for, according to Fernando, he was not present at the first meeting, at least, for reasons of security. Despite the distrust, Rafael Gómez volunteered to attend the meeting, which took place on the banks of the San Pedro River, and this is where Rufo ordered the organization of a new local committee, to include key members of both groups, and to serve as the nucleus of an expanded provincial committee, with representatives from Sanlúcar, Jerez and San Fernando. At this time, however, not only was the latter committee more hope than reality, but even Rufo's critical role in the political practice of the Party was still undefined. Before 1958 there had been a different 'linkman' from the Political Bureau (as it then was) whose code name was Juanito; and in the summer of the year following Rufo's first visit there arrived yet another such emissary, who called himself Pepe. No one knew who he was, then or later, and he only visited them once. He went first to the home of Fernando Guilloto, who, thinking him an agent provocateur, feigned ignorance (Fernando had been released for lack of evidence); and then to that of Juan Franco. His message? That someone would come from Catalonia and say, 'I come from Pepe, and he asks to be remembered to you'. In fact, Pepe turned out to be something of a John the Baptist, for the linkman he announced was none other than Jesús, or Benítez Rufo, who returned to El Puerto in the Spring of 1962.[4] This visit, it will be remembered, coincided with the first strike to be coordinated at the level of El Marco as a whole, and it is this moment, under the impulse of the commissions in the vineyards, which saw the effective formation of a provincial committee.

THE POLITICAL PRACTICE OF THE PROVINCIAL COMMITTEE

The first full local committee in El Puerto brought Antonio Camacho, Antonio Cárdenas, Rafael Severino, Rafael Ribeiro, Benito Herrera and Rafael Gómez into the leadership of the local Party, and was later expanded in

---

[3] This happened on the occasion of each of Franco's hunting trips to the region. For the same motive, some people were pulled off the streets for preventative detention, and could be seen walking the pavements in the following days with their heads shaved.

[4] In the meantime, as mentioned in Chapter 11, Rufo had visited Sanlúcar in the summer of 1961, which makes 'Pepe's' cryptic message appear rather superfluous. But it must not be forgotten that Rufo was also feeling his way and finding out whom he could trust. The only way he could avoid arrest (which he did successfully for all these years, as we saw in Chapter 1) was by exercising extreme caution.

1964 to include leaders like Paco de las Flores and Antonio Alvarez. For many of these men membership in the local committee in El Puerto was the springboard to the greater glory of the provincial committee, which in its beginnings was almost uniquely composed of militants from El Puerto such as Rafael Gómez, Paco Artola, Rafael Ribeiro, Juan Franco and Emilio Hermono; and although the first provincial committee was in constant contact with such leaders of Sanlúcar as Emilio Fábregas and 'the carpenter', they did not serve on it. Rafael Gómez was the secretary-general of the committee, and he immediately sought to extend the Party organization throughout the province, and especially in Algeciras and in such mountain *pueblos* as Arcos de la Frontera, Algodonales and Alcalá de la Valle. But while Gómez worked to make the committee an effective command centre for the province overall, he was aware that the heart of the struggle lay in the vineyards and was careful to cultivate his contacts with the leaders of Sanlúcar. Indeed, there can be no doubt that the combination of his political realism with Benítez Rufo's professionalism did much to make the local Party organization so effective in these early years.

Benítez Rufo ruled with a hard hand. So hard that Manolo Romero was twice expelled from the Party for indiscipline. But Rufo also knew whom to trust, and Manolo's house was one of the few places where he was disposed to hold political meetings. In fact, he timed his visits to the region so as to be present at nearly all the meetings of the provincial committee, where he delivered the Party Line, and commented on the political situation both locally and nationally. Rufo was more convinced than anyone of the importance of the struggle in the province of Cádiz, and especially in El Marco, of course, which was by far the most conflicted region; and never stopped pushing for more extended strikes and confrontations. One important extension of the struggle in these years was into Jerez, which traditionally had never been a very militant town. The first contacts were inauspicious and made almost casually through a man called Escalera, who was a heavy plant operator on one of the road construction crews. Not only was Escalera's job useful in contacting the mountain *pueblos*, but through him Rafael Gómez came to know Pepe Rosa and the small group of Communist sympathizers in Jerez itself. Pepe was quickly brought into the provincial committee in order to cement this extension of the network, and when Rafael Gómez left to work in Barcelona in 1968 he was chosen to replace him as secretary-general of the committee. This proved to be an important change in more ways than one. The committee was reorganized, with a specific allocation of roles to the secretaries of organization, propaganda, labour and finances; and Rufo, who for his own reasons was anyway a frequent guest at the house of Carmen de la Platera in Jerez, finally moved his 'headquarters' to the town. At the same time, and more importantly, Pepe Rosa seemed to push for more spectacular political actions and results, which was sometimes resented by the leaders of the vineyard workers, who doubted that a bank employee could truly understand the nature of their struggle. But in fact this aspect of the change had less to do with Pepe's personality than with the changing character of the local Party overall, and hence of its leadership.

From about 1966 a new generation of militants began to join the Party in El Puerto and Jerez. Unlike the first leaders, they often had some training as administrators, builders or mechanics, and so were more 'intellectual' than the 'primitives'; and, moreover, they had been blooded in the rising struggle of the commissions during the middle sixties. Hence, at the same time that the strategic decision to create a mass party was filtering down from the Executive Committee to regional organizations throughout Spain, a new local leadership, drawn directly from the labour movement, began to push for more mobilization and a different style of struggle (see Chapter 7). This change was reflected in the composition of the provincial committee, which by 1968 included not only the 'old guard' of Rafael Ribeiro, Paco Artola and Emilio Fábregas, but also men from the commissions such as Pepe Jiménez, Antonio Alvarez and Miguel de la Madrid (with Federico Iglesias in close collaboration), and the 'intellectuals' such as José María García and, of course, Pepe Rosa; and similarly in the local committee of Jerez where Antonio Palacios and Pepe Rosa were joined by Juan Sánchez, Manolo Fernández Mata, Pepe Pérez and Pedro Ríos. At the same time, 1966, Miguel Marroquín took over the organization of the Communist Youth, and after recruiting intensively in Sanlúcar, San Fernando, Trebujena and Algeciras, succeeded in raising its numbers from eight to one hundred and twenty-eight. Such was the effervescence of political activity in these years that by the end of the decade the Party was operating more or less openly in El Puerto especially, where its some three hundred militants enjoyed an almost awesome respect amongst the working population. By this time *Mundo Obrero* was being sold on the streets and in the buses, and although many of the Party leaders had been identified, the Party's capacity for mobilization made the police reluctant to move against them. Indeed, before very long El Puerto as the *foco* of regional dissent became something of a national scandal, and it was at this moment that the oligarchy of El Marco brought pressure to bear on the Franco regime to bring in the Political–Social Brigade (as recounted in Chapter 10).

In this connection it is interesting to compare the judges' version of this rapid growth of the organization as manifest in the sentences delivered by the Tribunals of Public Order (Juzgado:1971a, 1971b). In this version the key figures of the Party in El Puerto were Antonio Alvarez, Antonio Cárdenas, Francisco Artola and Manuel Espinar, who in 1967 began to proselytize for the Party and recruit new members, such as Miguel Marroquín Travieso and Andrés González Herrera, and use the skills of the printer José Antonio (Pepe) Jiménez to run off pamphlets and other propaganda materials in the workshop of José María Perea España. The sentence continues with further details of who recruited whom and when, and although representing a rather loose and often quite hypothetical account, in its own way it does reflect the rapid extension of the organization through the classic mechanism of personal networking. Thus, the judges have Antonio Cárdenas recruiting Federico Iglesias and Miguel Muñoz, and, in similar fashion, Paco Artola recruiting Francisco Marín (who operated one of the Party's stencil machines in his apartment in Jerez) and promoting further contacts in Jerez through Pepe Rosa; while in Sanlúcar, Manolo Romero, who joined the Party in 1964, apparently recruited Nicolás Gómez Ruíz (Pancaro) and Eduardo Sánchez Fernández in 1965, Francisco Delgado Gordillo in 1966, Manuel Sánchez Fernández in 1967, José Raposo Rodríguez in 1968 and José Francisco Rodríguez Calvo in 1969. Notwithstanding the inaccuracies of these sentences, then, not to mention their arbitrary nature, whereby the few pieces of information and misinformation available to the judges are loosely constructed into a story of conspiracy, they do provide a simplified and metaphorical map of the extending networks of the political opposition.

PERSONAL NETWORKS AND PARTY ORGANIZATION IN EL MARCO

The first of the great protagonists of the working-class movement in El Marco was Emilio Fábregas of Sanlúcar, yet his relationship to the Party apparatus was always ambiguous and finally conflictual, to the point where Emilio now denies ever having belonged to the Party at all. Many witnesses contradict this, not only on the evidence of the Party dues he undoubtedly paid, but by his presence on the provincial committee with Rafael Severino, Paco de las Flores and Rafael Gómez. Indeed, some assert that Emilio had more contact with Party leaders at national level than any of the local leaders, by virtue of the important posts he held within the Vertical Syndicate, and that he often met directly with Rufo; but others, while admitting this, suggest that he nevertheless always kept his distance from the Party apparatus and the Party line. For leaders like Antonio Alvarez, this independence is seen as a virtue; but others suggest that it merely betrayed a lack of commitment to the cause. They do not doubt his talents. He could have been the Marcelino Camacho of the rural workers, if only he had fully assumed that cause. As it was, the more disenchanted argue, he behaved in a contrary fashion, arguing for strikes when there was nothing to be won, and arguing against them when the conditions were clearly right. Emilio's view is that he was often unprepared to commit the vineyard workers to a strike which would merely benefit the abstract objectives of the Party; and, similarly, when his denial of Party membership is countered by his attendance at the Party congress in France, where he had travelled disguised under a wig, Emilio objects that he went as a representative of the rural commissions, and not as a Party member.

Emilio had not always been so distant from the Party, and it is suggested that his estrangement began when Pepe Rosa took over the provincial committee and began to insist that he toe the Party line more carefully than he had in the past; but as important (as will emerge in Chapters 11 and 12) was his personal rivalry with Manolo Romero and the increasing depth of the differences between them, which were forced into the open by the wave of arrests at the beginning of 1970. Although some fifty militants were arrested throughout El Marco, including five from the provincial committee, Emilio himself was never picked up because his comrades covered for him. In short, all those who, like Paco de las Flores, Paco Artola, Paco Cabral, Emilio Chulián and Manolo Romero and his brother Juan, found themselves in gaol, had the presence of mind to insist on Emilio's 'vertical' credentials, as a way of leaving him free to act for the Party. And it is in this conjuncture that Emilio stands condemned on three counts. First, it is argued that had he given a proper lead to the militants of Sanlúcar, the repression would not have focused on El Puerto, where the leadership of the Party was concentrated, and some of the damage to the political apparatus of the Party could have been avoided. Second, although it was the loyalty of his Party comrades which saved him, he straightway afterwards abandoned the Party in its hour of need; and third, he repeatedly refused to attend the Tribunal of Public Order in Madrid in order to testify on behalf of his comrades, and had to be obliged to do so by threatening revelations which could implicate him in the legal process.

Needless to say, perhaps, the events were not quite this straightforward. Not all agree that he abandoned the Party, although he could not be said to have done much for it. His reasons at the time looked plausible enough, when he argued that his 'vertical' responsibilities gave him too high a profile to afford to be seen consorting with known Communists; and although Benítez Rufo amongst others expected him to take a leading role in reorganizing the Party, he insisted that he wanted to continue working in the old way, inside the Vertical Syndicate, but now with the collaboration of new leaders who would necessarily have to replace those lost (temporarily) to the repression. Everything was in any case very confused at the time, and communications had broken down; and Emilio's break with the Party was not sudden but became apparent only gradually as he failed to attend successive meetings of the rump of the leadership. But as the Party had had great confidence in him, some leaders felt deceived, and by the time of one of the meetings he did attend in 1971 they had turned against him, and so turned on him.[5] Some suggest, then, that it would have been better for him

---

[5] Bitterness breeds scurrilous comment, and unconfirmed reports circulated of the favour shown to Emilio by the oligarchy of Jerez which extended him credit for the purchase of land, and of a certain sum of money which went missing. Such stories can certainly be dismissed as sour grapes. But one thing which did rankle with the militants of the

to have been arrested, so that such ambiguities might never have arisen; for by the logic of the situation, and by the time of the Vertical elections in 1975, Emilio was indeed in open confrontation with the Party, which led some to suggest that he had become an 'enemy' of the working class, which was never true. This was anyway not a universal opinion, and in more recent years, and under a democratic regime, it was mooted within the Party that some attempt should be made to 'recuperate' Emilio; but the political will to build such a bridge was lacking, and it was thought that even were it there, too much water would have flowed under it.

The other major protagonist of the movement in El Marco was Antonio Alvarez (see Chapter 7), who, like Emilio, began his political militancy in the commissions, but who, unlike Emilio, took his career in the Party very seriously indeed. He rose sharply through its ranks to membership of the provincial committee, and from this commanding position he took the struggle out onto the streets. He appeared to have the full support of Benítez Rufo, who was pleased to have spectacular protests that would look well to his mentors in France, and Alvarez was equally pleased to inflate his reports of such protests, so that 'if it was a thumb, he said it was an arm'. And Rufo could better advance his own objective of constantly increasing the rhythm and scope of the struggle by playing to what others came to see as Alvarez's vanity. So, contrary to the complaint against Emilio that he was holding the struggle back, Alvarez was accused of forcing it forward, although it must be added that such accusations were not patent before the repression of 1970, when, in the bitterness that ensued, everyone was looking for reasons for the reversal. It was only then that the clear ascendancy of Alvarez within the movement became a cause for concern, and that criticisms began to be levelled against his 'personalism' or egotism. But if what Alvarez said was 'God's word', then many militants are prepared to admit that this was as much the fault of the people who listened to him. There is no doubt in their minds that at that time Alvarez was a brave and honourable man, and a strong and sympathetic one, but his need to be out in front was clearly matched by the willingness of others to put him there.

If the repression in Sanlúcar mainly brought problems for Emilio Fábregas, despite the fact that he remained free while others went to gaol, the repression in El Puerto undoubtedly damaged the Party itself, which became divided between two distinct groups, one led by Antonio Alvarez and the other by Paco Artola. The mutual accusations began in prison, with the two sides blaming each other for their predicament, and then spilled into the outside world when Alvarez tried to impose his line on the militants

Party (and which I can confirm) was a press photograph showing Emilio giving an *abrazo* (or hug) to Generalísimo Franco. What is certain is that Emilio became more and more convinced of the durability of Francoism, and hence of the political importance of his role in the Vertical Syndicate.

who remained free, but who were confused and disorientated by what could only be seen as a clear split in the provincial committee. In both Sanlúcar and El Puerto the personal networks attached to different political leaders clearly acted to condition the political practice of the Party, but the latent contradictions between Party organization and personal networks did not become manifest until the repression struck. The differential effects of this repression in the two *pueblos* are easily explained by the peculiar position of Emilio Fábregas, who, despite his long years of syndical leadership, lost the confidence of his own network when he was tried in the fire and found wanting. Had it not been for what those he represented saw as his pusil-lanimity, then the organization in Sanlúcar may well have split between the distinct networks of Manolo Romero and Emilio, much as it split between Paco Artola and Antonio Alvarez in El Puerto. At the same time, the work-ing-class movement and the Party in Sanlúcar continued to be closely iden-tified in terms of both their leaders and their tactics, whereas in El Puerto it might be argued that the leaders who joined the Party from the movement lost touch with the real political constraints acting on their syndical practice, which still remained the basis of the democratic project.

RECONSTRUCTION AND RECRIMINATION AFTER THE 'FALL'

Not all the leaders of the Party were arrested in 1970, and those who were left free moved immediately to reorganize the Party. The very first day after the main wave of arrests in El Puerto, Federico Iglesias went out to contact the remaining members of the local committee, while José María García as the only survivor from the provincial committee (and still the only one with a car) went to Sevilla to seek advice from Fernando Soto and the comrades from the provincial committee there. The organization in Jerez had suffered less, and Manolo Romero Ruíz, Juan Sánchez, Pepe Perez and Rafael Pintor met to organize collections of money to support those in prison, and to this end made contact with El Puerto again. About a month afterwards Benítez Rufo arrived, and a meeting took place in the chalet of José María García in the mountains, where Rufo studied the situation and delivered his verdict. Certain of the comrades were strongly censured, and Pepe Mena (remember Pepe?) was brought in from France to head an 'emergency committee' com-prising José María García, José Marroquín and one or two others. This committee was fully operational by October 1971, and *Mundo Obrero* was again being distributed, which at least gave an impression of political ac-tivity. Then as the first of those detained began to be released, either because like Paco Cabral they had been absolved or because like Miguel Marroquin they had only to serve very short sentences, the committee was expanded to include these men, as well as Miguel Campo and José Ruíz Caballero from Trebujena and Manuel Verano from Sanlúcar. It was Federico Iglesias and Miguel Marroquín who had recovered many of the contacts, travelling throughout the region on Miguel's motor-scooter, and they continued to cover the Party's communications even after José María García had finally been arrested in 1971.

Naturally, everyone was afraid following the arrest of virtually the whole of the provincial committee, and many had no stomach to continue the struggle. The burden of reorganization in the initial months had to be carried by very few people, and they they tended to become exhausted and demoralized. Federico Iglesias was aware of having to hold out until the first of the committee members began to be released from prison, but all his efforts only earned him increasing criticism from the Party, and he retired from the struggle early in 1972. In fact, despite the heroic commitment of many of the militants, and the apparent invincibility of some stalwarts of the Party like Rafael Ribeiro, there is no doubt that the repression had succeeded in throwing the Party into complete disarray, and the rhythm of the struggle was barely perceptible. The change was felt dramatically in Sanlúcar, where Emilio Fábregas was suddenly no longer a leader of the movement; but, at the same time, here as elsewhere, the repression opened up a space in the Party for a new generation of militants, and as Emilio faded from the foreground, men like José Infante, Sebastián Ribeiro and especially Manolo Verano rose to take his place. Many of the old guard in the town dropped from political view, partly from confusion, partly from fear, and when Manolo Romero was released in 1972, none of the former comrades would speak to him, even though wherever he went in his first months he drank for free, in a collective display of what Manolo calls 'clandestine affection'. But then he met with Manolo Verano, who introduced him to the new men of the Party, many of whom had joined while Manolo was in prison. Heartened by this encounter, Manolo once again formed his own cell and began to recruit. The organization of the Party had been badly damaged but not destroyed, and slowly the Party's ranks were swelled by the struggle's second generation.

By 1973 most of the leaders of the local Party, such as Pepe Jiménez, Paco Artola and Antonio Alvarez, were being released, and in the same year Rafael Gómez returned from Barcelona at the request of the Party in El Puerto. Then Pepe Mena and Rafael Gómez worked together to construct a new provincial committee composed both of men of the old guard who had served their terms and of new men, such as Manolo Verano, whom the repression had pushed up through the ranks. Benítez Rufo had a hand in this, of course, and some say now began to act in a more arbitrary manner than ever before, pushing aside loyal elements like Fernando Guilloto and Benito Herrera, and bringing younger men like Miguel Marroquín onto the provincial committee. This was a question not of generations, however, but of the divisions which continued to rack the Party in the years following the arrests. On Rafael Gómez's return he had attempted a reconciliation, and had held an informal meeting with Pepe Jiménez, Paco Artola, José María García and others to see what could be done. But the divisions which had begun in prison were difficult to erase. They had begun with mutual recriminations for allowing the police to capture the propaganda apparatus (someone had talked), and had continued with Antonio Alvarez's insistence that they should deny the content of their 'confessions' in court and allege that they had been extracted under torture (which was true in some cases). Not everyone agreed, and the disagreements were pursued outside the prison, where the police used them further to divide and disorientate the Party. Then, given Alvarez's clearly preeminent position and his great popularity, all the money and food collected for the sustenance of the prisoners was taken to his house, which acted as a informal headquarters of the resistance, and this bred more resentment amongst his rivals; while Alvarez himself would brook no challenge to his own person but tried to entrust the reorganization of the Party on the outside to his own emissary Miguel Muñoz, on his release. In effect, whatever the specious issues, these were more like personal quarrels than political divisions, and they were especially shocking to men of proven courage and purported communist ideals; although in fact many of these men were simply syndical leaders, who had joined the Party because it was the only political vehicle for fighting a dictatorship which forbade freedom of assembly and free trade unions. Nonetheless, it is particularly apt that the men of the Party refer to the impact of the arrests as 'the fall' (*la caída*). They themselves use the term with no hint of religious irony, but it was indeed like a fall from innocence and grace; from unity and solidarity, and militant perfection, to a divided story of human foibles and weaknesses.

Following the fall, and during the transition to democracy in Spain, the divisions within the Party were temporarily resolved by Alvarez's continuing ascendancy. He not only dominated the provincial committee in alliance with Manolo Espinar, but succeeded in imposing his own line on the local committees, on the local organizations of the commissions, and in most meetings he attended. He insisted, as always, on pushing the struggle forward, and came into direct confrontation with Paco de las Flores, who was by then the national president of the vineyard workers within the Vertical Syndicate, and who refused to launch a strike at Alvarez's behest. His preeminent position was partly owing to his control of the most powerful commission operating within the Syndicate (that of sherry manufacture in the *bodegas*), which was well organized, very militant and replete with Party members; and partly owing to the organizational characteristics of the local Party, which had always drawn the majority of the provincial committee from El Puerto, and which depended for resources on its Party apparatus. In addition Alvarez had the support of Benítez Rufo, who now never met with the local committees, and this left Alvarez, Espinar and Marroquín free to set their own agenda and decide strategy without any significant resistance. So although there were reasons to censure Alvarez, the provincial committee did nothing, and he continued to appear not merely as a symbol of the struggle but also, by extension, as the principle of unity of the Party itself. Moreover, it is said that he was not above the machinations of clientelistic politics, and limited the enrollment of new members to his own supporters, who, although they may have had little interest in the Party or the movement, did attend meetings and exercise their right to vote. Finally, in 1979, Alvarez was elected mayor of El Puerto, but just two years later the Party he thought he controlled obliged him to resign; and although he was never expelled from the Party, he himself resigned from it shortly afterwards, and took with him some sixty-four of the newer members. More surprisingly, he also left the commissions, but continued to work as a foreman in the *bodega* Caballero.

THE LOCAL PARTY IN THE TRANSITION
TO DEMOCRACY

The local Party had remained in disarray until 1973, but the working-class movement in the form of the commissions had maintained the impetus of the struggle for democracy. By this time democratic councils (or Juntas Democráticas) were coming together throughout the country, and the Party leaders began to meet with their counterparts in the local citizens' movement, such as Rojas Pinilla and Rafael Escuredo. Rafael Gómez was made the Party's delegate to the council, leaving Antonio Alvarez free to dedicate his time to the commissions, and as such was the first man in the province to speak publicly in the name of the Party, at a joint meeting of the local democratic council and the united platform (*plataforma de convergencia*). During this time of pre-recognition and transition the Party even maintained an office in El Puerto, where anyone could enter to discuss Party politics, and with the prospect of democracy coming ever closer a certain air of festivity overtook Party activities, which appeared to heal the old wounds. Hence, not only were there strikes and demonstrations, but there was also a Party fair, put on to raise money to support the strikes and indeed the Party apparatus itself. The last day of the fair turned into a kind of communist celebration, with the police standing idly by and powerless to prevent it, just as they were no longer able to prevent the open distribution of *Mundo Obrero* in the vineyards. Finally, just before the meeting of the Central Committee of the Party in Rome in June 1976, the local committee of the Party in El Puerto held a public meeting precisely in order to present themselves to the public and so make themselves 'legal'; and in the months before legalization many new members were recruited, the membership within the province rising from about 500 in 1976 to 4,500 by early 1977.

But with the advent of democracy in the society at large, the Party, too, began to put a little democracy into its own principle of democratic centralism and held elections to the political posts within the Party, which was enough to dispel the illusion of unity conjured up by the transition. In El Puerto the effect was immediate, insofar as the first democratic meeting of the 317 militants of the local organization triggered a move to unseat Manolo Espinar as secretary-general of the local committee, and the ensuing debate brought all the old recriminations to the surface. A further meeting was held to decide the issue, with Benítez Rufo present, and to the surprise of many and the chagrin of some he came out against Espinar, and, by implication, Miguel Marroquín and Antonio Alvarez, thus inaugurating the open struggle for power inside the Party. As it happened, Miguel Marroquín was elected to replace Manolo, but found himself in direct confrontation with the new secretary-general of the provincial committee, Horacio Lara, who brought pressure to bear on him by ordering him out of the *pueblos* where he was organizing, and directing him to work much farther afield. As if by a signal, all manner of means such as false accusations, bureaucratic manoeuvres and blackmail were then levelled against him, and he was even suspended from the Party for some six months;[6] and though he was finally absolved by the regional conference in Sevilla, its refusal to order an investigation into the motives behind the accusations against him led to his resignation from the provincial committee. The further details of the fight are not of direct concern, except to note that by now the struggle was structured by the confrontation between the provincial committee and the local committee of El Puerto: and the crux of the matter was that as long as Miguel was secretary-general of the local committee the new powers at provincial level could not force Antonio Alvarez out. As could be expected, Miguel finally resigned not only from this post but from the Party in 1981, the same year that the Party obliged Alvarez to step down as mayor.

Antonio Alvarez argues that neither the Party nor the commissions properly understood his role as mayor of all the *pueblo*, and not merely of specific constituencies within it. Following his ouster as mayor, he ran as an independent in the municipal elections of 1983, which provoked something of a scandal amongst his former Party comrades, who saw it as a kind of heresy and alleged that his fellow candidates included two ex-Francoist mayors and construction bosses who together were involved in shady real estate deals. Alvarez replied that he was running on an independent ticket only to counter the excesses of the provincial committee under Horacio Lara. Thanks to the support he still enjoyed amongst the *bodega* workers and amongst some Communists, Alvarez was the only candidate on the list to be elected, but he declined to take up his seat when the Party won a

---

[6] Such local power struggles must have been occurring across the country in these years. For instance, at the same time that Miguel Marroquín was fighting for his political life (and that of Antonio Alvarez), Fernando Soto was under heavy attack by similar means in Sevilla.

majority on the council. From Horacio Lara's point of view, this merely represented one of the last spasms of Party parochialism, which was characterized by a suspicion of the so-called opportunists and a corresponding reverence for the old guard of Communist militants. Thus the Party in Sanlúcar, and Alvarez's faction in El Puerto, simply had difficulty in absorbing the political and cultural advances expressed in a progressive provincial committee like the one in Cádiz.

There is no doubt that Lara is at least halfway right insofar as these very particular disputes do reveal certain critical problems experienced by the national Party in the years since the transition to democracy. In effect, the Party's monolithic commitment to fight Franco's dictatorship, combined with a pragmatic political line which underwent a series of strategic shifts, precluded the elaboration of a sophisticated ideology, and this worked very well in conditions of clandestinity. In other words, while the dictatorship was in place, it was enough for the Party's project to be simply democratic. But with the advent of that democracy, then the struggle was no longer against the dictatorship *tout court*, but had to be structured by a different kind of project which proposed a distinct model of society; and it was in this context that divisions emerged between the old guard and the 'renovators' (*renovadores*), and were pursued with all the mutual distrust and recrimination evident in El Marco de Jerez itself.[7] Moreover, the situation was exacerbated by the attempts of the national leadership to reform the Party, and in particular Carrillo's proposal to transform it from a 'Party for the masses' to a 'mass Party' through the suppression of the cell as the basic organizational unit, and the creation of the territorial groupings (*agrupaciones territoriales*); for in the view of the Party in Sanlúcar, for example (PCE:1979), the meetings of the groupings tended to be monopolized by young arrivistes and intellectuals, by those with most 'culture', so that 'instead of doing it we just talk about it'.

According to Claudín (1978;1983a), although this order of problem is certainly more widespread in democratic conditions, its seeds were present

---

[7] The problem of the traditionalists and the 'renovators' can also be illustrated by the events in Sevilla (referred to in footnote 6), where a local committee of *carrillistas* (after Santiago Carrillo), supported by four other local committees, was similarly in dispute with the provincial committee. It all began in 1980 when Fernando Soto lost his fight with the chief of the renovators and secretary-general of the provincial committee, Juan Bosco Díaz de Urmeneta, and so he and the *carrillistas* had to retire to the local committee. They then called upon the Executive Committee to adjudicate, and the province was visited by a delegation comprising Jaime Ballesteros, Francisco Romero Marín, Enrique Curiel and Simon Sánchez Montero, who refused to discipline the local committee, thus provoking the resignation of the provincial committee. In this way, the faction which opposed the official Party structure of the province succeeded in ignoring the political line of the provincial committee by going over its head to the national headquarters in Madrid. Following the resignation, the Central Committee sent a more permanent delegation to run the Party in the province.

as early as 1964, or even in the late fifties. But the recent divisions are not just a question of differences in ideas, or styles, but have to do with the egotism and opportunism which the old guard sees as characterizing the competition for posts in the town halls. In their view, this was more important than any debate over the content of Eurocommunism, and has left many of the old militants embittered at the lack of recognition of their long years of struggle and sacrifice. In the strongest terms, it was their sufferings in exile, imprisonment and torture which paved the way for the transition, but they themselves have now been put aside and forgotten. But in El Marco de Jerez, at least, not all of them were on the outside, and the local power centres which focused on the town halls, the commissions and the administration of the 'community work' resources (*empleo comunitario*) were many of them in the hands of the old leaders and their networks (or *camarillas*). It is true that this small mafia of the left, as its critics see it, has again extended the networks into the younger generation, but this was the second generation of the struggle, which had had some experience of clandestine work in the early seventies. The youth of today are the ones who are completely on the outside, so much so that they do not even enter the bars with their fathers. They, too, are often bitter, and nearly always unemployed, even though their bitterness may not be as eloquent as that of the old guard, who struggled for liberty only to lose their identity in the new freedom and find themselves without political meaning for the first time in their adult lives.

Inevitably, many of the problems of the Party in El Marco reflect the vicissitudes of the national Party following the transition to democracy, but nonetheless the progress of the local Party is far from presenting a mirror image of the national one; and, in general, Party identification and Party support have held up much better in El Marco than virtually anywhere else in the national territory, as was evident in the results of the most recent elections, the municipal elections of 1983.[8] Even in the national legislative

[8] The results of the municipal elections of May 1983 were as follows: in El Puerto 18,724 votes were cast out of a possible 36,807, with 6,139 of them for the Spanish Communist Party, so electing 9 councillors for the Party, as against 8 for the Socialists, 7 for the Popular Alliance, and 1 Independent (who was Antonio Alvarez); in Sanlúcar, 18,308 votes were cast out of 32,535, with 9,994 of them for the Party, so electing 12 councillors for the Party, as against 6 for the Socialists and 3 for the Popular Alliance; in Trebujena 3,635 votes were cast of a possible 4,357, with 2,324 for the Party, giving it 9 councillors, as against 4 for the Socialists, and none for the Popular Alliance. Jerez was the exception to prove the rule: 72,749 votes were cast of a possible 117,230, with 39,231 for the Andalusian Socialist Party, so electing 16 councillors, against 7 for the Socialists and 4 for the Popular Alliance.

Across Andalucía, the Socialists gained 352 councillors, the Popular Alliance 94, the Communists 70, the Andalusian Socialist Party 35, with 112 Independents. So between them Sanlúcar, Trebujena and El Puerto elected 30 out of the Party's total of 70 councillors for the whole of Andalucía.

In the legislative elections in Andalucía the Party won about 300,000 votes in June

elections of October 1982, which were nothing short of a disaster for the national Party, the vote held more or less steady in El Marco, and even went up in Trebujena, despite the poor reception given to the Party's agrarian reform programme, which was seen as abusive of the small-holders who are so numerous in Trebujena and Sanlúcar. To a degree this is because the local Party is clearly distinct from the Party nationally, insofar as its close identification with the assembly-based working-class movement led it to practise a more direct democracy at the local level, where the principles of democratic centralism came much closer to realization than in the Party in exile; and, as a corollary, its leaders tended always to be those natural leaders who, if they had not actually risen from the assembly, had to be able to carry an assembly on the strength of the intuitive trust the workers placed in them. If this were not the case, then it is doubtful whether the bitter divisions which emerged in the local Party following the 'fall' of 1970 would have surfaced in the way they did, or at all. At the same time, the very fact of that fall from innocence, which revealed that there was something rotten in the Party long before the transition to democracy, meant that the recent problems were seen not as a necessary result of democracy but as a legacy of the clandestine past, which could be overcome democratically. Had the national Party achieved a coherent consensus of this kind, then it might have avoided the electoral doldrums which presaged its division and decline.

of 1977; some 400,000 in March of 1979; and some 500,000 in the April 1979 municipal elections. But in the legislative elections of October 1982 the Party managed to hold only two of the seven seats it had had until then.

10

The other side of darkness:
the repressive practices of the
Franco regime

Is it fear that protects the vineyards? Of course. But as long as it continues to protect them, God bless it.

Alvarez de Toledo, *The Strike*

If you stumble, it means you're walking.

Paco de las Flores

THE NATURE OF THE REGIME that was to be ushered into history by the final victory of the Nationalist cause on 1 April 1939 was clearly signalled by the Law of Political Responsibilities of early in the same year, which included a clause on 'grave passivity', making even simple residence in the Republican zone a possible crime. Under the dubious legal umbrella of this retroactive law, anything from 22,000 (Carr:1982) to 200,000 (Al-varez:n.d.) Spaniards were executed in the following few years, and this wave of revenge was accompanied by the cruel economic coercion of countless others, who were either summarily sacked from their jobs or compelled to work long hours by the threat of political retribution (Candel:1968): by Article 11 of the Labour Charter 'any collective or individual action which prejudiced the rhythm of production was considered a crime against the State', and the translation of this principle into Article 222 of the Penal Code made any strike or labour protest tantamount to treason (FSM:1959). Any infringement of the principle was judged by military tribunals, which operated with terrible severity, and condemned strike leaders and activists to long prison terms of twenty years or more. Thus, taking into account the widespread presence of child labour, the Spain of these early years resembled nothing so much as a large concentration camp.

Although this widespread repression continued in later years, it tended to abate with the passing of time (Soto:1976). In the 1950s there were still thousands of political prisoners from the Civil War, and the final three years of the decade saw a further six hundred prison sentences handed down for political crimes (Maravall:1978). But there is no doubt that by this time the repression had become more selective, and bore more heavily on some regions than others. One such region was Asturias, where the regime applied its first states of siege as one instance of the close control achieved by its police (Miguélez:1976), and where the strike of 1958 provoked the arrest of some two hundred miners, many of whom were to spend large parts of their lives in gaol; another was El Marco de Jerez, where tens of Communist sympathizers were arrested in 1948, and where in 1951 almost a hundred anarchists from this and surrounding regions (Vilar:1976) were condemned to eight to thirty years, and two of them executed. In such regions, and in such small towns as El Puerto de Santa María, the working-class movement was more directly and more immediately exposed to the forces of order than were the incipient commissions in Madrid or Barcelona, and so learned to struggle in the raw; with the result, as Soto (1976) wryly observes, that though some may think too much emphasis is given to the question of repression, the thought is not shared by those who suffered it.

If in the immediate post–Civil War years the repression was mainly directed against those who had in one way or another opposed Franco's insurrection, as time passed it found a new focus in the working-class movement, and this became patent once strike actions began to be organized in the latter half of the 1950s. Not only were there the very numerous arrests which followed the strikes in Asturias and Barcelona, for example, but there were also the preventative detentions which occurred before the days of National Reconciliation; and in the trials which accompanied the arrests the prosecutors were quite prepared to fabricate evidence against those they had identified as the 'leaders', who were those with a background of resistance to the regime, by commission or omission. Torture, if of a rather crude kind, was routinely used against such men, who were later imprisoned or condemned to internal exile (FSM:1959). Even without the provocation of a strike, those workers who as shop stewards (or *enlaces*) attempted to defend the interests of their workmates were treated to the hardest work and denied overtime (Candel:1968); and the employers also looked to control their work force through discrediting, threatening or corrupting such representatives (Soto:1976). Less aggressive employers were encouraged by the Decree of September 1962, which gave them the right to sack any workers accused of participation in any kind of labour conflict, without obligation of further explanation (Miguélez:1976); and in 1963 the regime created the Tribunals of Public Order or TOPs (Tribunales de Orden Público) in order to combat political dissidence by the labour movement (terrorist activities and violent political actions still being prosecuted by court martial) (Payne:1985). This was the same year that the commissions had first begun to appear in the open through participation in the Vertical elections, and in their first four years these TOPs tried 4,317 cases (Carr:1982); while over the three years of 1964–6 some 1,800 members of the Vertical factory committees (or *jurados*) were dismissed from their posts

(Wright:1977; Maravall:1978). By this time, then, repression in the workplace could come through dismissal from the *jurado*, through dismissal from the job, or through purely political sanctions imposed by the TOP, which in addition to imprisonment and internal exile might try to halter syndical representatives by placing them in 'conditional liberty'. Even such an apologist for the regime as Selgas (1974) admits that these representatives were often the victims of discrimination and intimidation; and only a commentator such as Pike (1974), who had taken only the appearance of the Organic Law of the State of 1966 and the Syndical Law of 1971, without looking beyond their formal statements, could imagine that 'the wielders of political power' tended to respond to strikes 'as the kindhearted father in assuaging the grievances of children and dependents'.

The 1963 decree creating the TOPs had been triggered by the strike wave of 1962, and the strikes of this and the following year provoked arrests throughout the country. In El Marco the arrests reached as far as Trebujena with the detention of Miguel Campo and Paco Cabral, but none of the leaders were indicted, for lack of evidence. In Asturias, however, the police succeeded in planting informers in the strike meetings, which they never did in El Marco, and many of the leaders were arrested and exiled; so the strike of the following year had the clearly political objective of rescinding their exile. At first the regime looked to negotiate, in keeping with its policy at that time of tolerating and attempting to co-opt the commissions; but once the talks broke down it unleashed the most severe repression since 1934, arresting huge numbers of miners (Miguélez:1976). In general, while the rather confused policy of co-optation was in place, the repression might be directed to split the movement by hurting those who opposed cooperation with the Vertical Syndicate; and in El Marco the suspicions which fed the later split in Sanlúcar were raised by the fact that workers outside the network of Emilio Fábregas and opposed to his leadership complained on more than one occasion of mistreatment and beatings from the Civil Guard. But following the Vertical elections of 1966, when it was clear that the commissions were not for co-opting, the repression became increasingly widespread and indiscriminate.

In January 1967 a nationwide demonstration led by the commissions was followed by hundreds of arrests and the subsequent decimation of many provincial and regional organizations (Mujal-León:1983). By way of example, over the years 1967 to 1969 the coordinating committee of the commissions in the light engineering industry in Madrid was reduced from sixty members to just two (Maravall:1982); while in similar fashion, the provincial commission in Asturias lost all of its best men and was left virtually 'leaderless' (Miguélez:1976). In 1968 the Supreme Court finally declared the commissions to be an illegal and subversive organization (Maravall:1978); and the sentences handed down for membership, which never used to run for longer than a few months, were now extended to two to five years, on the grounds that the commissions were an instrument of a proscribed political party, the Communist Party of Spain. As the tide of industrial conflict continued to rise, states of siege were declared first in the Basque Country in 1968 and across the country as a whole in 1969–70 (see following section); and over the years 1968 to 1973 at least five hundred of the movement's leaders were imprisoned, while some two thousand syndical representatives lost their jobs (Maravall:1982). Even these figures seriously understate the extent of the repression according to Mujal-León (1983), who suggests that the regime, hand in hand with the employers, forced the dismissal of between thirty and fifty thousand shop stewards over the period 1966–75, and arrested many more; and Maravall (1982) seems to admit that the repression became ever more intense, with over four and a half thousand workers fired in the first two months of 1974 for political motives.

Maravall (1978) argues that the commissions made the work of repression easy by choosing to act openly, and so becoming increasingly vulnerable; and in this he follows, as in much else, the judgement of Amsden (1972) who asserts that 'what was fatal for the movement... was the way in which collective bargaining activities helped to single out workers' leaders for arrest ... during the 1969 State of Exception'. But it is equally possible to argue, as does Santiago Carrillo (1967), that the beginning of the open struggle of the later sixties was in fact a response to the offensive of the regime against the legally elected Vertical representatives. At the same time the repression was also facilitated by a down-turn in the national economy, which brought increasing unemployment and a wage freeze, and tempted employers to themselves provoke strikes so that they could fire the trouble-makers (Mujal-León:1979); and Miguélez (1976) agrees that there was a change in the employers' behaviour. Until 1967 they tended to demand police intervention and arrests when strikes threatened, with the subsequent dismissal from syndical posts and prison sentences; but over the years 1967 to 1971, when jobs were very hard to come by, they were content to operate a system of black lists, and control the work force through sackings, or the threat of them. So it was probably a combination of increased exposure through public activity on the one hand, and economic downturn on the other, which led to an increased incidence of repression, which now reached the provincial and national committees, and culminated in the arrest of nine leading members of the national executive of the commissions in 1972. There is thus no doubt that the repression hurt; but, paradoxically, far from destroying the movement, it may actually have contributed to raising its profile as the principal organization of the illegal opposition.

It was over this period of the later sixties that the movement's protests became more public in El Marco de Jerez, and here as elsewhere, as described in Chapter 7, this led to increased surveillance by the forces of order. In December 1966 a group of militants from USO (see Chapter 6) was arrested, but later released for lack of evidence, and in 1967 Antonio Alvarez was condemned to a year's imprisonment, which he never served. Then in 1968 the police arrested a group of Communists in Chiclana, where they had been apprehended *in flagrante delicto*, distributing broadsheets, and under torture one of these men (who later hung himself in remorse) gave the names of Antonio Alvarez and Federico Iglesias. Both were arrested and Federico was interrogated and beaten for three days, until they were released under pressure of the protest in the church at El Puerto. As Federico's wife had been in time to destroy any incriminating documents before their house was searched, they were finally absolved by the TOP for lack of evidence. More often, and in the case of less notorious leaders, the arrests that occurred were simply followed by ill treatment, and eventual release. Miguel Marroquín reports that he was arrested six times over the period he was organizing the Communist Youth, and many of the militants of Sanlúcar were routinely arrested during strikes, and equally routinely denied whatever they were accused of. In effect, they tended to see the repression in terms of the traditional antagonism between the working class of the countryside and the Civil Guard, and it is at least possible that it was this resigned attitude, along with the fortitude with which they took the beatings, which rendered the repression relatively ineffectual. For it is remarkable that over a period when provincial commissions throughout the country were being badly mauled, the organization of the movement in El Marco remained intact, and indeed became increasingly coordinated across the region. On the occasion of each strike and each 'sit-in', however, the police were watching and compiling their lists; and at the beginning of 1970, after the longest, bitterest and most publicized strike of the decade, this successful record of the movement suffered a damaging and dramatic reversal.

THE ASSAULT ON THE ORGANIZED OPPOSITION IN EL MARCO

With the declaration of a nationwide state of seige (*estado de excepción*) on the 24 January 1969, the Franco regime mobilized all its repressive apparatuses to crush the organizations of the labour movement once and for all. Thousands of working-class leaders and activists were arrested, tortured and condemned to long prison terms of up to sixteen years. Moreover, for the first time the assault was coordinated in order to strike hardest at the regional centres of working-class militancy, so that while 'certain centres such as those of Valencia and Sevilla experienced a full scale police campaign against the newly formed workers' commissions ... the more traditional centres of labour organization may have been less affected' (Amsden:1972). In El Marco de Jerez, under instructions from the civil governor, several activists such as Ramón Gaitero, were subjected to house searches late in the night on suspicion of holding 'subversive propaganda or documents of clear dissidence and hostility to the present political Regime'; but although the searches showed that some elements of the secret police were already operating in the region, the opposition in El Marco continued to appear relatively immune to repression – an illusion which was to last only until the beginning of the following year.

There seems little doubt that the assault on El Marco was provoked by the massive strike of December 1969 and January 1970, although in their majority the arrests did not begin until the strike was over. The main exception was in Trebujena, where Paco Cabral was arrested on 8 January 1970 for distributing the solidarity funds sent to the region by the movement throughout the country. But at the time this appeared less like a reverse and more like an extension of the 'El Puerto principle' of mass mobilization to Trebujena: the whole of the *pueblo*, including the women and children, marched to the barracks of the Civil Guard, and Lorenzo Marchena Villagrán was delegated to demand Cabral's release, and got it. In fact, the first wave of arrests began in El Puerto, and every one of the militants has his own story of how it began. One of the most picturesque of the many apocryphal stories suggests it all started with the discovery of the printing press for *Mundo Obrero*, which was hidden in the workshop of one Perea España. In this version, an old woman was on the flat roof (or *azotea*) of the workshop, hanging out her washing, when she was blown over by a strong gust of the cruel wind called the Levante, and fell through the skylight to die impaled upon the machinery. When the police entered the building to investigate the incident, all was revealed. No, no, others say, it was not an old woman but a young one, and very pretty at that; but her fall had nothing whatsoever to do with the 'fall' of the movement in El Marco.

In the event, the real story was if anything even more dramatic, and turned on the covert use the Communist Youth of El Puerto had made of the premises of the Organization of Spanish Youth, the Falangist youth movement. These premises were known as the Zodiac Club, and the Communist Youth were intent not so much on infiltrating the enemy organization as using its sports and club facilities, not to mention its stencil machine, which they put to work for their own propaganda purposes. If any opportunity appeared for recruiting for their own cause, it was well and good. Then on 4 January 1970, at a New Year's dance at the club, the celebrations became somewhat rowdy, and either some young Communists, or, as others have it, young Falangists who had become convinced of the Communist cause, broke up the dance and smashed the pictures of Franco and José Antonio Primo de Rivera hanging on the wall. The police immediately came to investigate and arrested the youths they thought were responsible, who included Jesús Espinar Galán and Manuel Sendra Palma. They in turn gave the police the name of Miguel Marroquín, who was the head of the Communist Youth, and who was arrested on 23 January. Miguel later denounced to the judge the police torture he underwent, but by that time, of course, he had already revealed the names of Antonio Alvarez and Antonio Cárdenas, who was responsible for Party organization. By his own account, Miguel reasoned that these were the men who were best able to resist, but while he was clearly right in the case of Alvarez, there is a broad consensus that Cárdenas, in the graphic language of the militants, was 'as soft as a meringue', and began to name names. This was the opening for which the Political–Social Brigade had been waiting.

Antonio Alvarez had taken a heavy beating, but did not speak. Once the police succeeded in extracting names, however, the militants began to fall like dominoes, as the police rapidly unravelled the local networks of the Party. Amongst the first names were those of Paco Artola, Paco de las Flores, José María Perea, Fernando Guilloto, Miguel Muñoz, Pepe Jiménez and José Aldana; and once the strike was over on 8 February, the police moved against them in force. Antonio Alvarez was already under arrest, of course, and had known they were coming for him. He could have escaped, perhaps, but very typically refused to run; and found the police waiting for him, and his wife calling them all the names under the sun, when he returned home one day. Once imprisoned he began to sing the 'International' to give some cheer to his comrades, but then the torture began, and Alvarez reports that he hammered his head through a glass door when he thought he could stand it no longer. At a later moment in his life he met one of the policemen who had wanted to kill him that day because he 'did not deserve to live', and asked him why. He got no reply.

Following Alvarez, some of the first to be arrested were from the agitation and propaganda apparatus. In one night they came for Paco Artola, Miguel Muñoz and Francisco Marín Guerrero, and Pepe Jiménez, who had been warned by his comrades that his time was up. Pepe finished work at five in the afternoon and returned home in the normal way. At half past eight there was a knock at the door, and he simply got up and walked out of the house, not to return for another eighteen months. He was beaten until six in the morning. These men 'fell' first because the police were eager to get their hands on the propaganda machinery, which was housed in the radio-repair shop of José María Perea España (the same workshop where the young, or old, lady fell to her death). Paco Artola knew he had to get the stencil machine out of there, and so as soon as the arrests began he took it to Jerez, to the attic of Francisco Marín, the Jerez printer who kept the proper printing machinery of the Party. But then it was learned that José María Perea had already talked, revealing the name of Pepe Jiménez and leading the police to the machinery in Jerez; so Paco had to rush off again and take the stencil machines to the Pago San Julián, a rural food store on the road between Jerez and Sanlúcar, where the police finally found some three such machines and hundreds of copies of the Party statutes. And the discovery of the machines meant that Alvarez, Cárdenas and Artola all received longer sentences than they might otherwise have done.

Once the arrests began, the Party automatically put in motion its mechanisms for getting money to the prisoners' families. It was an elaborate business. In one early instance, Paco Cabral had passed a considerable sum to Antonio Palacios, who passed it to his brother José, who had arranged for José Aldana (still looking for his place in history) to pick it up at a rendezvous in the vineyards, and take it to Antonio Camacho's bar. Shortly after the completion of this operation, José was himself arrested and taken before the office of the police commissioner in Jerez, where prisoners were being interrogated. He felt free to mention Antonio Palacios, knowing he had already been arrested some four days previously. It was February the thirteenth. But he was surprised when the commissioner ordered his men to bring Antonio up from the cells, and he immediately implicated Antonio Camacho, who had just been released after several days of interrogation. Camacho finally spent two years in gaol in Jaén. José, who was later released, was then thrown into one of the cells below the commissariat. It was so dark he could not see the walls, and extremely cold. A guard had the good grace to light a cigarette for him, and he learned what a dangerous place this was. All the cells were full of Communists.

In this way nearly all of the provincial committee of the Party and those in charge of the propaganda apparatus were arrested in very short order; as were the leaders of the Communist Youth, such as Manuel Sendra Palma and Jesús Espinar Galán, and, more gradually, the men of the 'works cells', such as José Marroquín Gómez, José Marroquín Travieso and Federico Iglesias (*Diario de Cadiz*:6.2.1970). According to all accounts, it was almost worse to be free than in prison, such was the terror sown by the actions of the police, who constantly signalled their spectacular presence in El Puerto with the wailing of sirens in the streets. As *Mundo Obrero* (21.2.1970) later put it, the Political–Social Brigade fell on El Puerto and 'acted like a band of fascists, with no legal mandate, but with the clear intention of instilling panic amongst the population'. The *pueblo* was not entirely passive in the face of the onslaught, and some one hundred workers sat in at the local church for forty-eight hours in protest, demanding an end to the tortures, the release of those arrested and the return of the Brigade to Madrid. There was even a demonstration in front of the town hall, despite the virtual occupation of the town by the Armed Police. But everyone was afraid and the panic amongst the men of the local committee of the Party was very real as each waited for his own arrest. Perhaps aware of this, the police took their time, and both José Marroquín and Federico Iglesias, who were the last to be arrested, admit that when the moment finally came they were already 'done in'. Of the local committee both Antonio Ortega and Benito Herrera escaped the dragnet, which captured twenty-seven militants from El Puerto altogether.

From El Puerto the police followed the trail to unravel the networks of

Jerez, Sanlúcar and Trebujena, in that order; but no one was arrested in Cádiz, where the clandestine organization of the Party was very small. In Sanlúcar, once news had arrived of the arrests in El Puerto, the leaders of the Party sat and waited their turn, which they knew would arrive before too very long. First to be arrested were Manolo Romero, Pancaro and Juan Viega on 19 February, and on the following day they were joined by Eduardo and Manuel Sánchez, José Raposo and Paco Gordillo. Although Manolo Romero was beaten, Eduardo Sánchez was not, and by his own account he owed his good fortune to the fact that the police already had all the names they wanted. Indeed, the much smaller number of arrests in Sanlúcar appears to reinforce the perception that the Political–Social Brigade had targeted the leaders of the Party in particular rather than of the working-class move-ment in general, and that they were well aware that the heart of the Party organization was in El Puerto. To some degree this squares with the account of Emilio Fábregas, who asserts that if no more people were arrested in Sanlúcar, it was because he argued successfully with the authorities that it was not the representatives within the Vertical Syndicate who were respon-sible for the strikes, but the Communists, of whom there were just a few. But others suggest that the only person protected during the 'fall' was Fábregas himself, who was actually with Pancaro and Manolo Romero at the time of their arrest, and who was saved by their testimony of his purely syndical credentials. In this connection, it was said, perhaps apocryphally, that on the very same day of the arrests in Sanlúcar there was to be a meeting of the social section of the Vertical Syndicate at provincial level, where virtually all the members of the provincial committee of the Party were to be present. In the event, Emilio Fábregas was the only one to appear.

The assault by the Political–Social Brigade on the opposition in El Marco came at the end of a very long and successful strike, which had involved a careful coordination of the struggle both inside and outside the Vertical Syndicate, and, crucially, a campaign to collect the funds which could finance this struggle. In the face of these developments, the oligarchy of El Marco began to understand for the first time that even though their political power was secure for the time being, their long-term economic interests were cer-tainly capable of being hurt by this working-class movement; and so they called in the economic favours and political support owed them by the regime, alleging, not without reason, that this movement, and the strike itself, were directed by the Communist Party. With the arrival of the Brigade the vineyard owners were eager to collaborate in its work by pointing out the principal suspects, on the assumption, which was again not unwarranted, that the chief syndical leaders were also Party militants. In other words, once they had denounced the 'Red threat' in El Marco, the oligarchy used their political power to wreak revenge on the workers for their victorious strike. This conclusion is corroborated by the fact that the forty men of the

Brigade who had been called down from Madrid were not ordered to work immediately, their commandant, Juan Creix, preferring to wait for the end of the strike and the 'demobilization' of the striking workers.

At the same time the struggle in El Puerto, especially, had been advancing very fast and had presented an increasingly open challenge in the form of mass mobilizations and demonstrations. The celebrations of 1 May in particular were unmistakable evidence of the Party's expansion and the movement's growing confidence. In retrospect, as indicated in Chapters 7 and 9, there were some who were prepared, for better or worse reasons, to seek a scapegoat in Antonio Alvarez, who as unproclaimed leader of the province had forced the rhythm of the struggle to the point where the regime had to respond, if only to save face. In other words, Alvarez's triumphalism had failed to measure the real balance of forces and had led the movement into a premature show of strength. But if he appeared to believe that the movement was unstoppable, the fact was that until that moment it had not been stopped; and, indeed, had continued to advance even after the widespread repression heralded by the national state of seige of early 1969. And Alvarez alone was clearly incapable of leading the vineyard workers into a two-month strike, or of achieving the kind of national and international solidarity effectively generated by that strike. He himself admits that the local movement had grown hard to control, and there is no doubt that once the Political–Social Brigade was on the spot, but still straining on a tight leash, it was incensed by the impudence of the broadsheets that were appearing every day on the streets. Hence the resigned quality of the quotation from Paco de las Flores which appears at the head of this chapter and suggests that anyone engaged in this kind of struggle had to 'fall' sooner or later. Paco's quarrel is not with the struggle itself but with the Party code, and Benítez Rufo's insistence, that on arrest all Party members had to avow their Communism rather than deny it. In his view, this piece of bravado simply meant that many more good militants were arrested than the circumstances required.

IN THE AFTERMATH OF THE FALL

Very few of the movement's leaders in El Marco now remained free. Most of the members of the provincial committee of the Party had been drawn from the local committee of El Puerto, which had suffered worst; and the rump of this committee had anyway to be dissolved for fear of further arrests in the wake of the interrogations. Once the arrests had begun, the leaders in charge of provincial Party organization had met to decide what could be done and had agreed on the attempt to save the propaganda apparatus in Jerez. At the same time, Pepe de la Rosa and Manolo Espinar had fled El Puerto for the safe house in Jerez where Benítez Rufo used to stay, and from there escaped to France via Madrid. By this time José María

García believed himself to be the only one of the principal leaders still free and walking the streets of El Puerto. In fact, Benito Herrera, the key figure in the Party's propaganda operations, had also escaped arrest: so well had his identity been protected that not even José María knew of him. Antonio Ortega was also free, and although Rafael Ribeiro had been arrested, he was released almost immediately. Moreover, within three months or so, some of the comrades who had been charged with less serious offences began to be released on bail, and in this way José Marroquín Travieso, José Marroquín Gómez, Federico Iglesias and Fernando Guilloto were soon set free. But everyone was afraid, and the atmosphere within the *pueblos* of El Marco fraught with anxiety. In El Puerto just four men, José María García, Federico Iglesias and José and Miguel Marroquín (Travieso) reluctantly took on the task of reorganization; but elsewhere the movement was momentarily stilled. When José María took propaganda materials to Trebujena in the usual way, Paco Cabral refused to meet with him, which, in a man of renowned personal courage, was a reflection of the general demoralization which had fallen on the movement in El Marco.

The local Party organization was badly damaged, and moreover the Party was divided inside and outside prison (see Chapter 9). Nevertheless, the solidarity of the workers of El Marco with the prisoners was impressive. None of those in prison ever had to eat prison food, nor did their families ever go hungry. Collections were organized, and Radio Pirenaica called for contributions, which came in from all over the world; and these funds were used not only to feed the families but also to pay the bail bonds. In the meantime the legal process continued, and the prisoners appeared before Public Order Tribunals in the spring of 1971. Their sentences were stiff but not severe. In El Puerto, Antonio Alvarez, Antonio Cárdenas, José María Perea España, Paco Artola and Pepe Rosa (in his absence) were condemned to four years each; Miguel Marroquín to three years; Pepe Jiménez, Francisco Marín, Manolo Espinar (in his absence) to two years; Miguel Muñoz to eighteen months; Fernando Guilloto to one year; Federico Iglesias to six months; Jesús Espinar to one year, and Manuel Sendra to six months. In Sanlúcar, Manolo Romero was similarly condemned to three years; Eduardo Sánchez to fourteen months; Manolo Sánchez to one year; José Raposo to eight months; and Nicolás Ruíz Gómez (Pancaro), Paco Rodríguez and Paco Gordillo to six months and one day. In addition they were all suspended from any public posts and sacked from their jobs, and had their suffrage revoked (the latter not seeming too serious a sanction in Franco's Spain). In Trebujena, the sentences were of the order of nine months, except in the case of Miguel Campo, who served over a year. In the event, Miguel Campo, Pepe Jiménez and Antonio Alvarez shared the same small cell for some fifteen months.

José María García was finally arrested in September 1971, and he insisted on being taken to Cádiz, where most of his comrades were, so that he could explain how much damage the quarrels inside prison were doing to Party morale on the outside. But as the police failed to extract any information from him during his interrogation, he was released after just fifteen days. For this he had to thank the quick thinking of Antonio Ortega, who on hearing of his arrest had rushed to his house, which he found stacked full of copies of *Mundo Obrero*, which he then removed. So by the following month they had managed to make the emergency committee operational, and propaganda began to appear on the streets again, if only because José María distributed it. This caused some consternation amongst the police, who thought that the Party organization had been completely crushed. But they need not have worried. During the time that Manolo Romero, Antonio Alvarez and the rest were locked up in gaol, there was not one strike or protest of any kind anywhere in El Marco de Jerez.

There is thus no doubt that the repression experienced in El Marco at the beginning of 1970 was effective in slowing the rhythm of the struggle to a temporary stop. But although the region had not suffered anything of the order of this onslaught before, it still came to obey the general pattern of such repression, which had always succeeded in stopping the movement temporarily by the arrests that were routinely made after each strike, only to see it surge forward again in the following months. In other words, the movement grew despite the repression and indeed in the expectation of it. But if the repression did not succeed in containing the movement, it none-theless conditioned its development in certain critical ways. The most im-portant of these was the way in which the repression of simple economic demands could transform them into more overtly political demands, some-times in the course of a single strike. By way of example, the arrest of strike leaders could lead to further strikes in solidarity, and demands for amnesty; while the internal exile of such leaders might provoke political strikes to back the demand for their return (as occurred more than once in Asturias). If the new demands were then repressed in their turn, the leaders of the movement could the more easily argue for the necessity of basic trade union rights, such as freedom of assembly and free collective bargaining, if any improvements in wages or conditions of work were to be won at all. And as the movement grew and began to voice precisely such democratic de-mands, and to take them onto the streets, so the regime reinforced its repressive apparatuses at the same rate, raising the number of the Armed Police, for instance, from 20,000 to 34,000 over the years 1968 to 1975, in order to train and equip a new range of riot squadrons (Vilar:1977).[1]

---

[1] The total number of policemen in Spain amounted to about 106,000 armed men, which meant that there was one policeman for every 340 inhabitants, making the Spanish the most policed people in Europe. In addition to the Armed Police mentioned here, there was the Civil Guard, which numbered 63,000 men, with a budget in 1976 of twenty-seven billion pesetas (about four times the budget of the Ministry of Information and Tourism), and, of course, the notorious Political–Social Brigade. Both the Civil

Hence, it was what one tradition of social scientific discourse might call the 'dialectic of demands and repression' which catalysed the progressive transformation of syndical demands into strictly political ones, and guaranteed the political and finally democratic thrust of the movement (Soto:1976). But before rushing in where angels fear to tread and concluding that the repression was a good thing for the cause of democracy, it should be remembered that in the balance with this dialectic must be placed the terrible human waste of the thousands of good democrats destroyed by the Franco regime.

Guard and the Brigade were in principle subordinate to the Ministry of the Interior (Gobernación), but the Civil Guard depended for its organization, instruction and arms on the army, while the Brigade was always commanded by a general, with a colonel as the Director-General of Security.

11

Contingent connections: the relationship between the workers' commissions and the Spanish Communist Party

The Communists did not invent the workers' commissions. But when they emerged we saw them as something original ... as a highly effective means of struggle, and we made every effort to spread that struggle.

Santiago Carrillo, in *Nuestra Bandera*

Finally the Communist Party has found a way into the workplace. After half a century of looking for one, it now has its syndical 'transmission belt'.

Victor Alba, *El Partido Comunista en Espana*

THIS IS THE STORY of the making of democracy in Spain. Its basic empirical premise has been that its two principal protagonists were the workers' commissions and the Spanish Communist Party; and this premise has been defended on the grounds that these political actors were not only the first to enter the historical scene in opposition to the Franco regime but also the standard bearers of the struggle, around which other opposition organizations could begin to rally. Its main analytical assumption, on the other hand, has been that the strategic success of these actors was owing to their combination of legal and extralegal struggle as it evolved in the institutional context of the Vertical Syndicate; and this has been justified by the partial conversion of the high ground of the institutional terrain of Francoism to democratic purposes. In other words, just as the relationship between Party and commissions composed the principal *organizational* axis of what came to be the democratic project, so the relationship among Party, commissions and Vertical Syndicate constituted the central *strategic* axis of the struggle. In the reality, it was the intimate insertion of both these relationships into the same strategic matrix which inspired the democratic process; but for heuristic purposes the organizational axis of Party and commissions will be discussed first, the better to understand the genesis and practice of their central strategy (as discovered in Chapter 12). At the same time, these intersecting lines of analysis will be recurrently located, as always, in the context of El Marco de Jerez, the better to appreciate the historical challenges and contingencies implicit in the organizational and strategic composition of the democratic movement.

THE CONTINGENT CONNECTIONS BETWEEN PARTY AND COMMISSIONS

The development of the democratic movement in Spain did not depend so much on the separate growth and operation of these two organizations as on the relationship between them, and an analysis of this relationship is essential to an understanding of the piecemeal construction of the democratic project. In this connection, it is tempting to search for a direction of causality which can easily define the relationship, and establish either that the commissions were crucial to the growth of the Party and to its preeminent political role in the opposition, or that the Party provided the leadership and critical logistical support to workers' commissions which would have otherwise remained inchoate and uninspired. But such an approach is mistaken first in assuming a relationship of externality between commissions and Party, whereas in reality the demands which drove the democratic movement had to have majority support, and the leaders who put those demands, Communist or not, had to have emerged from the movement itself if they were to retain the confidence of those they 'directed' (compare Chapters 2 and 6); and second, in forcing the complexities of the relationship into the procrustean bed of historical determinations, and hence in failing to capture the contingencies of a relationship which changed with each subtle shift in the overall conjuncture.

This plea for contingency runs counter to the extant accounts of the relationship at national level, which may either accept more or less uncritically the version of the Party itself (Mujal-León:1983), or on the contrary may pretend that the Party had really very little to do with the growth of the democratic movement anyway (Maravall:1978); but which in both cases ignore the specificities of different regional contexts and the ways they could condition these contingencies at local level. The problem here is twofold. In the first place it is one of imbalance, insofar as Party propaganda tended to concentrate on some struggles to the detriment of others, and to the almost complete exclusion of the countryside in general. Hence, it was not until the Party's Eighth Congress that Santiago Alvarez delivered a *mea culpa* in this respect (PCE:1972), and added in quite uncharacteristic fashion that 'during all this time, yes, the combative workers of the Marco de Jerez and other parts of Andalucía have been struggling and holding high the banner of this heroic rural proletariat'.[1] In the second place, it is one of

---

[1] But to show that some things never change (recalling the argument of Chapter 8), Santiago Alvarez also asserted that when the national strike came the peasants of the countryside would invade the large landed estates.

inattention to the real evolution of the relationship between commissions and Party on the ground, and in particular the ways in which it was mediated by the networks of local leaders who played such an important part in both organizations. Thus, in the case of El Marco de Jerez, it has already been seen (Chapters 2, 6 and 7) how the dynamics of the movement created a certain kind of commitment to the struggle which was distinct from the ideological line of any party; how, later, the directly democratic content of the movement, with its assemblies, prevented any easy control by the Communist Party; and how the movement influenced and changed the character of the local Party (Chapters 8 and 9), making it different in many ways from the Party in exile. But equally, it has emerged that the Party reached out to leaders in the different *pueblos* of the region, many of whom were not and never would be of the Party; played a key role in coordinating the struggle across the region; and drove the movement forward during the sixties (Chapters 9 and 10), raising syndical leaders to political roles, and catalysing the transformation of syndical into overtly political demands. These different aspects of the relationship between commission and Party were articulated by the networks of local leaders, all of whom had to win, and some of whom finally lost, the trust of those they led. For this, if for no other reason, the relationship was a contingent one.

THE BEGINNINGS OF THE RELATIONSHIP

Communists and Socialists had worked together in the UGT in the 1930s, and in the initial post–Civil War years the Party worked to resurrect the Socialist union, but without success. The Socialists in exile strained at any idea of cooperation with the Communist Party, and forced a return to a UGT directly tied to the Socialist Party (PSOE) (Camacho:1980). Meanwhile the Communist Party continued sensitive to the need for an independent syndical base, but dubious of its chances of success in the harsh circumstances of the forties; and, as recounted in Chapter 8, was finally convinced by Stalin to work within the Vertical Syndicate of the Francoist regime. This decision was taken before the appearance of the first commission but had nothing like the kind of immediate impact which Ibarruri et al. (1964) suggest it did in their triumphalist account of the strikes in Barcelona in the spring of 1951. Had it done so, there would have been no incentive to create the Party's own syndical organization, the OSO (*Oposición Sindical Obrera,* or Workers' Syndical Organization), which, although it continued in existence into the sixties, never enjoyed any significant degree of mass support.

The first recorded use of the phrase 'workers' commission' by the Party is in a long article in *Mundo Obrero* (15.4.1955), where one small paragraph reveals that 'in the majority of the struggles in the factories and workshops we have seen workers' commissions spring up in the course of the struggle itself . . . shop stewards should not only not hinder, but on the contrary must do everything possible to encourage these commissions, seeking their support and collaborating with them'.[2] And in a later article (*Mundo Obrero*:15.6.1957; commenting on the renovation of collective bargaining which had already been advertised in the Syndicate's newspaper, *Pueblo*), the Party immediately saw the tactical significance of the change, insofar as it 'provided an opportunity for the workers to create or reinforce their Workers' Commissions, which have played such a positive role in the struggles in Viscaya and Cataluñia'. So it seems that Carrillo, as quoted at the head of this chapter (Carrillo:1962), had it about right in suggesting that the chief virtue of the Party was in recognizing the political potential of the commissions as the primary cells of the independent syndical movement; and only later would it join with Christian and even Falangist groups in theorizing their permanence and coordination (Camacho:1980). In other words, the commissions emerged with no prompting from the Party, but it was the Party's recognition of them which tempered the political will to extend and coordinate their presence.

Similarly in El Marco de Jerez, the commissions were not created by the Party, which simply responded to what was there; although, through its propaganda apparatus, the Party was already encouraging the commissions to participate in the new collective bargaining procedures in 1958, and Radio Pirenaica had already been promoting participation in the Vertical elections for some time. The Party in exile had become aware of the movement in El Marco at the time of the strike of 1959, which had included not only Sanlúcar but also Chipiona and Rota, and had instructed Fernando Guilloto to contact the leaders. Fernando's comrade Carlos Arébalo remembered a representative from the vineyards, who sat on the social section of the Vertical Syndicate and whom he had previously met in Rota. This was Emilio Fábregas. They sought out his very humble house in Sanlúcar one Sunday, and went to a bar, where Fernando immediately broached the business of the day. This was the Party, on the one hand, and, on the other, the need for a better organization and a broader coordination of the commissions. According to Guilloto, Fábregas immediately joined the Party, something he himself vehemently denies; but whatever the truth of this, they arranged a further meeting between Fábregas and Benítez Rufo, which took place in the summer of 1961 in the Plaza Jerez of Sanlúcar. Despite a degree of distrust on the part of Fábregas, who was reluctant to put all the

---

[2] This reference dispels any doubt that might remain over the myth of the first commission appearing in the mine of the La Camocha in 1956 (see Chapter 6). In this connection, too, Mujal-León (1983) invokes Fernando Claudín's authority for saying that the phrase was first used by the Party in 1955, but does not tell us where. Moreover, he suggests that at this time the Party was already arguing for making the commissions permanent, and this is incorrect.

eggs in one basket, this was the historic first meeting between the then leader of the commissions in El Marco and the Party's linkman in the region.

Despite the interest shown by the Party, by many accounts Rufo himself was unconvinced by the commissions, and when he was told how the strikes of 1962 had been organized in the vineyards and in the shipyards he apparently gave orders that this form of struggle was not to be repeated. The same sources gleefully recall how Rufo had very soon to eat his words, on orders from the Executive Committee; but this may simply reflect the eagerness of the local syndical leaders to establish the primacy of the spontaneous struggle in the region. Foremost amongst these advocates is Emilio Fábregas, of course, who himself attended a meeting of the Party in Paris in 1963, along with leaders of the commissions in Sevilla such as Fernando Soto and Eduardo Saborido. In this piece of local lore, it was his account of the struggle in the vineyards in the preceding years which convinced the Party not only to collaborate with the commissions but also to promote participation in the Vertical Syndicate! This is clearly wrong, but it does illustrate the widespread conviction that in the evolution of the strategy of the struggle the Party learned its lessons from the local leaders, and not vice versa.

THE PARTY'S SUPPORT OF THE NASCENT COMMISSIONS

At no time did the Party claim that it had created the workers' commissions, but rather insisted that it was simply encouraging and diffusing what the working class had created for itself through the struggle (*Mundo Obrero*:15.8.1964). Thus, in the Party's view the commissions had been generated spontaneously, first as temporary, and then as more permanent organizations; first self-constituted by the most conscious and militant workers, and then delegated by the direct democracy of the assembly (*Mundo Obrero*:15.2.1964). But Party militants were everywhere present on the shop floor and on the building sites, lending their support to these grassroots commissions, and providing a precarious institutional cover from their elected posts within the Vertical Syndicate (see Chapter 12) (Maravall:1982). In short, the Party was on the spot when the workers' movement gathered momentum, and it counselled its militants to work with the commissions, so 'making available its not inconsiderable clandestine network of contacts and organizing facilities to encourage organization and communication on as broad a scale as possible' (Amsden:1972). Moreover, in sending its activists to flesh out the commissions at local and provincial levels it developed many new cadres in the process (Mujal-León:1979), and hence as the commissions grew, so did the Party. Beyond this logistical support, the Party also offered strategic orientation, despite the vagaries of its own political line (see Chapter 8). Thus, many of the major decisions in the life of the movement, such as the mass participation in the Vertical elections and the open struggle of the later sixties, were formally taken by the Party, as the commissions themselves had no forum to do so. In this regard, perhaps the most crucial contribution of the Party was in coordinating the operations of an organization which until the seventies 'never really exceeded the provincial scale' (Amsden:1972).

Not all commentators see the role of the Party in this regard in such a positive light, although this appears to be more a question of validating their anti-communist credentials than of achieving analytical distinctions. By way of example, Ayucar (1976) saw the growth of the commissions as a good thing 'until one day the Communist Party . . . realized what the commissions, blessed by the Church and tolerated by the government, could achieve in working class circles, and infiltrated them. The Party's own illegality favoured its purpose'. In this version of events, when the leaders of the official syndicate saw that the commissions had become a 'subversive apparatus' they withdrew their sympathy and support, but 'it was already too late' (Ayucar:1976, p. 358). Similarly in Alba's (1979) account, the course of the commissions' history is acceptable until 1963, when the conduct of that year's strikes still demonstrated that they were not led by any party. But, he adds in a phrase remarkable for its historical compression, 'at the end of 1964, the Party realized that the workers' commissions were taking root, and decided to take them over'. Once the Party had suddenly seen the light in this way, it apparently manipulated and terrorized the assemblies in order to get control of innocent commissions which were until that moment made up of right-minded Catholics, and then demanded spectacular protests which undermined the confidence of the workers, and made them putty in the hands of the Party. In reality, of course, the Party's powers were nothing so supernatural.

In El Marco de Jerez it is generally agreed that the commissions were born of the conditions and needs of the workers of the region in the fifties, and came together spontaneously in embryonic form in the vineyards (see Chapter 6); but the Party was quick to interpret these needs and the aspirations for a better standard of living, and immediately encouraged the coalescence of the commissions by sending its best men to organize and coordinate them. Its support was especially important in the organization of strikes, and it not only gave tactical advice but also used its extensive contacts to provide economic sustenance during periods of prolonged struggle. However, the view of the emerging relationship between commissions and Party in the region tends to vary from *pueblo* to *pueblo*. In Sanlúcar, the skilled workers of the vineyards have it clear that they were already operating their commission before contact with the Party, and as all of the commission with one exception joined the Party, the commission in effect became the Party; and moreover the Party organization was extended to Trebujena through the commissions of these two *pueblos*, and through the person of Manolo Romero, who prides himself on having founded the Party in that town (although Miguel Campo would want to dispute this), and who remained in charge of Party organization in Sanlúcar until his arrest at the time of the 'fall' in 1970. In El Puerto, on the other hand, the commissions are seen as dependent on the Party, which came first and led the struggle. In that town, it is asserted, 'pure syndicalists just don't exist'; while in Jerez neither the Party nor the commissions were very well organized in the first instance, but became so as the movement within the region became increasingly coordinated in the sixties.

In general, the role of the Party in providing logistical support is not disputed, and even Emilio Fábregas admits that the commissions became properly organized only after the Party had entered the struggle. The Party indeed created commissions in some places, and everywhere coordinated them; and in the sixties actively sought out syndical leaders for more political roles. But in Fábregas's view the intention of the Party was always to build the Party, and in moving to take over every embryo of working-class organization it took commissions of a heterodox political persuasion in its own particular political direction. In short, the Party used the commissions for its own ends, and hence in Fábregas's syndical view, always asked too much of the movement. El Marco was expected to come out in solidarity with the miners of Asturias, even if there was no serious expectation that the miners would offer similar support to El Marco. The political discipline the Party tried to impose on local labour leaders was evidence of its true purpose of taking over the political leadership of the entire region. Against this, others such as Antonio Alvarez argue that the movement was never under such strict control of the Party as was suggested by the dictatorship. On the contrary, it was often the movement which had to push the Party forward, and convince it through its syndical practice of the efficacy of the commissions. In other words, the role of the Party was simply a question of historical necessity. Party and commissions grew in parallel, and the Party contributed its activists to the movement. Many militants of the movement baulked at joining the Party, mainly and quite understandably out of fear. But as the movement grew, more and more militants did join, as it became increasingly clear that the Party presented the only effective political option to the dictatorship.

In this connection, it is apparent that, at the local level at least, the question of leadership is the key to the relationship between the commissions and the Party, insofar as the leaders of the commissions, and of the Party (and finally of the social sections of the Vertical Syndicate) are by and large the same men. It can be argued that this was because the Party either placed its activists at the head of the movement or recruited the movement's natural leaders into its own organization; but whatever the truth of this (and once again, it is contingent rather than determined), the leaders of the commissions also came to have majority representation on the local and provincial committees of the Party. And even in Jerez, where for some time the organization of the movement lagged behind that of the other *pueblos*, it was the same group of men who provided orientation at the time of negotiating new contracts. To a degree, the leaders of commissions and Party were the same because there were so few leaders overall, and the initiatives of operation and action had necessarily to come from them. Thus in Sanlúcar, there were perhaps twelve such leaders in all, who carried the struggle forward during the sixties, and there the leaderships were almost identical; but even in El Puerto, which had a more educated and political population, there was a high degree of overlapping of leaderships by the end of the sixties. But if there was a high degree of identity between the leaderships, it was never in fact complete, because there were always some syndical leaders who were not of the Party. Hence the provincial coordinating commission in the sixties was composed of fourteen leaders, eight of whom came from the Party and six of whom remained independent; and on occasion this resulted in splits which made the effective coordination of strategy difficult. Nevertheless, the process of identification was so far advanced in 1965 that when Soliz Ruíz convened the first and only National Congress of Rural Workers in Madrid in that same year, the nine syndical representatives from the province of Cádiz went armed with a paper prepared from the Party's propaganda materials and used the occasion to argue for a radical agrarian reform. So it happened that on the same day they were presented to Prince Juan Carlos, they were also accused of being Communists. Their paper was immediately censored, and they themselves were escorted all the way back to Jerez by the police, who hoped to trap other 'Communists' by this manoeuvre.

THE COMBINATION OF ECONOMIC DEMANDS AND POLITICAL STRUGGLE

In 1964 the Party was still talking of its own Workers' Syndical Opposition (or OSO), and of the workers' commissions in the same breath (*Mundo Obrero*:15.2.1964; 15.8.1964), but shortly after this it stopped supporting OSO, which was finally disbanded in 1966 (Ayucar:1976). As must be abundantly clear by now, this is not the same as suggesting with Maravall (1978) that this was the moment when the Party 'jumped onto the bandwagon of the factory committees' (i.e., the commissions); and Maravall himself later revised his view to admit that Party cooperation with the commissions must have started as early as 1957 (Maravall:1982). In fact, it started earlier yet, but OSO had continued until its precarious existence could no longer be justified. As Santiago Carrillo later recalled at the Party's Eighth Congress, 'At one time we promoted clandestine syndicates until practice proved to us that this phrase is a contradiction in terms'.

Once Santiago Carrillo and the Executive Committee of the Party in exile had opted wholeheartedly for the commissions, then their syndical practice became the basis for the Party's democratic project. In a major publication of 1965 (Carrillo:1965) Carrillo exhorted both Party cadres and commissions to concentrate on the detailed formulation of economic demands in each and every factory and industrial sector, and was explicit that the struggle for economic demands would lead to the struggle for political goals. By using collective bargaining to stimulate a set of demands which became increasingly political, the Party could bring the labour-repressive institutions of the dictatorship into the centre of the syndical arena, and so automatically extend the struggle. At the same time, this transformative strategy found expression at the level of political organization in the division of political labour between the syndical practice of the commissions, on the one hand, and, on the other, the permanent political leadership to be provided by the 'conscious vanguard' of the Party. The commissions were to be simply the representatives of workers' assemblies with no outside political activities, and the Party could protect its militants on the ground by placing them in the commissions, which had a broad base and were more difficult to suppress, especially in times of economic expansion and scarcity of skilled labour (Linz:1973). The Party meanwhile would continue with its work of agitation and political propaganda (Carrillo:1965). For this reason Camacho (1980) could recall that 'in the times of clandestinity the majority of the communists who worked in the commissions did not work in the organization of the Party itself. The Party, for reasons of security and because of the huge work-load in the commissions, considered that to militate in the commissions was equivalent to doing so in the Party'. But while this may have been true at the heart of the national organization, it was different in the regions. Here the Party always retained a certain number of militants who did not work in the commissions, but the huge majority of Party militants, and most of its regional leaders, were deeply involved in the syndical movement.

Despite this, the Party saw the commissions as providing the basis of a unitary syndicalism, where it would work with working-class leaders, whatever their political affiliation, and especially with leaders from the JOC and HOAC (see Chapter 6). Later in the sixties Carrillo would assert (Carrillo:1967) that 'the Christian conscience plays an analogous part to that played by Communist consciousness amongst ourselves'. In the same vein the Party criticized the UGT and the CNT of the Syndical Alliance, which was formed before the watershed year of 1962, for aspiring to a syndicalism in the service of a party (which in the case of the CNT was apparently the Republican Party). According to the Party, the syndical freedoms of the past were a good thing, but the divisions of the past were bad then and were bad now (*Mundo Obrero*:15.8.1965); and there was a place for the ideas and objectives of all groups within the unitary and democratic commissions. The Party's line of argument in this regard remained remarkably consistent over time, and if it appears self-serving and designed to disguise the Party's intent of achieving political control of the commissions, it should at least be remembered that the Party's orientation was not universally respected within the commissions:[3] if the Party was hegemonic in Sevilla and Cádiz, it was not initially so in Barcelona, where the FLP and Catholic groups allied to it were the leading political force.

In El Marco de Jerez, too, the relationship between the commissions and the Party came to be marked by the political division of labour between the syndical practices of the commissions, which put the economic demands, and the political tasks of the Party, which over time came to focus on the achievement of political liberty. But if at national level the Party always held back a number of militants who did no work in the syndical movement, in El Marco it was the same men who carried out the work of the commissions and the work of the Party. This does not mean it was in any sense the same work: the Party aimed to coordinate the practices of the commissions, but in order to do so it had to keep their operations as separate as possible from its own organization; so the men who militated in the movement had to play very different roles, and keeping them distinct one from the other came to be a constant challenge which many think was not duly recognized by the Executive Committee's linkman, Benítez Rufo, in his meetings with the local committees of the Party.

The task of the Party, according to its own leaders, was to prepare and coordinate political action. The Party had members within each commission who were responsible for the syndical line, and each week its committees would meet and hear reports from these representatives before deciding on the appropriate course of action. Many of its members on the commissions were recruited amongst those restless men who had become shop stewards in the Vertical Syndicate, which the Party saw as a kind of nursery for militants; and in this way the very same men might be found in the social section of the Syndicate, in the commission, in the factory cell and even in the local or provincial committee of the Party. Nonetheless, if the social force behind the movement found expression in the natural leaders of the vineyards and the *bodegas* and the building sites, these men often lacked

---

[3] The presentation of this problem in Maravall is, once again, rather misleading. He talks of the Party's attempt to form autonomous workers' councils (commissions) and groups of officially elected delegates (*jurados*) into a single union, so that the 'commissions were based on legal and illegal workers' committees'. But in practice, these 'two' committees, as he calls them, were always the same committee (or commission); and Maravall has a clear political purpose in revising history in this way, as is evident when he continues that the 'UGT, which had taken part in the movement of the autonomous workers' councils, never accepted absorption into the structure of the commissions, which was controlled by the Communist Party and whose intention was to relegate the UGT to historical oblivion'. In fact, with the limited exceptions of the Basque Country and Asturias, the UGT had no significant political presence in the country at this time.

the information and contacts available to the Party, not to mention the political training of the Party leaders. This is, of course, the Party view, and assumes there were no differences of interest between Party and commissions. Emilio Fábregas, who was often very aware of such differences, did not admit to the Party's omniscience; and although the Party committee would always meet the day before its meeting with the representatives of the commissions, in order to fix the agenda, as Emilio has it, Emilio came to attend these meetings and, by his own account, often succeeded in out-manoeuvring the Party. For the most part, however, the Party leaders were better informed, and their leadership made for more effective political decision making.

Until 1962 the commissions of El Marco had been largely spontaneous and had tended to dissolve after each strike action; but from this time the Party began to seek out those leaders who emerged naturally at these moments, and explain the need for a greater direction and coordination of such strikes. In this way, the commissions themselves were made more permanent, at the same time that the political division of labour between commissions and Party, or between the *obrero* and the *politico* in the language of the movement, became clearer. Antonio Alvarez recalls that when he was first approached by the Party in this year, he immediately saw the advantage of political support and, especially, legal advice; and with the help of the Party he began to study the future organization of a more permanent commission in the *bodegas*. And once Federico Iglesias had been elected to the Vertical Syndicate, the Party began to send him to various *pueblos* to help establish their incipient commissions. The Party already had people there with experience of Party work, but none with a background in the syndical struggle; and Federico went as a member of the commissions to give instruction to the commissions. No one knew he was a Party member.

As this political division of labour grew clearer, however, there began to open up a progressive difference of perspective between the commissions and the Party. This was inevitable given the different political spaces they inhabited. The commissions, after all, were more and more deeply inserted into the structure of the Vertical Syndicate and therefore drawn into the legal and institutional aspects of the struggle (see Chapter 12); whereas the Party continued as a clandestine organization, with all the direct dangers consequent upon this. The paradoxes of a clandestine Party promoting legal forms of struggle are painfully obvious in the person of Emilio Fábregas, who had to work through the legal channels, and to do so had to collaborate over the years with the Party, and even attend a Party Congress; but who vehemently denies ever having belonged to the Party, and bitterly resented the control the Party tried to exercise over him. In his version of events, when the syndical leaders became aware of the Party's political manipulation, they tried to distance themselves from it; but his reference is not so much general as to the particular person of Paco de las Flores, who was sent to keep an eye on him. Paco, on the other hand, argues that he was merely the linkman between the Executive Committee (in the person of Rufo, for the most part, although Paco himself did visit the executive in exile in both 1964 and 1966) and Fábregas, who was difficult to contact, given his many posts in the bureaucracy of the Vertical Syndicate. The difference between them was simply that he came from the Party to the commission, and Fábregas came from the commission to the Party, but without much conviction; and they were anyway both against the Party line on more than one occasion, usually when the Party demanded a strike at an inopportune time, or for abstract motives of solidarity with the miners of Asturias. As Fábregas put it to Paco, 'No Party has the right to play with the bread of the working class'. And that was precisely the point of the difference of perspective: that Fábregas's syndical objectives did not always match the political objectives of the Party, as presented most often by Rufo. So Fábregas and Rufo often had their differences, but always in private. Neither in the civil society of the time nor in the movement itself was there any room to carry on a public debate.

PARTY CONTROL OF THE COMMISSIONS IN THE PERIOD OF OPEN STRUGGLE

From the middle of the 1960s the Party opted for a strategy of open struggle in order to build a mass organization. In part this decision was a response to the growth of the commissions across the country, and the first step of the strategy was to encourage these commissions to come out into the open; and the following years saw the creation of sectoral and intersectoral commissions, and area and national coordinating commissions, although the national secretariat remained clandestine in obedience to the policy of 'protecting the head but working openly at the base'. Nonetheless, the commissions suffered heavily from the repression of the later sixties (see Chapters 6, 7 and 10), and this tended to increase the influence of the Party, which was the one organization within the commissions which had a national network, allowing it to tighten control over the policy-making bodies and coordinate and distribute solidarity funds from inside and outside Spain (Mujal-León:1983). This in turn heightened the tensions that already existed between the Party and other groups such as USO, which now withdrew from the commissions, alleging that they were now a mere 'transmission belt' for the Party; while the UGT criticized the Party for seizing control of the organization. According to Maravall (1978), the commissions were now dominated by the Party, although left-wing Catholic organizations continued to exert considerable influence.

In the face of the repression the Party was also assailed from its left, when Maoist groups advocated a move to strictly underground activity, combined with an extension of the terrain of the struggle from the factory floor to the society at large; but the Party replied that it was essential to mobilize the workers and go on the offensive, or risk losing contact with the masses altogether (Mujal-León:1979). Eventually the Party line of combining legal platforms with open mobilization won the day, and it was able to proceed to seek alliances with middle-class organizations as part of its democratic project. The extreme left was adamant that a 'State-monopoly capitalist system' could only advance to a socialist one, and that trying to attract the middle classes was both a waste of time and a capitulation to the bourgeoisie; and this dispute was germane to the contrasting views of the commissions as the embryo of a new proletarian party, on the one hand, and, on the other, as a 'socio-political movement' which made no attempt to distinguish members from non-members (Mujal-León:1983). The Party's view was vindicated from 1973 onwards, when the commissions recuperated their militancy and operational capability, and continued to maintain a high profile through legal channels.

The decision at national level to create a mass movement to engage in a more open style of struggle was reflected in El Marco in the recruitment and rapid promotion of popular leaders from the most active commissions, and in the rising rhythm of strikes and protests which accompanied this transformation of the Party. The provincial committee was broadened to include Antonio Alvarez, José Marroquín, Pepe de la Rosa and Manolo Espinar, amongst others; and the Party was constantly on the lookout for new leaders with a capacity to mobilize the workers in their sector of industry. Antonio Cárdenas did a lot of the recruiting, but it was Benítez Rufo himself who pursued the overall strategy with most vigour, seeing the recurrent strikes as a regional prelude to the Party's long invoked and fervently desired peaceful national strike. At the same time other leaders such as Federico Iglesias, impressed by the results that Alvarez had achieved in the *bodegas*, volunteered their services; and Federico actively sought and got the job of organizing the commissions in the building industry. But if it was his decision, it depended on backing from the Party, which arranged his post in the Vertical Syndicate and instructed him on how to proceed. Antonio Alvarez himself, who had been a simple shop steward, was first noticed by the Party the day he confronted the Syndicate's lawyer at the meeting in the Syndicate's headquarters in the Plaza Arenal in Jerez (see Chapter 7); and he was then propelled forward by the Party to become provincial leader of the commissions and undisputed leader of the movement in El Puerto. In this way, the influx of young and combative leaders not only changed the composition of the provincial committee, which became weighted with representatives from the most active commissions, but also came to change the very character of the local Party itself.

Not everybody thought this was a good thing. Pepe de la Rosa was not convinced of the virtue of removing trained Communists from the provincial committee in order to bring in messianic leaders who did not have the discipline of Party cadres. In this connection, it is understandable that Rufo tried to attract Fábregas to the mass Party, but, as has become clear, he was reluctant to cooperate, and only did so *por los cojones*. In the event he did support Rufo in the first two strike calls he issued, but resisted the third; and after that he was always more aware of the obstacles to any strike than the advantages. So he was displaced from the centre of Rufo's strategy, and replaced by Paco de las Flores, Manolo Romero and José Aldana; and Emilio Fábregas began to turn his not inconsiderable energies to his representative work within the Vertical Syndicate. Then, as the struggle became more radical, with the Party pushing for more mobilization and more strikes, the split between Fábregas and the Party grew wider, culminating in his complete ostracism after the 'fall' of 1970. At that time he was even estranged from the commissions, of which he was the local founding father, because, as he said, 'they tried to make him join the Party'. Although this was not true, or at least was a gross simplification, it was indeed a true measure of the disillusionment of the syndical leader. Such leaders were schooled in mobilization and negotiation, and were not really Party men, and much less revolutionaries. So it is possible that the Party was too sectarian with Emilio Fábregas, and, to a lesser extent and at a later moment, with Antonio Alvarez. But in the end the answer to these questions has little to do with dogma, and yet less to do with personal morality. Rather, it is inscribed in the nature of the relationship between the commissions and the Party.

The classic division of political labour between Party and commissions, which in the case of El Marco had also found a further but no less concrete expression in the division of labour between El Puerto and Sanlúcar (see Chapter 3), became blurred after Fábregas's ostracism by the movement, which, moreover, happened to coincide with Paco de las Flores's retirement from the struggle with a bad back. Then, after 1973 especially, the relationship between commissions and Party came under close scrutiny and was the object of often acrid debates about the need for a fully independent union of the working class, which the commissions could never be while they appeared to remain in tutelage to the Party. Little by little the close links that had been forged between them in clandestinity were severed, and once again the commissions became a more heterogeneous force, which included many left-wing elements not associated with the Party. It is true that a great number of the militants and a large majority of the national leadership continued to be Party members; but the Party no longer aspired, formally at least, to direct the commissions or decide their strategy. In much more recent years there have been splits between the Communist militants inside the commissions and the Party itself which would have been almost inconceivable in the context of illegality and clandestinity. In the meantime, Emilio Fábregas continued to wait for a way forward after the 'fall', and went on with his work inside the Vertical Syndicate. Although tentative attempts at reconciliation took place, the basic differences of perspective persisted and they came to nought. Since the 'fall' he had been arguing that the commissions should be more independent of the Party, and to a degree felt vindicated once this position was adopted by syndical leaders of national renown such as Marcelino Camacho. But the good old days of the bad times of the dictatorship would never return.

CONTINGENCY, COMMUNISM AND THE DEMOCRATIC CAUSE

Thus the relationship between commissions and Party was never without its ambiguities and contradictions, which were a direct result of the contingent connections which drew them together in the democratic struggle. Contingent connections made for contingent outcomes, and, in particular, it is the organizational axis of Party and commissions which tended to reinforce the translation of the originally economic demands of the commissions into the political demands for freedom of organization and the right to strike which came to be promoted through the open struggle of the Party. This fundamental point means that the historical role of democratic actors such as the commissions and the Party did not depend on their democratic credentials or intentions in particular (and especially not those of the Communist Party); nor in general was the democratic project constructed in the image of a 'national democratic community' (Anderson:1983). On the contrary, the democratic project contained and expressed the contingent outcomes of a specific political process, and so could not correspond to any single idea of democracy. This is not to assert that individual actors were not conscious of struggling for democracy. Indeed they were. But their consciousness was formed through the complex choices they confronted within this *process* (see Chapter 15), and so could not reflect any overarching political *plan*. This argument applies *a fortiori* to the roles of the commissions and Communist Party as they evolved in strategic relation to the Vertical Syndicate and Francoist legality; and this will become clearer in Chapter 12, which completes the analytical bridge to the wider empirical assertions and more comprehensive conceptual framework of the final section.

12

Fighting with two faces:
the strategic combination of legal
and clandestine spaces

> The commissions have arisen on a terrain determined by the State itself. Only by overcoming the obligatory syndical structure in different ways and at different levels, have the commissions been able to emerge, develop and resist. In this way, a syndical structure imposed with the idea of controlling the working class has been transformed (despite itself and through the dialectics of the struggle) into the operational and mass base of the labour movement of today.
>
> Fernando Soto, *A Ras de Tierra*

As EL Marco de Jerez entered the decade of the fifties not a voice could be heard. The whole region was covered by the misty silence of Francoism. Outside of the vineyards, there was nowhere for the workers to meet, until it occurred to them that the Vertical Syndicate itself was a proper place to sit and talk; and from there it was but a small step to the thought that by seeking a more permanent place in the Syndicate they might gain some small benefit for themselves and their companions. Until that moment, although the Syndicate had been present in the region, it had not even fulfilled its own operational norms. The economic sections of the employers had simply packed the social sections of the workers with men they knew they could manipulate, and when it became time to negotiate a new contract these men were called together to rubber-stamp the new agreement. As much for this reason and for others of history, the few that remained of the older generation of anarchist leaders would have nothing to do with the Syndicate, and adamantly refused to 'collaborate'. But with the advent of elections within the Syndicate (see Chapter 5) new and natural leaders who had gained the confidence of the workers (see Chapters 1 and 2) began to organize slates in order to make representation within the Syndicate more effective. In retrospect it can be seen that these slates were the spawn of the workers' commissions, which might never have germinated had the employers not ignored the rules in such cavalier fashion.

As early as 1949 the Communist Party had urged the workers to make the Vertical Syndicate 'a breeding-ground of demands', and had suggested that Party activity within the Syndicate 'would inevitably lead to the denunciation of its class character and to the unmasking of the hierarchs nominated by Franco' (*Mundo Obrero*:20.10.1949). In El Marco, the original demands had to do with little more than the fulfilment of existing contracts (see Chapter 6), but nonetheless the newly elected shop stewards immediately suffered for their temerity, and here and elsewhere the lack of syndical guarantees led to the loss of jobs and even imprisonment. Moreover, according to Alvarez (1967), in many places it was just such repression which provided the final impulse for the formation of workers' commissions, which could in turn provide support and guidance for representatives inside the Syndicate. In this way, some of the first commissions were formed of shop stewards and representatives on the *jurados*, some of ordinary workers and some of both together; but in any event, political work by natural leaders within the Syndicate preceded the formation of the commissions. On the other hand, once the commissions were in place, they could promote their own candidates in the Vertical elections, as they had been doing in El Marco from 1956; and with the promulgation of the 1958 Law of Collective Contracts these same commissions of El Marco immediately moved to occupy the legal space the law made available, and so achieve more advantageous contracts, just as the resolution of the Party's Central Committee of that year suggested they should (Linz:1973). And however distinct the development of the commissions in different regions of the country, what they always had in common at the grass roots was precisely this strategy of electing their members to posts within the Vertical Syndicate in order, in the first place, to negotiate better pay and conditions (Wright:1977).

In this connection it is worth insisting that the new generation of natural leaders confronted an equally new legal and institutional terrain, primarily in the form of the Vertical Syndicate; and it was this terrain which conditioned both the formation of the commissions and the strategies they chose for advancing their demands. It has already been suggested (and the argument will be taken up later in this chapter) that the central strategy of the combination of legal and extralegal struggle was in part a reply to the difficulties of launching strikes in conditions of clandestinity (see, e.g., Chapter 2); but it is clear that such a strategy could make sense only in the specific institutional setting which was the Vertical Syndicate. It is for this reason, if for no other, that there was so little organizational and strategic continuity between the labour movement of the thirties and that of the fifties and sixties. The latter was obliged to operate on a distinct and initially disadvantageous terrain; but the organizational forms and strategic discoveries which eventually allowed it to do so contributed to the construction of a democratic project in a way the old unionism of the UGT and CNT was unhappily unable to do.

INSTITUTIONAL COVER AND CLANDESTINE STRUGGLE

Commenting on the Vertical elections, the Communist Party had suggested that the 'workers unite and form a solid block, and make the most of the very few rights which Francoist law gives them in such elections' (*Mundo Obrero*:31.1.1954). But as the commissions began to form in El Marco the workers went further than this, and from the first moment they entered the Syndicate they used the cover this afforded them to recruit militants and organize strikes. At first not all of the representatives on the *jurados* would attend the secret strike meetings, but the number of activists increased once the incipient commissions in the region had made contact with the Party, which also encouraged its militants to work inside the Syndicate. In this way strikes could be mounted without immediate danger of police repression, and as the movement grew the Syndicate also provided legal channels for the militants to maintain and coordinate their contacts within an extended organization. Federico Iglesias, for example, is explicit that the Syndicate provided the alibi for his work in the commissions at regional level, and if questioned by the police he was simply carrying out his duties as president of the social section of glass, ceramics and construction; and for this same reason he could legally spend time with other leaders at provincial level such as Pedro Ríos, Paco Cabral or Emilio Fábregas. Furthermore, Manolo Romero dared to allege in interview (*Diario de Cádiz*:14.12.1969) that one of the reasons for the strike of 1969 was the lack of any assembly of the vineyard workers in Sanlúcar, which had created a certain distance between them and their representatives in the Syndicate; this mythical distance being a precise measure of the 'legal' distance the leaders liked to keep between themselves and the recurrent strike actions. So José Aldana has it exactly right when he observes that the commissions worked inside the Syndicate not to undermine it, but rather to use it as camouflage for their clandestine activities, which they could then carry out with greater security.

This point has not always been understood. Mujal-León (1979) commented that the 'commissions' activists could penetrate the vertical syndical structure set up by Franco, but it was not that easy to take over the structure'; and turning his attention to the Vertical elections of 1975 (Mujal-León:1983) added that they 'still did not establish the utility of infiltrating the Vertical Syndicate'. But he could only reach this conclusion because he saw the Communist Party as wanting to 'step in and take control' of the Syndicate, which, given that all but the lowest-level posts were appointed, was never a realistic political possibility. On the contrary, in reality it was the very structure of the Vertical Syndicate which allowed the commissions to build their organization piecemeal, through the gradual and uneven replacement of employers' men by more genuine representatives linked on the outside to commissions which were slowly developing a coherent set of economic and later political demands. Even in the late sixties in Asturias, at a moment when the Provincial Mining Commission had won almost universal recognition as the real representative of the miners, and so could denounce the Syndicate, it did so not in order to eliminate it but rather to 'expand the possibilities it offers for putting demands, and to contest the "political line" which runs it' (Miguélez:1976). The legality enshrined in the Syndicate not only contributed to the commissions' survival but also continued as a central element of their strategy.[1]

By maintaining and using this legality the militants of the labour movement could work simultaneously within the parallel organizations of the Syndicate and the commissions (Linz:1973), and thus straddle the gap between legal and illegal activity. In effect, the *jurado de empresa* became linked to two 'syndicates', the official Vertical Syndicate, on the one hand, and the commissions, on the other (Amsden:1972); while the whole panorama of labour conflict throughout the country came to be characterized by this double presence of the commissions, which could decide demands and construct platforms outside the Syndicate at the same time they negotiated contracts inside it. But this ambiguous strategy was only deemed effective insofar as it contributed to strengthen the clandestine organization of the commissions, and so this double struggle was in fact weighted on one side. This was clear to Santiago Carrillo in 1965 (Carrillo:1965), when he addressed the question of the legal cover for what he came to call extralegal activities, and warned against the dangers of legalism: while it was correct to make use of 'the legal possibilities which the Syndicate provides, small as these might be, as a complement and a support to our extra-legal tasks ... the extra-legal struggles of the workers ... are the essential thing'.[2] Hence the strategy of the movement was to 'link with daring and intelligence the formal aspects of the so-called ruling legality to the very "trumping" (*desbordamiento*) of this legality' (Soto:1976).

---

[1] As there has been reason to observe before, even though the Communist Party in exile was cajoled by Stalin into adopting a strategy of infiltration of the Vertical Syndicate in 1948, many years had to pass before such a strategy became effective at national level. So the Party is indulging in wishful thinking when it attributed the strikes in Barcelona in the spring of 1951, for example, to its success in the Vertical elections of December 1950. There is no way such strikes could effectively have confirmed the 'tactical changes decided by our Central Committee in 1948 in order to correct the sectarian errors committed previously when we did not use the so-called legal possibilities' (*Mundo Obrero*:15.2.1954).

[2] In similar vein, the *real* 'workers' councils' are not those created by Solis within the structure of the Vertical Syndicate, but the workers' commissions themselves.

The struggle waged by the commissions was double in two senses: not only was it both legal and extralegal, it also used syndical practices to advance political demands. Maravall (1978) notes the culmination of the latter duality in the broad-based platforms of the 1970s, which drew together demands for wage increases and better conditions of work, on the one hand, with political claims for freedom of assembly, free syndicates, amnesty and the right to strike, on the other; but, in fact, economic demands had entailed political claims from early in the life of the movement (see Chapter 11), and it was precisely the link between its legal presence and its clandestine activities which gave this movement the sinew to hold to these claims. In other words, insofar as these political claims came to compose the core of the democratic project, then the syndical strategy of the labour movement underpinned the project as much as its syndical demands first spawned it. In both respects, the impulse given to democratic aspirations and process was a contingent rather than a necessary result of grass-roots syndical activity; but there would have been no such result at all were it not for the natural leaders whose commitment made the combination of the legal and extralegal politically feasible (a point I return to later in this chapter and in Chapter 15). Soto (1976) recognizes this when he suggests that

> the high percentage of syndical representatives dismissed and imprisoned gives ... some indication of how many men struggled by taking advantage of these legal channels; and it is from this dialectical connection between commissions and syndical representatives, from this fluid relationship, that the most stable part of the working class movement has been drawn and consolidated.

THE PROGRESSIVE INFILTRATION OF THE VERTICAL SYNDICATE

There is some uncertainty amongst the commentators over the origins of the Communist Party's strategy of infiltration of the Vertical Syndicate. Maravall (1978) refers to Dimitrov's speech on the infiltration of 'mass fascist organizations' to the Seventh Congress of the Comintern in 1935; while Ayucar (1976) has unearthed a document of April 1941, probably written by Mije, which noted that in some regions of the country the Falangist syndicates had developed quite rapidly, and proceeded to recommend the use of these syndicates to 'put the demands of the workers, using new methods and a different language ... and all the legal possibilities for work amongst the masses, so that the revolutionaries be not isolated from the bulk of the workers'.[3] According to Ayucar this indicates that the infiltration

---

[3] The document, entitled 'Guidelines for the Organization of the Party in the Interior of the Country', was given to Isidoro Diéguez by the Delegation from Mexico (Ayucar: 1976, p. 104).

of the Syndicate was Party policy long before the meeting with Stalin in 1948 (see Chapter 8), but the case is far from proven, insofar as in the very same document it is also recommended that the Party 'maintain the cult of the old syndicates amongst the workers, developing the idea of syndical unity on the basis of the UGT and the CNT'. What is certain is that the guerrilla was not disbanded until the 1948 meeting of the Political Bureau of the Party, which took place just a month after the meeting with Stalin, who had insisted on the dissolution of the clandestine syndicates and on the infiltration of the official Syndicate, as the most sure way of maintaining contact with the masses and avoiding 'infantile leftism'.

Whenever the policy was adopted, it took time to implement it. In 1954 the Vertical Syndicate was preparing its National Congress of Workers, but the regional meetings convened to establish the agenda were tending to escape its control, with demands for a minimum wage and a forty-hour week. At this time the Party was still exhorting its militants to 'take hold of whatever is new in the developments inside the Vertical Syndicate ... at times without letting it be known who we are' (*Mundo Obrero*:15.4.1954); but the local Party cadres were slow to understand what was being said in *Mundo Obrero* and on Radio Pirenaica about struggling inside the Vertical Syndicate, and possibly the only reason that El Marco was some way ahead of the rest was that the Party there could learn from the syndical practice of the commissions of Sanlúcar. Even so, it is generally agreed amongst such men as Juan Franco, Rafael Gómez and Paco Artola that not until 1962 did the local Party fully appreciate the advantages of infiltrating the Syndicate, and actively begin to promote it; and it was not until this year that the linkmen from the Executive Committee in exile, such as Rufo in Cádiz and Juan Menor in Sevilla, began to push the initiative. Once the decision was taken, the results were spectacular, and in the Vertical elections of the following year, 1963, the commissions of El Marco took the Syndicate by storm, capturing the presidencies of the social sections of all the major industrial sectors (as recounted in Chapter 6). There were Emilio Fábregas in the vineyards, Antonio Alvarez in the *bodegas*, Pepe de la Rosa in banking, Pedro Ríos in glass and ceramics, José Domínguez in fishing, José Alvarez in hotels and tourism, and Rafael Ribeiro in commerce; not to mention the vice-presidencies held by such men as Paco de las Flores.[4] All these men were Party militants, who marched into the headquarters of the Syndicate, located at that time in an old hotel, and took over an office each.

In the light of these events, which must have been repeated in some degree

---

[4] At this time it was Emilio Fábregas and Paco de las Flores who symbolized the presence of the working-class movement inside the Vertical Syndicate. It was they who nominated the representatives to the National Social Security Institute; and Paco de las Flores succeeded in negotiating compensation for injured workers, which had never been paid before.

in other regions of the country, it appears strange that Maravall (1978) should suggest that the process of infiltration did not begin until 1964; but this is probably explained by the priority attention he gives to Asturias in his analysis. In that region the repression of the fifties was so severe, and the consequent hatred of both the police and Syndicate so deep, that 'while other places were practising infiltration since 1948, in Asturias this did not even begin until 1957' (Miguélez:1976); and as the repression then focused precisely on the representatives elected in 1957, 'it was practically not until 1966 that the miners adopted the policy of infiltration as a form of mass struggle'. In particular, the commissions in Asturias advocated abstention from the Vertical elections in 1963, unless their deportees were returned. Elsewhere it was precisely the not inconsiderable successes achieved in the 1963 elections which stimulated both commissions and Party to wage a much more serious campaign in 1966. From the beginning of 1964 the Party was talking of the struggle of the commissions inside the Syndicate as the 'great political battle' (*Mundo Obrero*:15.2.1964).

The Vertical elections of 1966 were preceded by a veritable electoral campaign. On the one hand the regime in the person of José Solis Ruíz, the secretary-general of the Syndicate, who even in 1963 had still had a somewhat ambivalent attitude towards the elections, used all its propaganda ploys to encourage participation; and on the other both the commissions and the Party sought full participation for their own purposes. In part, they were reacting to the 1965 attempt to entice militants of the CNT into the Syndicate and so 'reform' it by giving individual syndicates an appearance of greater independence (see Chapter 4); and in part they were convinced that this was the moment of the 'great leap forward'. So the Party and the commissions[5] ran their campaign through workers' assemblies (which now became a reality) and meetings of every kind, and achieved the highest level of mobilization in almost thirty years of Francoism. Just before the elections the Party denied vehemently that to vote was to collaborate, and insisted that Party militants keep a careful watch on polling day to prevent pressures and fraud. The day itself saw a turn-out of 83.3 percent of the labour census (Amsden:1972), and although fraud there certainly was, the commissions nevertheless scored a notable victory, not only winning 40 per cent of the syndical posts in Madrid, for example, but also scoring well in the north, despite the intense campaign for abstention waged by the UGT, the Socialist Party in exile, and the CNT. Their success was seen first, in the campaign

---

[5] Although there was considerable local variation, in general it was the commissions which organized slates and votes and got their men elected, with the Party providing logistical support. In many instances, as in the case of the building workers' commission under Federico Iglesias in El Puerto, the organizing commission and the social section turned out to be identical after the election.

The Syndicate brought its own campaign to El Puerto, too, but when Solis's representative got up to speak he was booed out of the meeting.

itself, which through the assemblies held in the most unlikely places, and even in the Vertical Syndicate itself, had proved to be an authentic school of democratic practice; second, in the immediate results, which were impressive enough to convince the regime to postpone the elections of 1969 until 1971, and even then with the number of posts open to election reduced by 50 per cent; and third, in the openings it provided for the strategic use of economic demands and wage negotiations, which were reflected in the rising pace of industrial conflict in the subsequent ten years (Maravall: 1982).

Unlike the Communist Party, the UGT and the CNT would not run in the Vertical elections on principle, arguing that this would lead to the co-optation of the movement and the legitimation of the regime. The USO, on the other hand, continued to participate both nationally and in El Marco, where the brothers Ramón and José Gaitero of Jerez played an important syndical role. The result of the UGT's and CNT's boycott was that they both lost touch with the new working class of the cities; and even though Maravall (1978) argues that the UGT position found strong support in Asturias and the Basque Country, it was only in the Basque Country that it made a difference in the 1966 elections (Miguélez: 1976). But the Communists came to exercise more and more influence within the movement because their 'willingness ... to use the channels provided by the regime, in contrast to the Socialists ... combined with their organizational skills and the ambivalent admiration of the left Catholics for them, had opened the door of labour to them' (Linz: 1973); so that in both Andalucía and Catalonia, for example, the anarchist hegemony of the early decades of the century had been almost completely supplanted by Communist-led commissions by the end of the sixties. Within the Vertical Syndicate itself, the main opposition to the progressive infiltration of the institution came from its functionaries rather than from the employers, who came to be concerned not so much with the presence or absence of commissions, or with their ideological colour, as with the prospects for striking a wage deal that would stick.

INFILTRATION AND THE REPRESSIVE RESPONSE OF THE REGIME

As early as 1962 the Communist Party recognized that shop stewards and representatives on the *jurados* were susceptible to repression, and especially sacking and imprisonment, but nonetheless defended the viability of the overall strategy (*Mundo Obrero*: 15.4.1962). In the subsequent four years some 1,800 elected syndical representatives were dismissed from their jobs (Amsden: 1972); but this was a relatively small proportion of the total number of 220,000 such representatives across the country, so that Carrillo could boast in 1967 that 'Solis and the "political line" have no idea how to rid themselves of the unwelcome presence of thousands of genuine activists, working as shop stewards and on the *jurados* and social sections of the Syndicate' (Carrillo:1967). But the worst of the repression was still to come, and was foreshadowed in 1967 in Asturias, where it bit so hard that many argued for a return to clandestine struggle, so introducing divisions within the movement (Miguélez:1976). Many of the commissions were preoccupied by what Soto (1976) later called the 'defective or incorrect guideline which made the repression easier by separating out the more combative leaders . . . who were thus more easily hit with sanctions, sackings and imprisonment',[6] and the Party admitted that 'some of the hierarchs of the Syndicate certainly belong to the Political Social Brigade', and recognized that some workers must think that electing their companions onto the Syndicate was 'tantamount to sending them to prison' (*Mundo Obrero*:15.7.1969). Although it went on to argue that the situation had changed to the point where direct and brutal repression was no longer possible, it was to be proved wrong in immediate and spectacular fashion by the state of siege, and the wave of repression which washed over regions like El Marco de Jerez. In addition to the arrests and the suspension of habeas corpus, all known militants of the movement and their suspected sympathizers were suspended from their syndical posts; and less militant workers were discouraged now that economic demands had given way to overtly political confrontation. The Party, however, continued to urge participation, and over 80 per cent of the labour census voted in the elections of 1971; so that within two or three years it was apparent that the repressive measures had succeeded only in slowing down the process of infiltration, rather than stopping it.

INFILTRATION AND THE DANGERS OF CO-OPTATION

The strategy of infiltration was steeped in the kind of dangerous ambiguities which Santiago Carrillo alluded to in 1967 when he asserted that

> there can be no doubt that our task is to develop and consolidate those legal and extra-legal forms of unity of the workers [but] that task is not simple; on the contrary it is complicated and difficult. In these complications and difficulties there is all the difference between a policy of collaborating with the Vertical Syndicate . . . and using for the revolutionary struggle the legal possibilities, which is the tactic advocated by our Party. (Carrillo:1967)

---

[6] Not only were more and more activists dismissed from their syndical posts, and more often than not their jobs, but the hierarchical and vertical structure of the Syndicate also acted as a partial barrier against infiltrators, while its procedural rules limited candidates in elections to workers who had been employed for at least two years, and had never resigned from or been ousted from the Syndicate.

The Franco regime for its part was quite conscious of trying to induce such collaboration through participation on the *jurados*, and to promote it further through the collective bargaining encouraged by the 1958 Law of Collective Contracts; while during the first half of the sixties the chosen strategy of Solís Ruíz was to attempt to co-opt the emergent commissions into the structure of the Vertical Syndicate (see Chapter 4). In general the commissions were perfectly well aware of the dangers of such absorption, and indeed the very emergence of the commissions responded to the impelling political necessity of maintaining intact an autonomous organization *outside* the Syndicate, which might then work more effectively inside it; and the only collaboration they allowed was of the conflictive kind. Nevertheless, as Selgas (1974) notes, 'even though the commissions... act with markedly political objectives and even though their members when they enter the system do so with the preconceived intention of destroying it, there have been numerous cases of workers who on becoming representatives within the Syndicate have been won over by it, and have opted, in a sincere fashion, for the legal road'. In reality, Selgas's rather sanguine conclusion refers on the one hand to the 'individual appetite for syndical posts which mean pay without work' (Candel:1968); and on the other to the syndical representatives' sometimes disguised purpose of controlling a piece of the Syndicate's 'vast welfare, education and recreation apparatus' (Amsden:1972). In other words, although the Syndicate did indeed offer institutional cover for extralegal activities, it also succeeded in co-opting many of the movement's activists, usually through allowing them a series of expenses which exceeded any income available to them in their work.

In El Marco de Jerez concern over the problem and possibility of co-optation centred on the person of Emilio Fábregas. Every one of his companions knew him to be an honourable man and a born leader, who struggled tirelessly in the service of the workers of the region. But at the same time, they were all aware of how he seemed to succumb to the perils of professionalization as he rose in importance within the apparatus of the Syndicate. He began as something of a firebrand, but such was his success that he soon had an office in Cádiz, a secretary and an official car, and 'took aeroplanes as if they were buses'. Once he had abandoned his base in Sanlúcar he began to lose touch with his own people, and was soon speaking to them more on the radio or in the newspapers than face-to-face. He still received individual workers, and was recognized as effective in solving their problems (and at the same time in reproducing the traditional pattern of clientelistic relations); but by this time, as the number of positions he held allowed him to live from his expenses, he was no longer himself a worker, and this inevitably conditioned his attitudes and finally his person. In short, he became wedded to the job rather than the struggle, and soon this 'man of the thirty allowances' was spending more and more time in Madrid, 'watching Real Madrid and Atlético Bilbao' and 'walking in and out of Solís Ruíz's office as if it were his own'.

Ironically, in the early days it was always Emilio who warned against the dangers of the 'inside track', and counselled constant vigilance and aggression. But his long career led him to admire 'the apparatus these people have', as he told it to Antonio Alvarez, who remembers him as a potential leader of national stature, but one who never had, or finally lost, a vision of the political future. Indeed, once he became president of the Institute of Social Security (Instituto Nacional de Previsión), even his syndical commitment was blunted, although he retained his leadership of the syndical representation of the entire region until the very last moments of the dictatorship – never really believing perhaps that Francoism had feet of clay.

Emilio's version of his career is quite different. It begins with his election as the local president of the social section of the vineyard workers in El Marco in 1960, which only served to convince him of the need for higher office, if he was to look after the interests of his men, who worked not only in Sanlúcar but also in the very different contexts of Jerez, El Puerto and Trebujena. So, even though this was far from his original intention, with the help of contacts in these *pueblos* he was elected provincial president in the same year, alongside the other representatives of the section, all of whom came from Sanlúcar. As the next step he was elected as one of four representatives from his section to the newly constituted Workers' Council of the Syndicate (see Chapter 5), each of the twenty-eight or so social sections of the province sending two to four representatives who, he admits, tended to be the most ambitious and educated men of the movement in the region. By 1966 he had become first vice-president and in 1970 president of the council, and the effective head of the movement in the province, although every advance was achieved by election, never by appointment, and often against the wishes of the Syndicate's officials.

Once president of the council he also sat *ex officio* on other national bodies representing agrarian interests, became vice-president of the National Institute of Social Security and vice-president of Professional Training, and was able to win the confidence of progressive lawyers and economists, whom he used to advance the struggle. More crucially, he and five other representatives from the council sat, again *ex officio*, on the Executive Committee of the Vertical Syndicate, which is where problems were solved and agreements made, in short, where the real political dealing got done. Against his will, and as a compromise candidate, he was also elected in 1970 as one of two provincial deputies, and the only workers' representative, to the national council of the Syndicate. In this way, both on account of the positions he occupied, and on account of the expertise he had accumulated in the field of social security, his position had become more or less impregnable, and although the authorities had no special liking for him, they found it impossible to force him out.

The men of El Marco who became disenchanted with Emilio's success clearly believe with William Blake that the way to hell is paved with good intentions, and that it was precisely the small enticements of travelling and subsistence expenses which succeeded in drawing Emilio out of his own environment and co-opting him; and by placing men like him in busy bureaucratic jobs the Syndicate could absorb their energies and neutralize their democratic impulses. Emilio, for his part, is more than ready to admit that he was completely tied up with Syndical business, and that he spent his life travelling from one meeting to the next; but if he was paid expenses, they never added up to more than a working wage, or if they did, he never kept more than was needful for family subsistence. He was never co-opted by these allowances, never did anything dishonourable, but always stayed true to the anarchist morality by which he was raised.[7]

There is clearly no effective way of resolving this debate at the individual level, and it is anyway no part of the academic's task to sit in moral judgement on the political actors who have happened to fall under his scrutiny. The point at issue is not individual or moral but analytical and general; and simply serves to demonstrate that the fight with two faces was inherently ambiguous because it was *structurally* ambivalent, predisposing the leaders of the movement to infiltration and co-optation simultaneously. And it is in this context that the feud between Emilio Fábregas and Manolo Romero becomes comprehensible. Both men were leaders from Sanlúcar with a long record of struggle behind them, and both worked within the workers' commissions. The split between them has been explained in terms of the growing differences which emerged from Manolo's political commitment to the Party on the one hand, and Emilio's syndical commitment on the other;[8] but it is now evident that this political division of labour was usual in the movement and necessary for it, and that the real tension lay in the process of infiltration and cooptation, which always contained the potential for personal and organizational disruption. This tension was productive for the democratic project insofar as the political actors had to strive to resolve the ambivalence inscribed within it; but the struggle sometimes exacted a high personal price from those who tried to do so.

LEGAL SPACES AND THE DEMOCRATIC PROJECT

At the same historical moment that the Falangist movement which was the F.E. de las JONS (see Chapter 5) entered into decline with the arrival of

---

[7] As final proof of his good faith Emilio notes that in the final Vertical elections before the transition to democracy he was again elected president of the social section of his own syndicate, president at provincial level, and president of the provincial council, which could not have occurred had he been a 'class traitor', as some more angry opponents were heard to allege.

[8] Once again, Emilio consistently denied being a member of the Party, although it is clear that over many years he collaborated with it, if with increasing reluctance. For this motive, others allege that he was indeed of the Party, that the regime knew of his affiliation but left him free because it suited their own interests. But this allegation hardly squares with another frequently voiced criticism, which was that he succumbed to the blandishments of the Syndicate because he had no clear political line.

Opus Dei members in the cabinet and the partial liberalization of the economy, another movement in the form of the workers' commissions arose to
take its place. But while the first movement was authoritarian in nature and
never aspired to lift the population from the political apathy and despair
of the post-Civil War period, the commissions composed a democratic movement which sought ever higher levels of political mobilization. In this regard,
like every democratic project in an authoritarian context, the movement
was built on faith in the future.

The emergence and growth of the workers' commissions occurred within
and because of the regime's overarching structure of labour control which
was the Vertical Syndicate; and once these commissions had achieved their
own autonomous organization outside the Syndicate, their strategy was one
of infiltrating the Syndicate in order to secure an institutional cover for their
own extralegal activities, and in order to deny the Syndicate legitimacy.
While commissions and Syndicate can be studied separately for analytical
purposes, in the real political process they were indissolubly linked and held
in a productive tension that can only be called 'dialectical'.

A key element of the strategy of infiltration of the Vertical Syndicate was
the decision to compete in the Vertical elections, which took place every
three years or so. By 1975 not only USO but also groups on the extreme
left had joined the Communist Party in fielding candidates for these elections,
and in this year the commissions claimed to have won some 70 per cent of
all the posts open to election. At the same time, because of the leverage this
gave the commissions in collective bargaining, political power at plant level
had shifted from the syndicates to the shop floor (Wright:1977); and in
this way the formal potential of the *jurado* (or factory committee) had been
partially realized, and an element of democracy within the authoritarian
State extended far beyond its original conception, although not beyond the
boundaries of legality. The strategy of 'entryism' thus proved a very effective
form of struggle against the Francoist State, as it created contradictions
within the corporatist centrepiece which was the structure of labour control
embodied in the Vertical Syndicate, and built a strong Communist Party
presence in the syndical arena, such as it had never enjoyed before.[9]

In this connection, Poulantzas (1976, pp. 80–4) appears to have it wrong
when he talks of the 'isolation' of the Francoist State, asserting that as the
popular masses were nowhere to be found in the state apparatus, there was
no concentration of contradictions in a 'single' apparatus as in fascism.
Precisely to the contrary, the whole trajectory of the democratic struggle
was defined by the progressive occupation of posts within the institutions
of the State, and in particular within the Vertical Syndicate, which was
central to this struggle. The paradox is patently one of an authoritarian and

---

[9] The adoption of such a strategy by the Communist Party was not without its historical
ironies, however, as entryism has been the strategy favoured by Trotskyist groups in
their efforts to undermine the 'Stalinist' Communist parties of the West.

corporatist State whose primary objective is to control the working class, but whose main instrument for doing so becomes the privileged arena of democratic struggle in the society, and the legal space which is invaded in order to push back the frontiers of civil society.

The extension of civil society was clearly not a political goal in itself, but rather the result of important political gains which were won by the syndical practices of the commissions and, in particular, the infiltration of the Syndicate. These gains included the democratic practice and schooling of the workers' assemblies; the vindication of democratic spaces within the institutional apparatus of the authoritarian State; and the creation of an effective if not legal tradition of free collective bargaining. In keeping with the analysis of Chapter 11, these were contingent political effects of the syndical practices of the commissions as they were conditioned by the specific legal and institutional terrain embodied in the Syndicate. But even if an emphasis on the contingencies of process, rather than the rationality of plan or programme, can effectively explain the discovery of the syndical strategy and its effects, it does not address the successful reproduction of that strategy, which was essential for the political gains it finally achieved.

Here the key is with the people who made the democratic project. Although the commissions were organizing 'legally', and although the Vertical elections were the workers' one formal opportunity to choose their own representatives, candidates to these elections could clearly not run on open platforms. The workers' votes therefore went to those candidates who had won their confidence in the process of the struggle itself, and no matter how badly the Communist Party or the employers wanted their men elected, the limits on their aspirations were imposed by the presence of natural leaders and the networks they had built between themselves. So the commissions were composed from the personal networks. But without the networks the central strategy itself would have lost all logistical viability and capacity for reproduction, in the face of the proven co-optative and repressive powers of the regime, because it was the networks which bound together the two *operational fields* of the strategy (legal and extralegal) and secured a consistent and unambiguous practice in ambivalent conditions. The organic and pervasive presence of the networks in this story, therefore, was intrinsic not only to the birth and growth of the commissions themselves but also to the coherence and reproduction of their central strategy. Thus, the link between legal and clandestine activities, between the two faces of the struggle, was not simply strategic nor merely theoretical, but very immediate, usually personal and constantly reproduced within the process of struggle itself. In El Marco de Jerez this process often began with two men talking in a bar.

PART IV

Political strategies and the democratic project

13

Democratic transformation and the transition to democracy: the political project of the labour movement, 1955–1985

> The regime was no longer able to attack in such blind and brutal fashion as before, but retreated from the advancing masses, pretending to negotiate with strikers and workers at the same time as it deployed its repressive forces to disband their organizations. In short, it now attacked not frontally but from the flanks, in an attempt to preserve or rather recover its hegemony.
>
> José Biescas, *España bajo la Dictadura Franquista*

MANY RECENT ACCOUNTS of the transition to democracy in Spain have seen it as beginning with Franco's death. But this story shows that history is not quite this simple. What began in late 1975 was the relatively rapid abrogation of Francoist laws and the construction of a new legality which sealed the final phase of the democratic transformation of the Francoist State; but the transformation itself began much earlier with the slow stirring of the Spanish people and the progressive emergence of new forms of political organization which finally achieved a radical change in the balance of forces in Spanish civil society. The transition cannot be understood, therefore, without taking into account this process of transformation; and the key political question is not so much the merely tactical one of how so much political compromise could have been achieved in so little time, as the strategic one of how such extensive organization could take place despite the severe restrictions imposed by one of the most repressive of modern dictatorships. Thus, although the transition to democracy in Spain represents a change in the form of State, in this story its investigation has focused on the political associations of civil society and their efforts to create and defend the political space for effective organization.

There is no doubt that the coalescence of a broad range of political associations, including proscribed political parties, church groups (and their youth sections), student organizations, intellectual caucuses and neighbourhood associations in a series of platforms and councils during the early 1970s made a crucial contribution to the cause of democracy (Carr and Fusi: 1981). At the same time, the regime had to contend not only with a recrudescence of student struggles in the universities, which had been a recurrent source of irritation since the late 1950s (Maravall:1978), but also with renewed nationalist projects in Catalonia and the Basque Country, which presented a direct challenge to the secular, centralizing tradition of Francoism. But while these developments certainly were not insignificant, neither individually nor collectively did they play so important a role in the transformation of the Francoist State as did the emergence and growth of an independent labour movement, which discovered its own sui generis form of organization in the workers' commissions.

This story has stressed the role of the labour movement for several reasons. For one thing, the labour movement historically precedes other democratic initiatives; the commissions began to form at a time when almost the only signs of life in civil society were the last spasms of suffering from the white terror. Twenty years of slow organization prepared the political conditions for a massive mobilization around key democratic demands at the moment of the legal and constitutional transition, and it was under pressure from this mobilization that first political parties and then labour unions themselves were made legal. And, last but by no means least, the growth of the movement was of critical strategic importance because it required the extension of the boundaries of civil society itself in order to contest the political space monopolized by the regime's corporate structures of labour control. Indeed, at least for the 1950s and 1960s, the success of the labour movement in colonizing these structures provided a yardstick by which to measure the advance of the democratic struggle.

Within the labour movement overall, the story has stuck faithfully to the birth and growth of the workers' commissions. It may be objected that the commissions alone did not make up the total of the labour movement, which in fact comprised many other union initiatives and organizations – and this is true. But the commissions were clearly the major independent organization, and they spearheaded the struggle, which was largely because their practices proved most effective in winning labour's demands. Moreover, the commissions continued to be important in the post-Franco period, and, as we shall see, they and the UGT (the General Union of Workers) played important roles first in pressing for, and then in defending democratic freedoms during the years of the transition. Hence, I now wish to take a 'retrospective' view of the political practices of the workers' commissions, and assess their contribution to the moment of democratic transition. It is clear by now that these practices were addressed not only to employers but, crucially, to the Vertical Syndicate of the Francoist State; and so this view will inevitably include reference to the political institutions of Francoism. But the emphasis here is on the political calculations and strategies of the commissions (leaving the more detailed examination of the corporatist strategies of the State to Chapter 14).

ORDERS OF EXPLANATION: ECONOMIC CONTEXT
AND LABOUR COMBATIVENESS

There is disagreement over the causes of the remarkable growth of the labour movement, depending on how much emphasis is given to purely economic factors; and (as suggested towards the end of Chapter 4) an emphasis on political practices is intended to avoid the dangers of 'economicism', which in discussions of the labour movement in Spain tends to reduce the explanation of the political process to the demands of capitalist development. But such an emphasis should not forbid consideration of the economy and economic policy-making in particular conjunctures; and the radical revision of economic policies in the fifties proved especially important.[1] While the State had remained committed to its posture of war economy and to the policies of autarky, the economy had performed poorly (Bruce:1972). By the end of the fifties it was clearly in crisis, with wages at subsistence level or below, and unemployment rising. The Opus Dei technocrats, who had replaced Falangist politicians in both cabinet and key administrative positions, responded to the crisis by giving the economy the kind of shock treatment which has by now become the traditional prescription of the International Monetary Fund; and as their so-called Stabilization Plan of 1959 reduced real wages by as much as 50 per cent, it was accompanied by a new Public Order Act. As indicated in Chapters 5 and 7, these initiatives followed closely on the Law of Collective Contracts, which by reforming industrial relations was apparently intended to link wage rises more closely to productivity increases.

Even in the conjuncture of the fifties, however, where policy-making is so clearly dominated by perceptions of economic performance, it can be argued that these important political changes came as much in response to popular pressure as to the requirements of capital. Labour had never been entirely quiescent, even in the forties, on the evidence of increasing strike activity in the Basque Country and Barcelona in 1946, and in the following year in Madrid, Catalonia and especially Bilbao, where there was a general strike; while the decade of the fifties opened with the transport boycott and general strike in Barcelona in 1951, and its reverberations in Asturias and Madrid. By 1956 coordinated strike actions actually succeeded in winning wage increases on successive occasions, and 1958 saw widespread strikes in Catalonia, Valencia and Guipuzcoa (Guinea:1978). The governments of the fifties were not unaware of the harsh social conditions which inspired such protests, and the Vertical Syndicate tried to set up its own District

---

[1] As it is the fifties which mark the beginning of the political process which will lead progressively to the democratic transformation of the Spanish State, they provide an appropriate context for debating different orders of explanation of this process.

Workers' Commissions and Neighbourhood Absorption Units as palliatives. But the coincidence of these labour protests with an upsurge in the student movement posed serious problems for a regime within which all such protests were strictly prohibited; so that (as argued in Chapter 7) the syndical reform of 1958 can in part be explained as a cautious tactical concession in the face of popular opposition.

Nonetheless, even were the history of the labour movement pursued to the point of recording every strike action of the fifties and the following years, the political process of the period can no more be explained by labour combativeness *tout court* than it can by the economy writ large. On the contrary, the key element in explaining the process is the construction of a political project which proves capable of mobilizing diverse groups and organizations within civil society against the continuation of the Francoist State. The project itself (as I argue in Chapter 15) was cemented by a rare amalgam of personal networks and political strategies; and the important point to make here is that both networks and strategies took shape through the syndical practices of the labour movement. The story has shown how this movement discovered not only the political form of the commissions but also their grand strategy of infiltration into the Vertical Syndicate. These syndical practices led the commissions to form *within* the Vertical Syndicate (which I discuss in Chapter 14); to move partially but not completely *outside* its structure to organize at sectoral, regional and national level; and then to move back *inside* with the concerted aim of infiltration – a complex manoeuvre which expressed a continuous combination of legal and extralegal activities and which could only be secured by the skein of personal networks. In short, the syndical practices of the labour movement revealed the architecture of the project through their key strategic discoveries.

In this connection, it has become clear that the main contribution of the Communist Party was organizational rather than strategic. Indeed, it took some time before the Party recognized the political potential of the commissions and jettisoned its own more traditional approach (see Chapter 8); while its political discourse remained poor and ineffective until enriched by the roots it put down in the labour movement. Even then, the voluntarism of the Party leadership in exile continued to call for popular protests of a kind which squandered much of the prestige won by the Party inside the country (Preston: 1976), where it was the pragmatism of its militants (reinforced by the personal networks binding them to the labour movement) which succeeded in putting its organizational and logistical resources to work. Party cadres provided a crucial political input at critical moments, but the Party was never a vanguard in the Leninist sense: it came to represent and defend an authentic democratic alternative only insofar as it accompanied the strategic initiatives of the labour movement.

Although the literature tells us that the commissions first appeared in the mine of La Camocha (Asturias) in 1956, I have suggested that in fact they emerged earlier (from about 1953 or 1954) in Asturias, the Marco de Jerez, and, one imagines, elsewhere (Ariza:1976; Sartorius:1976). And while the conventional wisdom is that the commissions were elected from workers' assemblies (and this attractive image of direct democracy does indeed have substance in the 1960s), they were much more likely, in these early days, to have been self-elected small groups which had gained experience and come together on the *jurados* of the Vertical Syndicate (see Chapter 5). In fact, the *jurados* were often the origin of the first commissions, which thus grew out of the very representative structure of the Syndicate (a point which is pivotal to the argument of Chapter 14). Moreover, the participation by the incipient commissions in the Syndical elections also begins in the 1950s, and it is from this time that we can begin to discern their control of the *jurados*. This participation therefore begins much earlier than 1966, the year when the commissions said they would participate nationally. Thus the commissions had begun to practice a strategy of infiltration or *entryism* into the structure of the Syndicate long before the commissions nationally had it as an objective, and long before the Spanish Communist Party realized the potential of such a strategy or was convinced of its effectiveness.

The first commissions, elected or not, emerged to put concrete and for the most part very local demands to the employers. Once the demand had been negotiated, the commission would disband. The initial legitimacy of the commissions was thus contingent on results, and only later would such legitimacy be rooted in the assembly (where workers from the shop floor, mine or vineyard came together to vote the representatives of their choice onto the commission). This pragmatic and 'possibilist' style of organization characterized the growth of the commissions, which, unlike other highly egalitarian instruments of labour organization in the European tradition, such as the Turin soviets of the early 1920s (Cammett:1967), responded to no political or ideological model of class struggle. In this way the commissions could begin to spread from the traditional sectors of labour militancy such as mining and steel in Asturias, textiles in Catalonia, and winegrowing in Cádiz, to the recently implanted industrial sectors such as automobile manufacture in Barcelona and engineering and construction in

Madrid (Ellwood:1976). Moreover, insofar as the commissions were originally concerned with *economic* issues (wages and conditions of work), their
initiatives met with the increasing complicity of the industrial employers,
who were willing to negotiate with the clandestine commissions, and so by-
pass the official channels, whenever a peaceful settlement appeared more
attractive than intransigence and repression.

The trajectory of the labour movement was closely conditioned by the
representational form of the Syndicate (as we shall see in Chapter 14). A
landmark in this relationship was the Law of Collective Contracts of 1958,
which was designed to open up the process of collective bargaining. In part
this was a response by the State to a situation of chronic economic crisis,
and the perceived solution of linking wage increases to productivity agreements; in part it was an attempt to stem the increasing number of unofficial
agreements. In addition, this initiative was also the State's answer to the
rising level of labour militancy, expressed in the increasing number of wild-
cat strikes across the country since 1956 (see above). But whatever the
reasons for the law, it was its results which mattered, and there is a fair
degree of consensus (Martínez-Alier:1983; Martínez Lucio:1983;
Roca:1983) that its principal consequence was the shift to decentralized
collective bargaining. There is also the sense that the real relations between
employers and workers went beyond the newly established legality; and
that assemblies, free negotiations and direct action became the 'modal pattern' (Martínez-Alier:1983) as the commissions came increasingly to occupy
the political space made available on the shop floor. Thus the 1958 law
gave a powerful impulse to the growth of the labour movement, which came
of age just a few years later with the massive wave of strikes which shook
first Asturias and then the rest of the country in 1962.

But while the move to institutionalize collective bargaining created certain
indispensable conditions for the growth of the movement (Fishman:1982),
it was not quite the sea-change in the direction of labour autonomy that
many observers seem to suppose. In the first place, all negotiations still took
place within the structure of the Syndicate (between the economic sections
and the social sections in the peculiar 'bureau-speak' of the regime), and all
labour contracts were still subject to the final approval of the National
Directorate of Labour (see Chapter 7). Moreover, the state still reserved
for itself the right to impose such contracts (the so-called NOCs – or oblig-
atory norms) whenever the negotiating parties failed to agree. Immediately
following the law there was a huge increase in the number of 'free' agreements, but very soon rising demands appeared to produce deadlock. By
1966 some 70 per cent of all pay settlements in the steel industry, for
example, were imposed by the Syndicate (Ellwood:1976). So even though
the commissions themselves more often than not sought compulsory arbitration (see Chapter 7), it was still the case that at this time industrial

relations were conducted within the general framework of the Syndicate. In this way, the labour movement grew most rapidly from 1962 to 1966, when the regime continued to believe that it could *co-opt* the commissions and use them to fulfil the objectives of the 1958 law.

The fact that the state did not immediately see the commissions as incompatible with its own objectives gave the commissions time to begin to organize at sectoral and regional levels, and then to establish a national presence. The first provincial commission – which brought together representatives from different factories – appeared in the light engineering industry of Madrid in 1964, and this was soon followed by similar organizations in other sectors (Guinea:1978). In particular, the commissions put down roots in those sectors (engineering in the Basque Country, steel in Madrid and Barcelona) where the majority of strikes were to take place in the later sixties and early seventies. The State's reply included the creation of the worker and management councils, which provided new channels within the Syndicate for the upward mobility and corruption of hundreds of labour leaders (Guinea:1978). But the attempt to live with the commissions was met by the increasing pressure of illegal strikes which were almost automatically translated into overtly political confrontations, focusing very often on the issues of amnesty for those leaders dismissed or arrested, and of the very right to strike itself. While the regime was even prepared by 1965 to make a cosmetic concession in this connection, too, with its ambiguous distinction between economic and political strikes, it was too late. The political trajectory of the movement had already changed. In 1966 the commissions came out as a permanent and national movement with a dual thrust (Ariza:1976): no longer committed merely to higher wages and better conditions of work, they now wanted democratic liberties, and this was something the regime could not tolerate.

While the commissions were not now prepared to settle for less than freedom of association and the right to strike, which effectively meant demanding the end of the dictatorship, what is interesting for our argument is that they marked their coming out by announcing their entry into the Syndicate, through their full national participation in the syndical elections of 1966. The initiative met with notable success, and the commissions won over 50 per cent of the posts in factories with more than five hundred employees (i.e., once again, in the more modern sectors of industry) (Ellwood:1976). In the short term, however, the initiative also carried harsh political disadvantages, since it made it that much easier for the police to identify the leaders of the movement; and this began to matter once the Supreme Court had finally declared the commissions illegal in the following year, 1967. This declaration heralded a wave of repression in the form of the dismissal of militants from the factories (Ellwood:1976), the expulsion of commissions' candidates from the *jurados*, increased police surveillance and, in 1969, a state of siege. In effect (as we saw in Chapters 6 and 10), the years from 1967 to 1973 were the years of the heaviest and most widespread repression since the early years of the regime.

From the time of the 1966 syndical elections until the death of Franco, the field of industrial relations was turned into a battleground. Paradoxically, the years of heaviest repression also saw the fastest growth of strike activity, from 179 strikes and 184,000 working days lost in 1966 to 3,156 strikes and 1,800,000 days lost in 1975 (Couffignal:1979). By the latter year Spain came third in the European table of strike activity – even though nearly all strikes were still illegal (Guinea:1978). The repression continued with the showpiece trial of ten of the commissions' top leaders in December 1973; but by the following year the first of the 'juntas' had been formed, the Junta Democrática (shortly to be followed by the Plataforma de Convergencia Democrática). Both of these alliances had their limitations, but as clearly interclass organizations they marked the definitive broadening of the labour movement into a popular struggle for democracy (Comin:1976) (see Chapter 15). The growing impetus behind this struggle led the regime to postpone the syndical elections, in trepidation that the commissions would sweep the board. In the event they did, and of the 274,466 shop stewards elected in 1975 at least 40 per cent were commissions' candidates, while perhaps as many as 40 per cent again espoused the position of 'reform without rupture' (Ellwood:1976). This last victory of the commissions in the syndical elections paved the way for the response of the labour movement to the death of Franco. It is reckoned that between November 1975 and April of the following year some three million workers mobilized in strikes, demonstrations, sit-ins and other forms of protest (Ariza:1976).

During the last years of the dictatorship the labour movement continued to suffer repression and reverses. But the fact that strikes remained illegal meant that the commissions' economic demands were inevitably translated into political ones, and their syndical practices into a heightened struggle for democratic objectives. In short, to the degree that their syndical practices exceeded the legal limits imposed by the regime they automatically took on political objectives and moved beyond the wage relation into the broader political arena. As the struggle continued, the commissions gradually prepared the conditions for a transition to democracy by schooling the working class in 'free' collective bargaining and in a sense of its democratic rights, so readying it for its massive mobilization at the moment of the formal and constitutional transition.

THE LABOUR MOVEMENT IN THE TRANSITION
TO DEMOCRACY

In December 1975 the first 'government of the monarch' looked little disposed to make profound political changes. But it faced one very immediate problem in the shape of the workers' commissions. So one of its first measures of the new year was a syndical reform which sought to introduce more flexibility and local autonomy into the Syndicate by making it independent of both State and employers. The economic and social sections would now be separate, but within the continuing unity of the Syndicate. But it was too late for such convoluted formulae, and the syndical congress which was to debate them never took place for the very good reason that the commissions refused to participate. What the government faced in place of dialogue was a massive increase in strike action across the country in 1,568 strikes which lost the nation 18,600,000 working days (a 1,000 per cent increase over the previous year) (Guinea:1978). These strikes had the plain political objective of winning recognition of union freedoms and, especially, of the right to strike itself;[2] and the massive mobilization of labour they achieved was decisive not only in sealing the fate of Martín Villa's syndical reform but also in precipitating the fall of the Arias government which backed it, thus making way for Suarez and what appeared to be a far more serious commitment to the democratization of the polity. And while the overall mobilization, as measured by strike activity, decreased in the following year (to 1,305 strikes and 13,500,000 working days lost) (Guinea:1978), this later mobilization tended to concentrate in the first months of the year, immediately before the legalization of the political parties, and then of the independent labour unions, in April and May 1977. In the light of these observations, the thesis is not that such mobilization made *continuismo* absolutely impossible; but rather that by conditioning the calculation of political costs it made *continuismo* impracticable, and reinforced the will to reform the polity.

The Suarez project certainly looked different, and his new Minister for Syndical Relations, Enrique de la Mata, seemed eager to enter a much more open dialogue with the commissions and other unions. This new realism in the relationship between government and unions seemed secured by the decree of October 1976 setting up the AISSP (Administración Institucional de Servicios Socio-profesionales), which offered at least a temporary solution to the problem of what to do with the patrimony and the thirty-two thousand entrenched functionaries of the Syndicate (Almendros et al:1978). They were to be transferred to this semi-autonomous agency, which would remain under the direct authority of the president. But in other respects the government was moving very slowly, and the bill on syndical association which found its way to the Cortes in November 1976 aroused suspicion in all the unions and outright hostility in the commissions. In this same month the

---

[2] At the same time (March 1976) the Junta Democrática and the Plataforma de Convergencia Democrática merged to form the Coordinación Democrática (or 'Platajunta', as it was popularly known). The commissions were also active in this new grouping, pressing for its expansion and the inclusion of nationalist tendencies in particular.

'day of peaceful struggle' brought two and a half million workers onto the streets (Ariza:1977) to add impulse to the reform process. But if there was a residual reformist reluctance on the part of the government, this was now seen differently by the commissions. It was not that the government intended to prevent the legalization of free unions, which was now seen as impossible to do; but rather, by impeding the progress of the commissions and at the same time promoting rival unions, that it wanted to guarantee a pluralist syndical movement and avoid at all costs a unitary syndicalism under the hegemony of the commissions.

At this time the continuing political project of the commissions was to build a single, unitary organization to represent the whole of the labour movement, which could draw on their accumulated experience; but the governments of the transition did all in their power to prevent this. The re-emergence of the socialist UGT (General Union of Workers) met immediately with government favours: it could hold its Thirtieth Congress, the first since the Republic, quite openly in April 1976, whereas the commissions' conference of July that year still had to be held secretly. The commissions were stridently aware of the government goal of pluralism in the labour movement, but at this conference they nonetheless constituted themselves as a traditional labour union, in implicit recognition that their original project was no longer viable. For a time the relative success of the COS (the Coordinator of Syndical Organizations), which had been set up in September 1976, maintained a semblance of syndical unity, but the actual legalization of the unions (by the Law of Syndical Freedom of March 1977), while it represented a political advance, also set the seal on the lack of such unity – in the face of what was to become a highly consolidated employers' organization, the CEOE (Spanish Confederation of Entrepreneurial Organizations). All remnants of the Syndicate were finally abolished in June 1977, the same month as the first parliamentary elections.

Another key initiative in the transitional governments' domestication of the unions was the extension of the electoral principle to the shop floor, leading to open competition between the majority unions (commissions, UGT, USO) for the support of the work force, and reinforcing syndical pluralism. It is significant in this regard that the UGT finally withdrew from the COS (the event which spelled the end of unitary syndicalism) over the issue of what to do with the workers' representatives elected in the last of the Francoist Vertical elections. The commissions and USO wanted to retain them because they were mostly their militants, while the UGT wanted them out; and, in similar vein, the commissions wanted individual candidates in the new labour union elections, which would have favoured the leaders recognized for their militancy against Franco, while the UGT wanted slates (Fishman:1982; Prevost:1982). Such disagreements only left more room for political manoeuvre to the governments, which succeeded not only in setting the legal framework for union elections but also in establishing legal procedures for the bargaining process itself. Moreover, it was not long before these governments themselves entered the bargaining process at the national level, something they could only do once the great majority of the work force had become organized in the two major unions, which were now professionalized and bureaucratized in traditional Western European fashion.[3] In this way the new liberal state, without attempting any direct control of the emerging union organizations, could condition their development, with the rules of the game being decided and legitimated in parliament, that most classic of liberal institutions.

In conclusion, it can be said that in the process of transition to democracy in Spain the honours were divided evenly between government and unions: the unions for their part won what they most wanted, which was legal recognition and autonomy; while at the conclusion of the legal process the government faced not a unitary syndicalism under the hegemony of the commissions, but a plural unionism in the modern European mould. At the level of labour organization such a result represents the same order of compromise that was achieved in the transition overall: not *continuismo*; not a *ruptura democrática*; but a *transición pactada*, which included the admission of parties representing popular interests to the electoral arena (where they lacked the impetus to win anything more than bargaining power from the first pair of free elections), and the mobilization of labour into a participatory system (as had been suggested by Arias Navarro in early 1974) in order to emphasize the break from the authoritarian demobilization of the Franco period (Valles:1979). But one other essential contribution of organized labour to the transition must not be forgotten, and this is the effective representation of labour achieved *by* the commissions *through* the Syndicate. It is true that with the democratic transformation of the State and the extension of civil society, new forms of political mediation became historically available; but for such mediations to be realized in some degree required the accumulated historical experience of 'free' collective bargaining between industrial employers and commissions. Thus labour organizations paved the way to democracy both directly and indirectly: the illegal infil-

---

[3] By the spring of 1978, and on the evidence of the syndical elections of late winter and spring that year, the UGT and the commissions were the two main rival 'majority' unions – the UGT claiming a membership of 2,020,000, and the commissions claiming 1,840,441 (Guinea:1978). In assessing the figures, it is well to remember that this was the high point of union membership, due in part to the multiple membership held by many Spanish workers who were simply hedging their bets. But the conclusion is inescapable that a little more than two years after the death of Franco, and but one year after the unions themselves were made legal, they had successfully organized some 35 per cent of the Spanish working population (Pérez Díaz:1979). Two or three years later the self-attributed figures are still high, but estimates based on sampling (ETUI:1982) gave lower scores, of the order of 897,000 for the commissions and 866,000 for UGT, with total union membership across the country standing at about 2,300,000 – which would represent a drop of some 20 per cent since 1979.

tration of the Syndicate created a tradition of 'free' functional interest representation on which governments of the transition could draw; while the popular mobilizations led by the labour movement contributed to liberalize the State and so restructure the relations between State and civil society along different strategic lines.

UNIONS AND GOVERNMENT IN THE POST-TRANSITION PERIOD

In the post-transition period the search for a stable model of industrial relations tended to proceed through parliamentary promotion of a changing pattern of neo-corporatist channels of union representation. The political arrangements which underpinned this pattern, and the ways in which they conditioned the trajectory of the labour movement in the period are material for Chapter 14, which discusses the political contents and political contexts of the distinct corporatist strategies during and after Franco. Here it suffices to suggest that, in the wake of a series of neo-corporatist and nationwide wage agreements during the late seventies and early eighties, the general political orientation of the big unions has tended to be even less radical than in the earlier years of the transition.

The commissions appeared for a time to become more closely wedded, in principle at least, to the native and conservative version of Eurocommunism, and the UGT was now more than ever a social democratic union in the West German or Scandinavian mould; while both unions were keen to comply with the wage norms of the agreements made between 1977 and 1983. Indeed, Fishman (1985) has talked of the 'enduring sources of support for a policy of negotiated wage restraint', and this support has appeared to grow yet stronger in recent years. In 1984 there was a 3 per cent reduction in real wages, while the new two-year national agreement signed at the end of 1984 pegged wage rises a point below the projected rates of inflation for 1985 and 1986 (Carson-Parker:1985), besides making it rather easier for managements to dismiss their employees. Little surprise then that a recent special edition of the business magazine *Euromoney*, noting that the average number of working hours lost to strike activity had declined from 133.5 million per annum in the years 1977–80 to about 70 million for the subsequent four years, could assert that 'the once feared militancy of the Spanish trade unions has ... faded' (Carson-Parker:1985).

For both big unions it has been a time of retrenchment with membership rolls falling, and the most obvious explanation for the relative quiescence of the unions is their organizational weakness. One reason for this is almost certainly the upward displacement of bargaining from the shop floor to the state or neo-corporatist level, the general effectiveness of such agreements making union membership appear increasingly redundant. This, it may be noted in passing, is not a phenomenon unique to Spain, and has been called by Regini (1984) a 'crisis of representation'. The effect is analagous to that noted by Gunther (1985) in respect of the Centre Democratic Union and the Spanish Communist Party, and the important concessions they made in the interelite consociational process that was so important to the transition. These concessions undercut their broader brief of interest representation, and led to widespread disaffection amongst their public constituencies. 'UCD and PCE leaders', he says, 'may be regarded as having sacrificed party unity in the interests of establishing a legitimate democratic regime'. In much the same way, the unions may have 'sacrificed' many of their members in the same cause.

Another reason, which in my view complements rather than contradicts this argument, is that alleged by Fishman (1985), who sees the moderation of the union rank and file not as a result of demobilization from above so much as of demoralization from below. In his view, the generally unsuccessful strikes of 1979 failed to provide an effective reply to the severity of the economic crisis, and so led to the rapid decline in union membership, to the point where only some 13 per cent of the work force remains organized. Such demoralization is easy to understand in a situation where, despite the significant contribution of organized labour to the transition, more than twice as many workers are now jobless than in 1977. Such high rates of unemployment themselves tend to contribute to union weakness, it is alleged elsewhere in Europe, and this argument applies *a fortiori* in Spain, where the rate of unemployment has recently climbed from 18.5 per cent at the end of 1984 to somewhere just short of 25 per cent at the time of writing.

In these circumstances it is understandable that even the Socialist Party, with the large parliamentary majority it won in the elections of October 1982, preferred to seek to expand the scope of bipartite and tripartite agreements, instead of legislating on issues such as hours of work, retirement age and social security benefits; and following the Socialists' sweep of the regional government elections of May 1983, the prime minister announced that although the government would continue to consult with the opposition parties, the 'true negotiating forces' for government were organized labour and organized management (Giner and Sevilla:1984). For all that, and despite the continuing if somewhat unstable neo-corporatist practices, they have never yet become institutionalized as the unique location for such national concertation. When later in 1983 the Socialist government failed to get the support of the commissions for its 'industrial reconversion programme', it simply reverted to parliamentary legislation to achieve its objectives.

In retrospect, the decision to legislate this programme proves significant, for it is industrial restructuring more than anything else which has raised union resistance once again, and made any judgements on the passing of union militancy in Spain appear somewhat premature. To a degree this is an expression of union dissatisfaction with government economic policy in general, and to a degree with the results of national concertation in particular. On the one hand, the Socialist Party platform of 1982 promised 800,000 new jobs, while 'reconversion' has meant cutting jobs in order to make industry competitive.[4] On the other hand, while unions have continued to comply with national wage norms since 1977, the promised returns in terms of employment, social security benefits and economic welfare measures have not been delivered. On both counts the unions face stable or declining real wages in a shrinking job market, and they have begun to protest.

The protests to date have tended to be led by the commissions, and have concentrated in the first main sectors targeted for 'reconversion', namely steel and shipbuilding. Thus from the end of 1983 there have been staggered strikes, local general strikes and even campaigns of civil disobedience at steelworks and shipyards, and some of these protests have turned violent. The UGT joined in these protests for the first time at the beginning of 1984, and at the end of this year the commissions refused to endorse the new national two-year pact, on the grounds that it was a sell-out of the workers' interests. But perhaps most indicative of the changing mood of the unions, even if the motive was not 'reconversion' but further restrictions on the pension eligibility of some sectors of the work force (which the government again chose to legislate), was the general strike of 20 June 1985. This was the first such strike launched since the first free parliamentary elections of 1977, and brought some 75 per cent of industrial workers and 65 per cent of service and transport workers out in protest (*New York Times*:6.22.1985). The strike bit hardest and was most violent in Catalonia and the Basque Country, where it had the full support of the 'autonomous' unions, and dozens of arrests were made. In reply, the government agreed to alter its plan, even though the bill had already passed the lower house. The unions, it appeared, might be down, but they were not yet out.

It is difficult to gauge the significance of events of this kind without the benefit of hindsight. What is certain is that the government will continue to accelerate the 'reconversion' programme in order to streamline industry in the uncompetitive sectors of steel, shipbuilding, textiles, clothing and footwear, in preparation for Spanish membership in the European Economic Community (which began on 1 January 1986). What are uncertain are the economic effects of this entry. In my view, membership in the EEC is a political prize, and an apparent guarantee of democratic survival, for which the governments of the transition have been prepared to pay almost any

---

[4] The government's own figures at the end of 1983 projected a loss of at least 65,000 jobs over the following three years (*Washington Post*:12.3.1983), and at the end of 1984 it added a further loss of 10,500 in State-controlled industries (*New York Times*:10.10.1984).

economic price. This price may be heavy in the short term. The Spanish structure of comparative advantage is much more similar to that of the EEC than those of Greece or Portugal, so that Spanish industry will enter into direct competition with that of Europe (Reig:1984), with further large-scale job losses in the susceptible sectors – which are precisely those the government is attempting to prepare through 'reconversion'. Moreover, it is foreseeable that such effects will not be spread evenly but will concentrate in the politically most sensitive regions, and especially in the Basque Country, where the fishing and dairy industries are also likely to suffer. In such circumstances the present weak condition of Spanish unions is much to be lamented. Not only do weak unions rarely make for good industrial relations, but, on the evidence of the past thirty years, organized labour may yet have an important contribution to make to the consolidation of democracy in Spain.

14

Corporatist strategies and the transition to democracy: the institutional terrain of the struggle

> Political forces do not exist independently of the state: they are shaped in part through its forms of representation, its internal structure, and its forms of intervention.
>
> Bob Jessop, *The Capitalist State*

CORPORATISM IN THEORY AND IN PRACTICE

AT A TIME when political scientists have come to accept that there is no realistic possibility of a general theory of the capitalist State or, more especially, its historical forms, they are still reaching for general statements about contemporary corporatist structures and institutions. In their majority these statements are clearly descriptive rather than theoretical, and are derived from studies of the advanced industrial nations of Western Europe and North America; but this does not prevent them being applied, by induction, to other polities such as those of southern Europe. This procedure belongs to a broadly Weberian methodological paradigm, which sanctions the construction of a corporatist ideal-type to be used in the comparative investigation of different national realities where the various synthetic elements of the type will be found to be 'more or less present and occasionally absent' (Weber:1959). While such an approach may yield an interesting description, it runs the danger of subsuming different cases to the type in uncritical fashion, without trying to explain the differences. This is a real weakness in a world where different corporatisms are likely to be highly specific, depending on national political culture, the form of State and the disposition of social forces in particular conjunctures. There is therefore still a need for theory, as long as it is recognized that this will seek to explain not corporatism, writ large, but distinct corporatisms, and their location in specific political contexts.

There is broad agreement that all corporatisms must be located in the field of relations between the capitalist State and civil society, and that to talk of corporatism is to talk of the *relationships* between State and civil society. Descriptively, corporatist arrangements can be seen as 'blurring' the division between the two (Goldthorpe:1984), but theoretically they are better understood as contributing to construct it (Schmitter:1985).[1] This supposes a complex approach to the State itself, which is understood not as the instrument of the ruling class, nor as a political arena equally accessible to all class (and non-class) forces, nor as a unified subject in its own right which floats free above civil society; but rather as 'an institutional ensemble of forms of representation, internal organization, and intervention' (Jessop:1982). By this definition, corporatism is clearly *not* coterminous *either* with the State itself *or* with the political system (and still less is it a socio-economic system distinct from both capitalism and socialism). More modestly, it is just one of the representational forms available to the capitalist State and has emerged historically in connection with different State forms. The key question, then, concerns the extent to which any one corporatism can be explained by its strategic location in the institutional ensemble of its particular State form.

In this perspective, corporatism belongs to the field of *mediations* which are contained politically in the institutions of the State, and which act upon the disposition of social forces and the class (and other) practices of civil society (Foweraker:1982).[2] More particularly, corporatism contributes to construct the institutional terrain where political struggle takes place, and so contributes to *condition the development of the social forces in struggle*. It is not denied, of course, that there may be a material economic or social basis for the interests held collectively by the interest associations of the civil society; and precisely because of this such mediations are seen to *condition* rather than *constitute* these social forces. But what is then at issue is the definition of such interests, their common perception and, crucially, their mode of expression. In this connection it is worth emphasizing that these interests must be conceptualized as active in civil society (otherwise it is difficult to see how they could ever be recognized as interests). On the other hand, corporatist arrangements are always the result of a State initiative, and their deployment represents a State *strategy* for managing political conflict.[3]

---

[1] Goldthorpe talks of the 'renewal of corporatism' as 'blurring...the line of division, crucial to liberal political theory, between State and civil society': In fact, this line of division is equally important in both liberal and Marxist theory, but would have no empirical reference were it not for the institutions of the State and the associations of civil society; and it is in this connection that Philippe Schmitter talks of corporatism as 'one possible mode of restructuring State-civil society relations'.

[2] In this article I argue that different (capitalist) State forms can be distinguished only by identifying the political content of their characteristic forms of political mediation (such as law, bureaucracy and violence).

[3] 'What corporatist institutions can be said to provide is a distinctive context within which the class conflicts of a capitalist society may be carried on' (Goldthorpe:1984);

Corporatism, then, can be present in different State forms and common to a wide variety of political conjunctures. But this is clearly not because it is in any way *essential* to the general and necessary functions of the capitalist State: such 'capital logic' kinds of argument will only return us to the illusions of general theory. It is rather because, as a State strategy, it is a recurring element in the construction or re-ordering of State–civil society relations. On the other hand, such strategies are unlikely to be entirely indeterminate, but will obey clear policy objectives which are themselves more or less realistic depending on the disposition of social forces in the particular political conjuncture. Corporatism as strategy is therefore determined primarily at the level of the conjuncture (some historical conjunctures being far more stable than others), and thus the political content of any particular strategy will always be an empirical question but never a completely open one.

These are the propositions to be explored in the context of the changing political system of Spain, where progressive shifts in the political conjuncture have been overshadowed historically by the peaceful but dramatic transition from an authoritarian to a liberal democratic regime. It is an empirical case which immediately throws questions of theory into high relief; for despite the widespread willingness to talk of corporatism in general, it is generally accepted (with no awareness of contradiction) that corporatism of the authoritarian and liberal democratic kinds are two distinct political animals, or at least political horses of very different colours. The distinction was first made explicit by Schmitter (1974) in a seminal article where he christened the two subtypes State corporatism and societal corporatism, and has since been taken up by Lehmbruch (1979a;1984) and more recently reaffirmed by Schmitter himself (Schmitter:1985).[4] In this regard it must already be clear that in my opinion corporatism cannot *itself* be either authoritarian or liberal, and there can be no theoretical justification for modifying general statements about corporatism by what is an ad hoc and ex post distinction. Moreover, to label the subtypes as State and societal is especially misleading because corporatism is always a State strategy which will be inserted differently into the institutional ensemble of the State, and contribute differently to structure State–civil society relations in distinct State forms in specific historical moments.

---

and they should be analysed 'in the context of possible political strategies in the face of social conflict' (Roca:1983).

[4] Lehmbruch (1979b) prefers to talk of authoritarian and liberal variants of corporatism; or, more recently (Lehmbruch:1984) and more innocently, of that industrial or sectoral corporatism, on the one hand, which has a long history, and, on the other, of that 'trans-sectoral concertation' which is relatively new. Schmitter (1985), in his turn, has most recently referred to the 'unfortunate etymological association with inter-war experiences in authoritarian *corporativismo*', which is capable of confusing discussions of the so-called neo-corporatism.

With these strictures in mind, I now proceed to compare and contrast the corporatisms of Franco and contemporary Spain as strategies for conditioning and containing the syndical and political practices of the Spanish working class, which is the principal if not the only strategic objective of the corporatisms of both periods. To this end, and as a simple heuristic device, I consider first the *differences* which have been drawn between them, before suggesting what they may have *in common*; but the argument will repeatedly focus on the political content and the political context of the distinct strategies. In regard of their content, the discussion will concentrate on the question of representation in order to demonstrate, among other things, the error of denying real representation to such a strategy just because it is not liberal; while in both corporatisms the representation of economic interests will be seen to be driven by the imperatives of the immediate political context. Finally, the differential insertion of these strategies into their distinct State forms will go some way to explaining the country's transition to democracy.

CORPORATISM IN SPAIN UNDER AND AFTER FRANCO: THE DIFFERENCES

From early in its history, and as a political response to the massive divide created by the Civil War, the Franco regime began to purvey a classic corporatist ideology of social peace, where Spanish society was portrayed as an harmonious pyramidal structure, with the State at its apex and the family at its base. The main body of the political pyramid was built from the administrative offices of provincial and municipal government, and from the most hierarchical and unitary of all the institutions of the State, the Spanish Syndical Organization, universally known as the Vertical Syndicate;[5] and although it is possible to argue for a variety of corporatist features which characterized the regime, the Syndicate proved to be the mainstay of Franco's corporatist strategy (see Chapter 5).[6] Its overarching presence was

---

[5] The Spanish Syndical Organization, or Organización Sindical Española (OSE), was called the Vertical Syndicate, or Sindicato Vertical, because it was designed to order the whole world of production according to vertical lines of command, which would supersede the old horizontal, or class, divisions (the use of the word 'class' was prohibited by the Franco regime). Thus, in principle, it organized both labour and capital in what were termed, respectively, the social sections and the economic sections; but while it aspired to the exclusive representation of labour, the employers continued to enjoy independent representation through their Chambers of Commerce and Industry.

[6] One such feature was the 'rubber-stamp' parliament itself, the Cortes; and it has been noted that whereas prior to the Civil War, the corporate groups and organized interests of civil society had been relatively weak, with the nationalist victory employers' associations, Catholic organizations and professional colleges were given special protection, until Spain became 'in a specific and non-conventional, non-fascist way, a traditional corporatist universe' (Giner and Sevilla: 1984).

felt in every workplace, and its rules and regulations controlled every aspect of labour relations, and many aspects of production itself. What cannot be disputed therefore is the *highly institutionalized* nature of the strategy, as it found expression in the Syndicate.

Since the transition to democracy the picture is very different, but a range of trans-sectoral practices have emerged for negotiating and implementing macro-economic and social policy. Although the policies being negotiated have included employment policies, social security targets, and sectoral arrangements for restructuring specific industries, the main thrust of these practices has been towards a national incomes policy, which, in practice, has tended to mean wage freezes or reductions. These practices have come to resemble familiar, Western European modes of corporatist intermediation, but in the way they have been promoted by the governments of the transition in Spain (and, in particular, by the Socialist government, in conscious deference to the Austrian model) they have a further and defining characteristic, which is their *complete lack of institutionalization*. Indeed, of all the names by which neo-corporatist procedures have been called in the literature, namely, patterns, networks, exchanges, arrangements, pacts, practices, tendencies, strategies and even episodes (Regini:1984), 'institutions' is the one which least fits the case of democratic Spain.[7] Invoking the Weberian notion of 'institutional charisma', which describes those institutional initiatives taken outside of any normative legal framework, it is possible to think of these practices as a kind of 'charismatic corporatism'.

The different degrees of institutionalization of the two strategies are intimately linked, in the literature (e.g. Giner and Sevilla:1984), to their distinct State forms. Under Franco all workers were compelled to associate in the Vertical Syndicate, and so in the majority their syndical activity was involuntary and imposed. In fact, it is no exaggeration to say that organized labour had been ripped from the womb of civil society and forcibly removed to the sphere of the one-party (some would say no-party) State, which attempted to control all the outcomes of industrial relations.[8] After the transition the political context was liberalized by political parties and par-

---

[7] The fact that corporate practices in contemporary Spain lack any sign of institutionalization is not, however, an indication that they are therefore 'societal' rather than 'State'. Although the State–societal distinction seems to be derived from *a priori* assumptions regarding the degree of institutionalization or the stability of the two subtypes (State corporatism, one supposes, being more institutionalized or more stable), it is hard to sustain the distinction in the face of the empirical evidence. The corporatisms of Austria, Sweden and Norway (all of them societal in this scheme of things) are highly institutionalized and very stable; whereas those of Mexico, Brazil and Peru (all of them State) are diverse, clientelistic, episodic and contingent.

[8] Juan Linz's famous characterization of the regime's 'limited pluralism' referred explicitly to elite–regime relations, and not to capital–labour relations (Linz:1964).

liamentary elections, and freedom of association found expression in several trade unions and, at first, in more than one employers' organization. Moreover, whereas Franco's strategy sought legitimation through the doctrine of social harmony and peace, the present corporatist practices are in general defended by an appeal to economic necessities and results (Roca:1983),[9] in addition to the legitimation of the liberal State per se, through the plurality of interest representation and a range of values linked to universal suffrage and a universal legal order. In short, the liberal State has sought to lend its authority to these practices in order to bolster the voluntary nature of class collaboration.

Pointing up the differences between the two regimes in this way is not difficult to do and can lead straight to the conclusion that in the Franco regime corporatism represented a 'strategy of domination' (Crouch:1977), in contrast to democratic Spain where corporatism is more a 'strategy of exchange' (Regini:1984). But such a simple contrast fails to take into account certain inconvenient facts such as the often voluntary nature of class collaboration under Franco, on the one hand, and, on the other, the limits that contemporary corporatist practices place on the expanding political pluralism of democratic Spain. This is not to suggest that the two political contexts are in some sense similar, which would be plainly absurd, but rather to insist that the critical differences between the two corporatisms lie not in their intrinsic characteristics but in their insertion into their respective State forms: in the contemporary context the relationship between *parliamentarianism* and *corporatism* (that is, between the system of political parliamentary representation and the system of organized economic interest representation) demonstrates the necessary existence in democratic Spain of alternative State representational forms; whereas the unitary, integral and bureaucratic character of Francoism effectively excluded such alternative forms. Franco's corporatist strategy represented a fixed and exclusive mode of mediating the capital–labour relation, and it was its exclusivity, not its intrinsic qualities, which proved its fatal historical flaw.

Discussing the differences between the strategies in these terms runs directly contrary to the received and radical wisdom which categorically asserts that Franco's corporatism was not *real* corporatism at all, and that corporatism only came to Spain with the transition to democracy. By insisting on the involuntary nature of Franco's corporatism, the absence of 'valid interlocutors and intermediaries', and the Chambers of Commerce and Industry which continued to represent employers, the Vertical Syndicate

---

[9] For Panitch (1980) this is more a question of degree than of kind: the ideology of class harmony and organic unity which underpins Francoism is simply reproduced in less explicit form in the contemporary strategies, and couched in the more technical and less philosophical language of the economists.

is condemned for representing neither labour nor capital, and is found to be 'an empty shell', a 'dead union' (Martínez-Alier:1983). In other words, with a Syndicate which offered no information, no genuine bargaining, and was totally politicized and corrupt to boot, 'Francoist corporatism meant the de facto decorporatization of a large subordinate sector of Spanish society' (Giner and Sevilla:1980).[10] Once the Syndicate has been denied a political role in this way, it can only be explained as 'an ideology', a 'mere decorative facade for force' (Martínez-Alier:1983). Thus, content to travel the axis between the two analytical poles of ideology and coercion, the vast and costly apparatus of the Syndicate becomes nothing more than an ideological legitimation for repression.

This attempt to deny Franco's corporatism the status of a political strategy seems to require two main objections, and both of them important to this argument. The objections are clearly linked. In the first place, Franco's strategy, institutionalized though it was, is not real corporatism because it is *all form and no content*; and in the second place, it lacks content because it contains *no real representation*. In my view, on the contrary (as I will argue), the degree of representation was real and constantly increasing; which in turn was largely due to the form of the Syndicate, which finally came to provide political spaces for key democratic initiatives. But before pursuing these observations, the argument will consider what the two strategies have in common.

CORPORATISM UNDER AND AFTER FRANCO: THE COMMON GROUND

At a sufficiently high level of abstraction, which is that of the relationship between corporatism and capitalism, all corporatisms have something in common insofar as they are representational forms which directly reflect the capital–labour relation (Martínez Lucio:1983), and seek to involve the economic-corporate interests of civil society as functional representatives in State-controlled policy-making and decision-taking, with a view to achieving higher degrees of class, or class-based, collaboration (Panitch:1980). Such a proposition is immediately recognizable by the intellectual comfort of its class reductionism, and its interest lies not in whether it is true or not, but in its assumption that corporatism in general is subject to primarily *economic* determinations, and has to do with defining, constituting, organizing, representing, and accommodating *economic* interests. For in Spain, both in the early years of the Franco regime and in the years of democratic transition, the design and deployment of corporatist strategies obeyed immediate *po-*

---

[10] In their review of the apparatuses and institutions of Francoism these authors do not even mention the Vertical Syndicate, not even as 'an institution of ideological legitimation'. The Syndicate was simply a 'sham'. By this account it is impossible to imagine how it could have survived for some forty years.

litical imperatives – although the disposition of social forces in these two distinct conjunctures was very different one from the other.

In the aftermath of the bloody Civil War, which, it is now generally accepted, was a class war, the principal and most urgent nationalist mission was to subjugate, domesticate and depoliticize the working class, which it did by military might, police terror, the constitution of the Labour Charter and the establishment of the Vertical Syndicate. During the years of the transition the different governments had to find a political formula for transforming a very militant, highly mobilized and undefeated working-class movement into bureaucratized trade unions in the Western European mould, so that bargains could be struck and pacts negotiated which could protect and secure the fledgling democratic regime. In both historical moments the first and immediate purpose of the corporatist strategy was to provide direct political supports to the regime in question; and both strategies were initiated during the constitutional construction of a new State form.

The element of continuity in the deployment of corporatist strategies, then, was not so much labour or capital as the Spanish army, which approved and underwrote Franco's corporatism (even though the Falange itself made no headway in penetrating the armed forces), and closely conditioned the corporatist practices of the transition. From the Pacts of Moncloa (1977) onwards these practices sought to restrain wages and avoid strikes in order to demonstrate *to the army* the moderation and responsibility of both unions and left-wing parties; while, in similar vein, the Law of the Harmonization of the Autonomies was designed to curb separatism and allay the fears *of the army* that democracy would mean the break-up of the Spanish State (Giner and Sevilla:1984). In short, the army is the principal 'intervening political variable' in explaining corporatism in Spain; and possibly the principal consideration in the agreements on incomes policy of the years 1977 to 1983 was the question of democratic stability, with the unions restraining their *economic* demands in order to secure their future *political* freedom (Roca:1983). If this was a 'strategy of exchange', it was an exchange of a rather special kind, with the unions which participated in corporatist practices sitting in proxy for the civil society as a whole, and trying to secure it from attack.

I believe this situation goes at least some way towards explaining the 'charismatic corporatism' of post-Franco Spain. The unitary and institutionalized corporatism of Francoism had 'reproduced class conflict within the heart of the State apparatus itself' (Jessop:1979)[11] and had made the continuation of Francoism politically impracticable. In other words, Franco's corporatist strategy had finally failed. In the post-Franco period, given the new political imperatives, the State had to be insulated as far as possible

---

[11] Jessop was talking of a theoretical possibility, and not of Spain in particular.

from the antagonistic struggles of civil society. Historically, the liberal State form has served this purpose well, but with the exceptional political pressures generated during the transition, and with the new regime too fragile to risk offending the 'powers that be' (*poderes fácticos*), such 'charisma' took an extreme form. The process of 'autonomization' was a similarly extreme constitutional response designed, again, to insulate the governments of the transition from the 'national question'.

This emphasis on the political determinations of corporatist strategies in Spain, which have emerged in the direct aftermath or presence of nationwide militancy and struggle, is not intended to render the question of *economic* interest representation redundant. Corporatism is a political strategy but is directed to the interests of civil society (in the Hegelian sense); and the definition and organization of group economic interests *within* civil society contribute to the configuration of the relationship between this society and the State. Only by investigating the *forms* of economic interest representation can we establish the political *content* of the corporatist strategies.

CORPORATIST REPRESENTATION UNDER FRANCO

If the Vertical Syndicate had no representative capacity, then it is simple enough to dismiss it as a fake strategy, which cannot be compared to present-day corporatist arrangements. But the evidence makes it difficult to sustain this view. Real wages have been falling and unemployment rising in the years since the transition, in a way they did not do during the latter years of Francoism (Fishman:1982; Prevost:1982); and whereas these years were characterized by de facto decentralized bargaining and (admittedly illegal) direct action, from the time of the Moncloa Pacts there has been an increasing tendency in democratic Spain for highly centralized wage negotiations, with less participation on the shop floor. I do not mean to suggest, quixotically, that syndical practices were more representative and plural in authoritarian decline than they were in democratic consolidation; but simply that the historical process requires a more modulated approach.

There is a natural reluctance within liberal scholarship to recognize representation within the Vertical Syndicate, if such representation is taken as tantamount to collaboration with an authoritarian and repressive regime.[12] In my view, this does not so much reflect a primitive insistence that the Franco period was simply a continuation of the class warfare of the 1930s, as a mistaken idea of the representation itself. It is not a question of liberal or parliamentary representation, through which a citizenry could exercise a choice of its political future, but of the definition and organization of economic interests, whereby any increase in material benefits or improve-

---

[12] For Panitch (1981) such collaboration is a key definitional element in all corporatisms, whereas for Lehmbruch (1979) it is a characteristic only of liberal corporatism.

ment in conditions of work could indicate successful incorporation and representation. Relevant in this connection is the huge welfare and education system of the Syndicate, which offered a range of services from health care to job retraining (see Chapter 5); and compulsory membership of the Syndicate did bring benefits in job security (Selgas:1974). Yet more significant than these formal advantages was the complex network of clientelistic lines of influence which permeated the massive and complex structure of the Syndicate, and channeled the resources at its disposal to favoured places and people.[13] In this regard, it was sufficient in most instances that the travel and subsistence allowances for official representatives paid twice as well as any available wage. In this way the combination of formal benefits and informal patronage was effective in incorporating many labour leaders by providing a practical and material response to their interests and demands.

If the Syndicate did not lack a representational *content*, nor can its *form* be dismissed as unimportant. The most visible aspect of the organization was the rigid and hierarchical bureaucratic structure which imposed its norms on every workplace in direct subordination to the Ministry of Labour (Amsden:1972); and its most visible actors were the higher authorities at national and regional level, who were all appointed directly by central government. But its form also included the factory committees (or *jurados*), which were set up over the years 1947–53, and which offered labour leaders valuable experience in the discussion of such issues as conditions of work, social security and job classification. Moreover, the relative freedom of election to these committees, and to a growing number of posts on committees at provincial and national level, provided an incentive to autonomous organization, and led to the eventual success of the workers' commissions in capturing many of the posts in the lower echelons of the Syndicate – despite the hierarchical principle which drastically reduced the syndical electorate for each successive rung of the structure.

As indicated in Chapter 13, the literature[14] is misleading on this point, insofar as it subscribes to the myths of the birth of the commissions in La Camocha, and their consolidation through direct election from workers' assemblies. As suggested then, the first commissions were in fact self-elected, and had first come together on the factory committees of the Syndicate. The commissions therefore emerged from the representational form of the Syndicate itself. Similarly, they had begun to infiltrate the Syndicate long before their newly created national organization announced it as an objective in

---

[13] In other words, the Syndicate used its powers of patronage to co-opt and corrupt. But corruption is no impediment to representation. On the contrary, it is possible to argue that there can be no effective system of corporatist–clientelist representation without it: 'corruption provides immediate, specific and concrete benefits to groups who might otherwise be thoroughly alienated from society' (Huntington:1968).

[14] Compare, for example, Ariza (1976); Comin (1976); Ellwood (1976); Sartorius (1976); Maravall (1978); Almendros et al. (1978); Mujal-León (1983).

1966, and long before the Communist Party realized the political potential of such a strategy. Thus, it was the very gamut of co-optation and representation operated by the Syndicate (and the factory committees achieved both) which created the political spaces for autonomous labour organization.[15]

These observations are reinforced by the historical process after 1958, the year when the regime moved to open up collective bargaining but only succeeded in decentralizing it – insofar as the commissions themselves succeeded in occupying the political spaces made available within the Syndicate, and consequently on the shop floor. Nonetheless, as we saw, syndical norms continued to govern the negotiation of all new contracts, while the number of workers contracted under compulsory syndical arbitration (in the form of NOCs) had risen to almost half a million by 1965 (Maravall:1982). Indeed, the commissions themselves often sought such compulsory arbitration, having found that these contracts were usually more favourable than those to be had from employers. In this way, as long as the regime continued to believe it could co-opt the commissions, a close working relationship could grow between commissions and Syndicate, which the regime tried to reinforce through the Syndicate's new worker and management councils. In fact, at no time did the high incidence of syndical arbitration demonstrate a lack of effective representation of labour. On the contrary, it is clear that the commissions were successfully using the legal form of the Syndicate in order to advance their demands.

In the event, the regime did not succeed in co-opting the commissions, however, and its attempts to live with them always came too late. This fact was inescapable by 1966, when the commissions came out as a national movement which demanded not only economic gains but also political liberties; and from this point in time the regime returned to the ruthless pursuit of its only possible response, which was more repression. Despite this repression, the commissions continued to expand their organization in the context of their continuing infiltration of the vast apparatus of the Syndicate.

According to the commissions themselves (Canadian Committee for a Democratic Spain:1973), they did not do this in order to destroy the Syndicate's institutional cohesion but rather to take advantage of its legal cover and institutional resources for the purposes of their own extralegal activities; and this close combination of legal and extralegal practice is something the Spanish Communist Party learned from the commissions and made central to its own revolutionary theory. So it makes little sense to assert that the *real* process of syndical representation was the autonomous organization of the working class by the commissions, which took place *despite* the

---

[15] One convincing demonstration of the representation achieved in this way was the expulsion of 1,800 labour leaders from factory committees between 1964 and 1966 (Wright:1977) (see Chapter 10).

overarching presence of the Syndicate, when it was the *representational form* of the Syndicate which created the political space for the early organization of the commissions, and moreover catalysed their later growth into a national movement – many of the contacts at provincial, regional and even national level being made through its partially elected committee structure. In short, just as the Syndicate certainly succeeded in co-opting many labour leaders, so the commissions succeeded in colonizing the Syndicate, and, in particular, its representative committees.

Thus, the point of the argument is not merely that over many years there was a close and symbiotic relationship between the Syndicate and the commissions, but rather that the commissions could never have discovered their distinct political practices were it not for Franco's corporatist strategy. Later, it is true, the commissions came to insist on their *right* to organize autonomously, and so came to spearhead the struggle for democratic freedoms. This struggle peaked immediately following the death of the dictator, with a ten-fold increase in strike activity from 1975 to 1976 (Guinea:1978), culminating in the 'day of peaceful struggle' in November 1976, which brought more than two million workers onto the streets (Ariza:1977). As I argued in Chapter 13, such a massive mobilization made a simple continuation of the regime impracticable. But the democratic momentum gained by this mobilization could never have occurred were it not for the representational form of the Syndicate; and it was the regime's own strategy which opened its institutions to colonization by civil society, so forcing a fatal breach in the authoritarian carapace of the State.

REPRESENTATION IN NEO-CORPORATISM

Chapter 13 suggested how the new liberal State managed to condition the development of the unions without attempting any form of direct control, with the rules of the game being decided and legitimated in parliament. In this way the governments of the transition could look to control labour *either* through the incorporation of the newly institutionalized trade unions, *or* through the newly constituted parliament; but there was no political prescription for the relationship which was to emerge between these two distinct State *representational forms*. Precisely for this reason, it is the changing contours of the relationship which provide the key to the character of the new corporatist strategy.

The first national wage agreement of the new era was the Moncloa Pact of 1977, which traded the promise of economic and political reforms[16] for global wage restraint. With the economy inflating fast, an incomes policy had become the top government priority, impelled by its concern that with-

---

[16] In the areas of the Military Code of Justice, rural tenancy legislation, and education and energy policies.

out a greater degree of economic control there could be no guarantee of political stability (with the military waiting in the wings). The government response was to agree to the Pact with the parties of the left, so excluding the employers' organization and the two big unions. The unions at first wanted to reject the deal, precisely because they had not been consulted; but finally consented, if with bad grace, in order to protect the social peace.[17] Constitutionally speaking this was not a parliamentary but an extraparliamentary agreement, as it was signed by all parties *outside* parliament; but it was parliament which legitimated it and parliamentary legislation which gave it teeth. In short, it was a parliamentary consensus which achieved the agreement.

The agreement set a pattern of parliamentary initiatives on incomes policy; and in 1978, with the benefit of hindsight, the commissions condemned it as a mistake and a 'victory' for the government of the Centre Democratic Union. This did not augur well for the social peace, and, in effect, strike activity rose rapidly in 1978 and 1979.[18] Indeed, the Centre Democratic Party failed in an approach to the unions to renew the Pact, but the near absolute parliamentary majority it had gained in the legislative elections of March 1979 allowed it to impose a new wage ceiling unilaterally. Moreover, at the end of 1979, the government was still strong enough to push through the Statute of the Workers, with the support of the Socialist Party and the UGT (who had negotiated such changes as they required), but in the face of strong opposition from the commissions. The law's Article 87 restricted national negotiating rights to unions with a minimum of 10 per cent of the national vote in the labour union elections (or a minimum of 15 per cent in any of the 'autonomous communities'), thus concentrating power at the top of the big unions, disqualifying smaller unions with local bases and making 'concertation politics' that much more possible.

The wedge driven between the two big unions was widened at the beginning of 1980 with AMI, the Confederal Target Agreement (Acuerdo Marco Interconfederal), which was signed by the employers, the UGT (under pressure from the Socialist Party again), but not the commissions, which tried to mobilize their members against it, for being too conciliatory. Nonetheless, AMI and AMI-II, which followed in 1981, rapidly raised the number of workers covered by national agreements, and dramatically reduced the number of industrial disputes.[19] In short, the opposition of the commissions had little impact: on the one hand, this was because workers were intimi-

[17] The commissions fell into line behind the Communist Party (with a significant minority still strongly opposed); while the UGT showed de facto acceptance without actual endorsement (Prevost:1982).

[18] With 11,551,000 working days lost in 1978 and 18,917,000 in 1979 (ETUI:1980).

[19] Such collective agreements, which had reached only 57.6 per cent of the work force in 1979, covered 92 per cent by the end of 1980 (ETUI:1982).

dated by rising unemployment,[20] and survey research has shown that they came to favour a less combative attitude to employers and government (the UGT making considerable gains in the syndical elections following its participation in the AMIs) (Pérez Díaz:1980; Fishman:1985); on the other, it was because it was still *parliament* which was leading the process of national concertation, and the Socialist Party, in particular, had lent its full support to the AMIs as the loyal opposition which was grooming itself for government.

No sooner was AMI-II in place than discussions began on a new and far more wide-ranging agreement, which was to be known as the National Agreement on Employment, or ANE (Acuerdo Nacional sobre el Empleo), which was once again designed to limit wage increases across the board, and even reduce the level of real wages. In return the government made some strong commitments on job creation and other issues.[21] But the true significance of the agreement was that it was the first since the transition to democracy to be signed not only by the government and the employers, but also by *both* of the major unions. Moreover, they all signed but the political parties did not. Such a development was consonant with the difficult economic circumstances and with the increasing consolidation of both employers' and union organizations; but the immediate motivation for the first authentically *neo-corporatist* agreement of the transition was the consternation created by the so-called *tejerazo* of February 1981, when parliament was invaded by disaffected elements of the Civil Guard in an attempted coup against the constitutional government. In the wake of this attack, ANE was endorsed in united fashion, by both UGT and the commissions, the latter hailing it as a Plan of Solidarity, when in reality it was not so very different in its essentials from the AMIs they had so roundly condemned.[22] In effect, the big unions took the overtly political decision to restrict their economic demands, and even incur short-run sacrifices, in order to protect the democratic system. They muted their demands to match the precarious political equilibrium of the country as a whole.

Thus, over the first years of the transition, *parliamentarianism* was the key to achieving national wage agreements, which were defended, if only

---

[20] The absolute number of workers employed had fallen by about a million over the years 1974–80 (ETUI:1980), while the level of unemployment had risen to 13.6 per cent by 1980–1, which meant two million idle workers (ETUI:1982).

[21] The government promised to maintain the same *rate* of employment until the end of 1982 (when the agreement expired), which meant it would have to create some 350,000 new jobs. This was an explicit *quid pro quo* for declining real wages. In addition, the unions succeeded for the first time in gaining official recognition as representatives of employees in the public sector (ETUI:1982).

[22] Even then the proposed endorsement of ANE led to acrimonious debate in the commissions' congress of July 1981, and about a quarter of the delegates remained intransigent (Prevost:1982).

implicitly, as leading to a more stable political system; and parliamentary initiatives seemed more than sufficient to condition union practices, with the crucial participation of the parties of the left. (Indeed, the links between these parties and the unions clearly proved crucial to the consolidation of Spain's democracy.) This appears to confirm the view that in the liberal State form it is 'permanent' parliamentarianism which underwrites 'temporary' neo-corporatist arrangements (Panitch:1981), the degree of legitimation achieved through parliament as the repository of the national interest providing the conditions for strategic success. But when parliament came under direct political threat, as it did on 23 February 1981, there was full participation in neo-corporatist concertation for the first time; and corporatist representation took direct precedence over parliament in the negotiation of the national pact. In other words, there was a *strategic displacement* of policy-making from the parliamentary arena to the neo-corporatist context at the moment of political crisis in order to regulate conflict and underpin parliamentary democracy. However, as Chapter 13 left clear, this effect has not been permanent, and neo-corporatist practices have not yet become institutionalized as the unique strategic location for such national concertation.

CORPORATISM AND STATE REPRESENTATIONAL FORMS

The apparently rapid transition to democracy in Spain had in fact been prepared over many years by the slow organization of the labour movement around the axis of the symbiotic relationship between the workers' commissions and the Vertical Syndicate. With the transition, new forms of political mediation became historically available; but the political realization of such mediations required the accumulated historical experience of the 'free' collective bargaining which had occurred between the commissions and the employers. In this way (recapitulating the conclusions of Chapter 13), the real representation achieved through the corporatist form of the Syndicate paved the way for the 'charismatic' corporatism of the latter years both indirectly and directly: the illegal infiltration of the Syndicate – often with the compliance of the employers – created a tradition of 'free' functional interest representation on which governments of the transition could draw; while the popular mobilizations led by the labour movement contributed to liberalization of the State and so to the restructuring of relations between State and civil society along different strategic lines.

Neocorporatist practices in contemporary Spain have evolved in an entirely ad hoc and expedient fashion, and so lack any legal or constitutional basis. This can be seen as a defensive strategy: with the lessons of the colonization of Franco's Syndicate still fresh in the political consciousness, such 'charismatic' arrangements have been constructed in order to protect the fledgling liberal State from the shocks of civil society; while, with both government and unions in the process of formation, it is anyway disingenuous to expect such neo-corporatist practices to be further institutionalized than the parties to them. But in a broader sense the new corporatist practices reflect the very process of negotiating the democratic pact for society overall. This, too, was achieved on an ad hoc basis, and depended closely on the agreement between distinct social forces to curb their short-term interests (and even modify their political beliefs) in favour of the longer-term development of the democratic project (Gunther:1985). Thus the new corporatist strategy, which was part and parcel of this process, was also 'charismatic' in the sense that it was defended by appeal to a higher and more general good.

But however flexible and temporary the practices of charismatic corporatism, they do in fact constitute a distinct and specialized form of representation; and, in general, such neo-corporatist strategies of whatever kind compose one of the *representational forms* available to the liberal State. Another such form is parliament itself. But this approach to the relationships between State and civil society does not entail an hermetic separation between distinct State representational forms. Over the early years of the transition to democracy in Spain it was the representatives of the parliamentary executive (government) who played the leading role in corporatist decision-making, with strategic corporatist initiatives being delegated to the legislative process; and although, wherever and whenever possible, the governments of the transition attempted to keep the difficult negotiations over national incomes policy in the sphere of charismatic corporatism (the better to conserve the institution of parliament as a symbol of unity and consensus), this strategy was only partially successful until parliament itself came under direct political threat. This threat impelled the *strategic displacement* which achieved full national concertation for the first time.

The question of corporatism as a political strategy of the State cannot be divorced from the institutional ensemble which defines the State form itself. This is evident from the comparison of the corporatist strategies in Spain during and after Franco. Both the descriptive distinctions (rigid and fixed as against flexible and temporary) and the supposedly analytical ones (authoritarian or State contrasted with liberal or societal) attempt to focus on the intrinsic characteristics of these corporatisms, conceived in isolation. Here, on the contrary, I suggest that these corporatisms be conceived as the strategies of particular forms of State in particular political conjunctures. In this perspective, Franco's corporatist strategy was eroded not because it was authoritarian or, still less, unrepresentative, but because it was *uniform*, in the sense of being inserted into a State form devoid of alternative representational forms. In the language of Jessop (1982), when this strategy entered into crisis with the colonization of the Vertical Syndicate, there was no political capacity for *switching* the privileged location of representation to a distinct representational form; unlike in democratic Spain, where a multiform State (with its parliament, charismatic corporatism and autonomous communities) has rapidly consolidated this capacity, especially in regard of the balance between corporatist and parliamentary practices. Indeed, on the evidence from Spain, it is not finally so much a question of 'switching' as of a shifting balance of mutual logistic support.

15

Personal networks and political strategies: Spanish civil society in the struggle for democracy

> This turning of real lives into writing is no longer a procedure of heroization; it functions as a procedure of objectification and subjection.
>
> Michel Foucault, *Discipline and Punish*

THIS IS THE STORY of ordinary people who worked to make democracy possible. They came together in personal networks to seek support for their immediate demands, and so discovered the piecemeal political strategies which came to create political spaces for the exercise of citizenship. It is therefore a story about political actors at the grass roots of civil society, and their commitment to making democracy, and in this connection it makes no sense to refer to Spain's transition to democracy without taking into account the long years of democratic transformation which preceded it (see Chapter 13). In other words, a guiding assumption of the story is that the achievement and consolidation of democratic arrangements at governmental level are rooted in the democratic maturation of actors within civil society; and democracy is thus to be defined as the practice of citizenship, or the achievement of an increasingly autonomous control of the political conditions of social life.

Hence, in contrast to many recent and current theories of democratic transition in southern Europe and Latin America, which concentrate on the State and on political engineering at the level of the State, this story thinks of democracy in terms of civil society first and the State second. In doing so, it imitates a constant preoccupation of the very diverse classical tradition of political philosophy (Locke, Rousseau, Marx, Mill, Gramsci), in order to provide a corrective to the rather lopsided view of democratic possibilities produced by the enormous effort dedicated to theorizing the State. Indeed, although the theories in question aspired to a global explanation of democratic advance and retreat, in practice they often reduced political analysis to an ex post and sometimes ad hoc commentary on regime shifts as and when they occurred. My own bias, on the contrary, is to focus on secular developments within civil society as a better historical gauge of democratic potential.

In this story, therefore, civil society is an original site of political strategies and democratic projects. It is civil society where the battle is lost and won; and this political battle canot be reduced to the binding imperatives of the national or international economic orders, in the way it often is in Statist theories of democracy. One such broad and influential school of thought (Lechner:1977; O'Donnell:1978,1979; et al.) has emphasized the structural conditions which undermine democratic institution-building, focusing on the ways in which the integration of Latin American countries into the international economic system has forced individual governments to adapt economic and political development to the demands generated by the evolution of this system overall. In this perspective, plural institutions were seen as fundamentally incompatible with the need for adaptation to, and further integration into, dominant patterns of capital accumulation. In short, such theories have obeyed a 'capital logic' (Jessop:1982). My contention, on the contrary, is that politics is never a mere reflection of the society or the economy, and while things economic are not unimportant (see the final section of Chapter 4), only politics can provide a proper explanation for democracy or its lack. But this then requires an alternative approach to theorizing democratic practice, which appears to demand a theory of civil society itself.

CIVIL SOCIETY AND POLITICAL CONTINGENCY

There is no shortage of contemporary empirical studies of social movements, political parties and elections by scholars interested in the question of democracy; and other political organizations such as student groups and the Church have also received some attention. But if civil society has certainly been studied, it has usually been so by way of its discrete effects and particular manifestations, without any corresponding preoccupation with theorizing what all or any of them contribute to the making of democracy. It is tempting to suggest that this is simply owing to the bias of recent theory; but this avoids the real difficulty of theorizing a wide diversity of initiatives which are politically and culturally specific. Indeed, the efforts to explain democracy through a general theory of the capitalist State, or through reducing politics to economic constraints and imperatives, themselves seek to avoid such specificities *inside* civil society by locating their principles of explanation *outside* of this society.

But the specificities of civil society would not create such an obstacle for theory were normative social scientific methods not imprisoned by their deterministic assumptions. In other words, if there is a (very proper) reluctance to theorize these specificities in terms of a common set of determinations, whether of a historical and structural sort or of the rational choice variety, this is more a result of the rigidity of the methods than of the intractability of the real world. Whether it is a question of class struggle or of rational choice, the sometimes obsessive inquiry into *why* things happen the way they do leads such methods to employ a privileged theoretical device in order to provide a general answer; but finding an appropriate and adequate device for explaining civil society has proved impossible. Here it is suggested that the first question to pose to the making of democracy is not why this happens but *how* it happens; and this question no longer requires us to travel the same deterministic axis.[1] On the contrary, the goal is not the discovery of a new set of determinations of democracy but rather a range of descriptive categories and analytical concepts which can isolate and relate the multiple contingencies operating in any one context, and reveal the strategic choices available to political organizations as they confront State agencies, other political actors in civil society and themselves.[2] And, in effect, this is the way this story has approached the making of democracy in Spain.

However, the refusal to adopt a privileged device which can descend onto the stage of history like some theoretical *deus ex machina* is not tantamount to a total rejection of the notion of causality. It rather suggests a 'decentred' analysis which attempts to capture the 'contingent necessities' (Jessop:1982)[3] of a specific conjuncture, and their outcomes, in terms of their various determinants. This apparent contradiction in terms indicates that while combinations or interactions of different causal chains produce determinate outcomes (necessity), there is no single theory that can predict or determine the manner in which such causal chains converge and/or interact (contingency). And if it is objected that such a resolution only addresses the logical properties of a theoretical discourse, then the argument may address

[1] It is not exactly that *why* is the wrong question, epistemologically speaking. Any attempt to analyse the world must assume that it is determinate and determined; but it does not follow that any single theory can comprehend the totality of its determinations without resorting to reductionism of one kind or another. And, in fact, the deterministic bias tends to lead to both reductionism and instrumentalism, which in turn tend to privilege a certain theoretical device (e.g., the social relations of production), or a certain empirical relationship (e.g., between bourgeoisie and capitalist State), respectively (compare Jessop:1982).

[2] To a degree, the choice of 'multiple contingencies' and 'strategic choices' in place of civil society writ large (or as a way of operationalizing the notion of democratic practice within civil society) is analogous to the refusal to deal with corporatism per se in favour of distinct corporatisms qua strategies emerging from the institutional ensemble of particular State forms (see the beginning of Chapter 14).

[3] While the discussion of 'contingency' owes much, but not everything, to the work of Bob Jessop, it must be emphasized that Jessop is almost uniquely concerned with the question of State strategies and does not investigate civil society as a site of political strategies in general, or of democratic practice in particular. Jessop's account of the State as an institutional ensemble of forms of representation and intervention, and its implications for our own story, are explored in Chapter 14.

the theorization of political process by moving to the more familiar field of structure and practice: structures cannot be said to exist in such a way that they can shape practices, but, on the contrary, exist in and through practices, which are the sites for the production, reproduction and transformation of structures.[4]

The notion of practice is very important to this inquiry into the making of democracy in Spain, which has focused on the kinds of people who made it and the ways they went about it; and these few theoretical premises are similarly important in clearing the analytical ground for the entry of human agency onto the historical scene. My aim is to achieve a style of analysis which is neither determinist nor voluntarist, and this has required a careful mapping of the construction of personal networks and the emergence of cross-cutting political strategies. Indeed, such networks and strategies are the two principal points of analytical reference in the telling of this story, and hence provide a dual point of departure for theorizing (or at least systematizing my observations of) democratic practice within Spanish civil society.

PERSONAL NETWORKS AND DEMOCRATIC PRACTICE

Personal networks are observable and traceable, and emerge within a common economic and cultural milieu (see Chapter 1). Nonetheless, like all social relationships they are matter for theory, and it is axiomatic in my approach that the expression of personal restlessness or social concern through membership in such networks already represents a political choice on the part of the social actor; and these personal networks are thus the site of the individual political choices which are the spawn of more complex

---

[4] This rather bare statement is simply designed, once again, to call into question the deterministic properties of common social scientific language. Amplifying the assertion, it can be said that *practices*, i.e., specific types of social relationships (economic, political, sexual, etc.) are carried on through particular institutions or apparatuses (e.g., State, party, trade union, church, family, firm) in particular historical situations. The development of complex systems of such relationships leads to *structures*, which acquire an effective degree of historical permanence. These are not, however, two ontologically distinct levels or regions (and above all are not related in an 'essence' to 'appearance' form): practices do not express structures in a mechanical fashion, and there is indeed no relationship of externality between the two.

A similar argument can be made about the nature of political strategies (a kind of political practice), which cumulatively structure the relationships between State and civil society: 'the current strategic selectivity of the State is in part an emergent effect of the interaction between its past pattern of strategic selectivity and the strategies adopted for its transformation. In turn the calculating subjects which operate on the strategic terrain constituted by the State are in part constituted by the strategic selectivity of the State system and its past interventions' (Jessop:1985).

strategic initiatives. Moreover, as many of these choices are governed by chance acquaintance and chance meetings (and constrained by tests of reliability and trust, which are as much a question of 'personality' as anything else), then the networks compose the social texture of political contingency at the very roots of civil society. The study of personal networks could then be seen to express an analytical preference for contingency over determination; but the real operation of such contingencies creates the political conditions for a strategic response to what Foucault might call the 'polymorphous techniques of power' (Foucault:1978). As the lines heading this chapter suggest, these techniques, articulated within the 'moving substrate of force relations', serve to objectify political subjects through the construction of their individuality, and so to dominate them. But the contingencies inscribed in the notion of networking tend to cut through the life-lines of this 'capillary power' (Foucault:1977a); while the political choices which construct the network represent the first steps in the political actors' shaping of their own subjectivity.

Let us pause for a moment and retrace our steps. My choice in writing of the making of democracy has been to focus on the people who made it, and to insist on the presence of individuals in the struggle for democracy. This approach inevitably raises basic questions concerning the role of individual ideas and choices in the development of a democratic project: Who are the subjects of political strategy? What occurs in civil society to make political actors? How do such actors come to perceive their scope for strategic action, their degrees of practical manoeuvre? And these questions cannot be answered without taking into consideration the achievement of political consciousness in its relation to ideology, and its importance in the moments of political and strategic choice. My own view, succinctly put (and I believe that it is the only democratic one), is that subjects produce themselves in the context of definite social practices (by stealing I become a thief, by loving I become a lover).[5] All subjects, and *a fortiori* all political subjects,

---

[5] This is not a widely held view. Jessop (1982), who has contributed so much to this discussion, himself retains the notion of 'interpellation' from Laclau (1977) and Althusser (1976, 1977a). This notion seems to suppose that ideology is 'in the air and everywhere', or, at least, outside of the individual. So individuals (who, mysteriously, have already been 'individuated' in Marx's language) are interpellated by different discourses which condition their subjectivity. Therefore, for these authors, and even for Gramsci, the constitution of subjects is a *passive* process.

If the production of subjects in both Althusser and Gramsci is seen as passive, this is because it takes place *through ideology* (a conclusion which was further vitiated in Althusser by the assumption of a 'pre-ideological' existence of individuals qua *trager* of social relations, who were 'waiting' to respond to ideological interpellation). I disagree, if only because there are no possible grounds for assuming ideological production by some subjects, while simultaneously denying it to others. Therefore I argue that the production of subjects by subjects takes place through political practice, and, in particular, through political and strategic choices. It is true that such choices do not take

are therefore historically specific. Moreover, the process of the constitution of subjects is always both *active* and *relational*, insofar as subjects become subjects through their relations with other subjects – subjectivity thus being a process of self-location in relation to others. In this connection the personal network (as it has been discovered in this story) is the first visible political practice at the grass roots of civil society, and the primary site of the self-constitution of political subjects – the place where individuals begin to become political actors.

These beginnings provided much of the material for Chapters 1 and 2, and are interwoven into the warp and woof of the entire story as it has been told here. What is called a *forma de ser* in El Marco de Jerez (Chapter 2) could as well be called a form of democratic practice which is broader and more historically resilient than any particular ideological expression it may assume; and this practice was founded in the networks built on personal confidence and trust. Moreover, without such networks it would be difficult to explain the formation of the regional leadership which did so much to make this practice strategically effective. Implicit in this account of the active and relational self-constitution of the subject is an equally active idea of consciousness as being generated through political practice,[6] and, especially, through the moments of political and strategic choice. In other words, these people who fought against Franco learned from their practice of the struggle and not from doctrine, and it is through practice that they began to exercise their citizenship. The notion of citizenship thus articulates a process of political learning, on the one hand, and, on the other, an increasing strategic capability (which represents an increasingly autonomous control over the political conditions of social life). The practice in question is not democratic, therefore, because it is 'liberating' (as measured by any absolute and humanist scale of values), but because it creates knowledge (in Foucault's terms) and so constitutes an advance in what Gramsci (1973) would call the 'war of position'.

Democratic process is thus a process of the constitution of democratic subjects, or the process of democratic maturation of the subjects of civil society. Thus, if power is exercised both over and through individuals

---

place in a discursive vacuum, and equally true that there will be different discourses available in the social formation which may be competing for the subjects' 'attention'; but it is the moment of choice which is crucial to the self-constitution of the subject. However, these choices (as I argue) are not necessarily, and probably only rarely, individual, because their defining quality is their social and relational content. So there is no place here for rational-choice theory.

[6] Discursive practices in particular are never divorced from political practices in general in the real processes of the exercise of political power and political struggle. In my opinion, this is one of the most important insights to be gained from a reading of Foucault. In other words, all political practices are simultaneously discursive practices, and vice versa; although it may be possible to justify separating them for heuristic purposes.

through the 'political, economic, and institutional regime of the production of truth' (Foucault:1980), which objectifies them, then they subjectify themselves by creating their own truth through their own political and strategic choices. (By extension, my own strategic choice in telling this story was not to flee the subjectivity of my informants, but to embrace it, and make analytical virtue of it.) The personal network then becomes a critical nexus of the grass-roots democratic struggle, because it is here that subjects constitute themselves, and simultaneously produce consciousness, in their relations with each other.[7] Thus, we noted in the course of the story that these networks were forged not on the basis of ideological traditions but in the struggle itself, and in particular through mounting strike actions (Chapters 1 and 7); and that the principle of cohesion which ran right through the syndical movement was certainly not ideology, understood as any kind of doctrine, but these same networks (Chapter 2), which underpinned the formation of the first proto-political organizations to oppose the Franco regime. This turned out to be strategically advantageous given the wide range of ideological convictions contained within the first workers' commissions (Chapter 6); but even the local organizations of the Communist Party were based on such networks (Chapter 9). Finally, not only did the networks precede both syndical and political organizations (even if the growth of these same organizations catalysed the extension of the networks), they bridged the two 'halves' of the central strategy of the opposition, which was the combination of legal and extralegal struggle (Chapter 9). Given what I shall argue is the essential ambivalence of democratic struggle (see below),[8] the consistency of this strategy could only be maintained by the personal networks which linked the two operational fields of the strategy.

---

[7] Interestingly, the mélange of linguistic analysis and semiotics known as 'discourse analysis' agrees that the constitution of subjects is *relational*, but this is possibly the only point of convergence between this analysis and my own. The argument goes that the production of meaning is the production of a system of differences (insofar as meaning emerges from the interplay of discursive oppositions). In this way, the relational constitution of subjects is simultaneously their differential constitution vis-à-vis other subjects. But, unlike the discourse analysts, I insist that, in practice, such differentiation takes place through making choices, and it is progressive choices which shape subjectivity. Hence, the subject cannot be the external reference for a discourse which it simply appropriates; and even if we consider the subjects' choices to compose a 'discursive practice' (compare footnote 6) it is still the subject who makes the political actor. If, as the discourse analysts tell us, there are no subjects prior to discourse, then, in this argument, there are no subjects prior to the moment of political choice.

[8] The ambivalence of the struggle corresponds to the personal ambiguity inscribed in the political roles of the protagonists of the struggle (as noted repeatedly in Chapters 11, 12 and passim). Here it is useful to refer to another notion from the discourse analysts' lexicon, which is that of 'intersubjectivity' or 'interdiscursivity', and which denotes the subject as an articulation of the various subjectivities corresponding to the diverse discursive formations present in the different political practices in which it is

Two caveats are in order. First, just as networks could knit the movement together, so they could contribute to its unravelling and splitting under the impact of repression (Chapter 10); and second, they were also effective in representing opposing social forces, such as the sherry oligarchy, at the level of the State (Chapters 3 and 4). Nevertheless, in this story of the emergence of a regional leadership in opposition to the Franco regime, they are the key to the capture of the strategic initiative. But at this stage in the argument it is important to distinguish between the political choices which bring individuals into the network and produce consciousness; and the strategic choices which direct the struggle, and which are capable of producing ideology (see Chapter 8). Political calculation enters the construction of political subjects and their democratic practice; but strategic calculation aims to vindicate and defend a new or larger political space within civil society. So while the notion of strategic choice certainly indicates intentionality, it does not assume a unified agent with an intention, if only because strategies can emerge from the interaction or opposition of contending or contradictory practices or organizations.

POLITICAL STRATEGIES AND 'WAR OF POSITION'

Strategic choices seek to create political spaces for the operation of the autonomous associations of civil society. Thus, the construction of a new political organization, the way demands are decided and put by a labour movement, the search for political alliances or an effective political division of labour between political parties and social movements, and consensus-building within or between opposition groups under an authoritarian regime will all involve such choices. In Spain, moreover, the strategy of infiltration into the Vertical Syndicate (to provide cover for the clandestine activities of the workers' commissions) succeeded in opening up a political space for democratic organization *within* the institutional ensemble of the State itself; as well as inventing the strategically effective fiction of a legal separation between striking workers and the commissions' representatives within the Syndicate (see Chapter 12). But the most illustrative space to appear under Franco's authoritarian regime (seen in Chapter 6) was the commissions' practice of direct democracy, once open assemblies on the shop floor began to define the bargaining strategy of the sixties.

If political strategies emerge from civil society, then they are inevitably constrained, in the first place, by the range of political actors present in this society, to the degree that they respond to existing political practices and

enmeshed (I am a Brit, a WASP, a trade unionist, a male, a democrat, etc.). My insistence on the *active* achievement of consciousness does not invalidate this notion (and may even strengthen it). For how else can we understand the subject of a (strategically) ambivalent democratic practice?

are shaped by a particular disposition of social forces in a specific con-juncture. For this reason (and for others which I will analyse below), such strategies will certainly express intentionality, but without necessarily spec-ifying a unified agent with an intention. In short, they must be understood as emerging from a matrix of multiple contingencies.

These observations are founded in the slow emergence of the commissions' syndical strategy from the immediate needs and personal networks of the workers themselves (refer to Chapter 6). As my informants never tired of telling me, it was something they did *a nuestro aire*; and, as such, represented an authentically grass-roots strategy which Gramsci (1973) would call 'or-ganic' (to distinguish it from strategies which are 'rational, arbitrary and willed', such as the Leninist theory of the vanguard and the seizure of State power). From the rise of the natural leaders, to the use of strikes as an integral part of the negotiating strategy (the commissions acting as both negotiating *and* strike commissions), to the inevitable translation of strictly syndical into broadly political demands, the commissions' strategy followed this same organic trajectory (see Chapter 7). Even the discovery of the central strategy of combining legal and extralegal struggle was spontaneous, insofar as it was rooted in the circumstances of clandestine struggle; while the lengthening agenda of political demands led to another natural division of political labour between syndical practice and political organization, which in El Marco de Jerez even found a geopolitical expression (see Chapter 3). The Communist Party took on the task of formalizing and disseminating the strategic discoveries of the labour movement, and for these purposes its pragmatism and opportunism were entirely appropriate characteristics (see Chapter 8): the exception to prove the rule was its doctrinaire insistence on the 'arbitrary and willed' strategy of the peaceful national strike, which predictably met with complete failure.

It is easy to make retrospective judgements of this kind, and, in general, it must be clear that there is no objective set of instrumental or *realpolitik* criteria against which the efficacy of different strategic choices can be mea-sured. All that can be asserted with confidence is that many such choices must be taken before different groupings of whatever origin or form begin to coalesce into the beginnings of a democratic project; and therefore the political content of any such project will be defined by the strategic choices which have entered its construction. Indeed, the emergence of a recognizable project will mean that certain strategic choices will have crystallized and found systematic organizational or ideological expression, as they had by the middle of the 1960s in Spain, which were marked by the commissions' strategic shift to open struggle and the Communists' commitment to the creation of a mass party (see Chapters 6 and 10). In this way, the people of El Puerto could claim their citizenship by joining the demonstrations led by Antonio Alvarez, because they could perceive themselves as part of a democratic project which was capable of removing the Franco regime.

Some argue that the crystallization of a strategy of open struggle was itself a response to State repression of legitimately elected syndical representatives; just as the broader and more progressive shift from syndical to political demands was certainly catalysed by the repression of strike activity. The repression can similarly be seen as responsible for indirectly strengthening personal networks within cellular and clandestine organizations (Chapter 2), for provoking mass mobilization (as in El Puerto in Chapter 7), and for conditioning the calculation of strategy, although not always in order to avoid such repression (Chapter 10). From this it appears that even State repression can be turned to account by effective strategic choices, although the continuing potential of this repression to inflict heavy damage on the democratic movement set severe operational limits on this possibility (which is clearly demonstrated in Chapter 10). But in arguing for the contingency of strategic calculation and strategic outcomes, much more is being suggested than a simple dialectic between opposition groups and repressive State apparatuses. Rather than a skeletal and Hegelian vision of the opposition entering into contradiction with the repressive principle of the State, I see political strategies as calculating and negotiating a vast range of possible political initiatives and responses – but in the specific political conditions imposed by the legal-institutional terrain which defines the relationships between State and civil society.[9]

In this perspective strategic choices of whatever kind are always conditioned by this terrain. This is not to deny that political movements and organizations which express the development of social forces may have a real and material (if mediated) foundation in common economic interest; nor is it to assert that this terrain is itself impermeable to political strategies, which would then meet a uniform fate in the procrustean bed of legal-bureaucratic rules. For these reasons this terrain (as argued in Chapter 14) is conceived as *conditioning* rather than *constituting* the range of strategic choice. Indeed, democratic initiatives in authoritarian contexts will almost automatically reject passive conditioning and seek to open up new political spaces by broadening the gamut of strategic choice. Hence, most political projects will have more than one strategy for advancing across this terrain, and engaging State agencies and opposing social forces in the 'war of position'.

The notion of a legal-institutional terrain (like so much else in political science) is a metaphor, which does not resolve the question of what divides and what joins civil society and the State. For once I disagree with Jessop (1982), who as a rule of thumb accepts that the line of division is the legal one between public and private, because this line is internal to the capitalist

---

[9] The notion of an institutional terrain is expressive because in this perspective (as explored in Chapter 14) the unity of the State is not given but is problematic and itself has to be constituted by specific practices.

State itself; and rather agree with Gramsci (1973) that the terms of the division are 'methodological and not organic', which is his way of saying that they are not given *a priori* but are always historically specific. In other words, there is a varying threshold of separation and proximity between the two, which is the result of different dispositions of social forces in concrete historical conjunctures: a moving frontier between the forces which exercise State power and which attempt to expand their basis of political support by incorporating and regulating private organisms; and the forces located in civil society which acquiesce in or resist such incorporation and regulation, and attempt to articulate their own strategies for extending the field of their autonomous operation. In other words, not only is this terrain a shifting one, but its institutional instability is germane to democratic struggle.[10] In fact, were there an immanent and fixed divide between State and civil society, no such struggle would be possible.

In this story, the legal-institutional terrain has been dominated by the Vertical Syndicate, which condensed the *global* corporatist strategy of the Franco regime (see Chapters 5 and 14). What is of most immediate importance here is not so much the Syndicate's powers of co-optation, through which the regime was able to advance a partially successful 'transformist' strategy, as its representational form, which (it was argued in Chapters 13 and 14) catalysed the birth of the commissions and conditioned their growth. In other words, the commissions found a legal space to organize in the *jurados* of the Syndicate, and it was this legality which anchored and potentiated their central strategy of legal–extralegal struggle (see Chapter 12). Moreover, when the regime attempted to broaden and modulate the strategy through the 1958 Law of Collective Contracts, it so altered the terrain that the commissions quickly found more space for their own strategic manoeuvres. In general (as was argued in Chapter 14), the overarching and global character of the corporatist strategy limited the regime's range of strategic choice, while the political line imposed within the Syndicate rendered it politically inflexible. In El Marco de Jerez the labour movement was confronted both by the uniform and ubiquitous presence of the Syndicate and by the uniform intransigence of the sherry oligarchy; yet it was in these seemingly most adverse conditions that the movement made its most important strategic discoveries.

The role of the Syndicate, and especially its representational form, as an object and location of democratic struggle offers a different perspective on the concept of 'mediation' and the forms of State representation and intervention. This is a useful concept insofar as it suggests that the State intervenes

---

[10] Foucault (1980) has insisted that in our studies we have to account for the 'constitution of the subject within an historical framework' (for which the notion of a legal-institutional terrain is one metaphor). At the same time he is very clear that 'states of power ... are always local and unstable' (Foucault:1978).

not only in things economic but also in things political, in its attempt to control the terms and parameters of political struggle. But this argument often supposes that the social forces in struggle (such as bourgeoisie and proletariat, for instance) are themselves fully constituted and 'always-already' present, which in turn supposes that political forces are capable of being formed through economic relationships. My own emphasis on the personal network as a principle of political cohesion, and on political and strategic choices in the growth of democratic practice, leads to the contrary conclusion: that all political forces, whether popular or class forces, can only emerge and exist through the political strategies and institutional forms which organize and project them. So on this point I agree with Przeworski (1977) that 'if classes are to appear in politics they must be organized as political actors... political class struggle is a struggle to constitute classes as political forces before it is a struggle between classes' – an observation which must apply *a fortiori* to the construction of popular political forces in the struggle for democracy.

But if class struggles and democratic struggles have this much in common, they are nevertheless distinct; and the specific contours of the legal-institutional terrain are especially important to popular and democratic struggles, which are nothing less than struggles between the people and the State.[11] Hence, democratic initiatives can advance across this terrain on distinct fronts, each of which addresses the relationships between State and civil society in different ways: first, the formal scope and institutional mechanisms of representation and accountability, and the formal definition of those entitled to participate in the democratic process; second, the substantive conditions in which popular control can be exercised; and last, the discursive constitution of 'people' as democratic subjects (Jessop:1982). In this particular story, the 'people' succeeded in constituting *themselves* as democratic subjects through struggling to achieve autonomous control over their own social life, and so prepared the terrain for the introduction of formal democratic arrangements at the level of the State; and it is generally useful to disaggregate democratic struggles in this way,[12] if only to dem-

[11] Such struggles may not *begin* in this way, and certainly not in the minds of the people in question; nor are such struggles necessarily unrelated to class struggles – as the case of El Marco makes very clear. 'In the field of political practices', says Jessop (1982), 'a wide range of popular (democratic) struggles can occur in isolation from the class struggle. The spheres of State/civil society and State/subject relations constitute the field par excellence for such struggles (*which may nonetheless have a class-relevance*)' (my emphasis).

[12] Jessop (1982) also suggests possible subhypothetical periodizations of democratic struggle, e.g., that as the extent and forms of State intervention shift with the passage from laissez-faire through simple monopoly to State monopoly capitalism, then there is a corresponding shift in the area most central to successful popular-democratic struggle as individual citizenship and parliamentarianism become less significant in comparison with membership of corporations and functional representation. But in

onstrate that formal democratic institutions do not (and cannot) guarantee that politics will be conducted in a substantively democratic manner – but may, for instance, be used to defend an authoritarian and populist regime. These observations can serve not only to reinforce the strength of my own definitions of democratic process and democratic practice, but also to evoke a hitherto unrecognized characteristic of democratic struggle, which is its essential ambivalence.

THE AMBIVALENCE OF DEMOCRATIC STRUGGLE

Both civil society and the State are potential sites of strategic choice, and hence of democratic practices; but in telling this story I have chosen to focus on the democratic practices of Spanish civil society (which, in my view, succeeded in placing the elite compromises and democratic pacts of the so-called transition to democracy on the historical agenda). This civil society has been portrayed here as a contingently woven web of political strategies, which may or may not be mutually consistent; while the State has been defined (in Chapter 14) as 'an institutional ensemble of different forms of representation, internal organization and intervention' (Jessop:1982). The legal-institutional terrain thus describes the specific and determinate field of strategic operations for democratic practice, where State and civil society meet; and although the political organizations of civil society inevitably have to wage their 'war of position' in conditions which are not of their own choosing, for their part they can (and must) take advantage of contradictions between State agencies, policies and forms of representation (and of the political spaces contained within those very forms). This complex chess game of constantly changing strategic options introduces a strong element of ambivalence into democratic struggle in authoritarian contexts: new political spaces may be created even within the State apparatus, but some degree of autonomy may thereby be lost; ways may be found to use the legal cover and resources of State agencies for extralegal and independent activities, but democratic actors may be co-opted or democratic goals distorted; repression of democratic initiatives may promote greater internal coherence within and among opposition groups, but their own organizations may simultaneously become more authoritarian in style. One consequence of this is that while democratic practice will always articulate specific political goals and therefore values, it cannot ever be conducted in complete accord with these values, absolute or otherwise.

my view this suggestion (provocative as it is) runs the danger of returning us to an [ethno]centrist and reductionist perspective on democratic practice, which is conditioned not so much by general periods of capitalist development as by specific conjunctures of political forces and characteristic forms of institutional mediation, and their insertion into the ensemble of the State.

In this story this general strategic ambivalence found its strongest expression in the commissions' strategy of infiltration into the Vertical Syndicate, and their combination of legal and extralegal struggle. As this strategy occupied exactly the same legal and political space as the element of co-optation implicit in the State's corporatist strategy, its operation inevitably introduced equally strong ambiguities into the political roles of syndical leaders like Emilio Fábregas, with all their accompanying personal anguish (see Chapter 9). Such ambiguities were similarly felt by many militants of the Communist Party, who were frustrated by the authoritarianism and corruption of the Party's democratic centralism (see Chapter 8), and who inhabited an historical time which did not allow them to enjoy the paradox of such a party making a crucial contribution to the achievement of liberal democracy. In the Spanish case, as has just been suggested, this strategic ambivalence was partially resolved, at any rate in the short term, by the operation of personal networks (clustering around their natural leaders), and, at a later stage, by the practice of direct democracy within open shop-floor assemblies.[13] And in general, far from constituting some kind of universal disadvantage for democratic forces, this ambivalence is the very stuff of democratic struggle, which is always a practice of the (democratically) possible.

What this means, once again, is that democratic process has to occur through a strategic practice, which produces more knowledge (through an undivided political and discursive practice) at the same time that it achieves more political power. Power is therefore not something that is ever won or lost definitively, but simply refers 'to a complex strategical situation within a particular society' (Foucault:1978). By definition, this characteristically strategic practice cannot finally be guided by appeal to absolute values of any kind, even purportedly democratic ones like 'freedom' and 'liberation', but only by political and strategic calculation. So, had the incipient commissions refused to collaborate with the Vertical Syndicate (as many of the old anarchists insisted they must), they could never have turned this instrument of working-class control into a privileged arena of democratic struggle. However, this is emphatically not to assert that values are therefore unimportant, or that they themselves have no place in democratic discourse. Much to the contrary, any democratic discourse will have to go beyond the questions of forms of representation and accountability to include the definition and dissemination of shared standards of official conduct and civic duties, which together it may call citizenship (Jessop:1982). But (and this is a strategically very big 'but'), whatever citizenship is *called* in the dis-

---

[13] Personal networks and open assemblies both worked to link and reproduce the distinct operational fields of the ambivalent strategy of infiltration and legal–extralegal struggle, as well as operationalizing the political division of labour between commissions and Communist Party (see Chapter 11).

course, it only *exists* in practice. In negotiating their political strategies on the terrain which links civil society and the State (and calculating their strategic options), democratic actors continue the education they began by organizing autonomously in the first place, and in their recurrent contacts with the legal system, the bureaucracy and the police, they learn concretely about the ways their social life is mediated by political process. This education is likely to be halting, contradictory and costly; but it is the only education in citizenship available in authoritarian contexts. In short, not only is it true that citizenship has to be achieved and can never be merely conferred; but citizenship is achieved through learning to live the ambivalence of democratic practice. Indeed, it is apparent, in bringing the argument full circle, that were it not for this ambivalence, then there would be no need to theorize the elements of political calculation and strategic choice on the premise of a 'contingent necessity'.

THE MAKING OF A DEMOCRATIC PROJECT

Throughout the telling of this story I have claimed that the people of El Marco de Jerez, and countless others like them, were making democracy. To make this claim I have had to suppose that the democratic process has more to do with democratizing civil society than with legal-political norms governing the operation of the democratic State (and this is what makes this story distinct from the great majority of recent studies on democracy and democratic process). Nonetheless, the claim of making democracy clearly goes further than simply keeping alive a vibrant civil society in harsh conditions. Such a society, as de Tocqueville forcefully argued, can provide a powerful political foundation for effective democratic rule where government is ruled by a democratic constitution; but there is no historical guarantee that government will be made in the image of civil society. On the contrary, the question of whether it is or not can be decided only by the political actors of civil society themselves; and my argument seeks to show that through the development of personal networks and political strategies these actors were not only practising citizenship in civil society but were also constructing a democratic project.

It may be objected that this was not so much a popular-democratic struggle as a class struggle, that was led by a sui generis form of working-class organization which was the workers' commissions. In answer I would agree emphatically that it was the labour movement which sowed the seeds of the democratic struggle, and that this struggle continued to have a clear 'class-relevance' (Jessop:1982). But to a great extent this was a result of the Franco regime's attempt to control civil society (and especially the working class) through its global corporatist strategy, which closely conditioned the initial possibilities for autonomous political action within this society (see Chapter 14). In other words, the predominance of the labour movement in the democratic project is a matter of political contingency, as are the strategic outcomes which translated its original syndical demands into a range of broadly political and finally democratic goals. But it is true that I have focused the story on the little studied and least understood aspects of the construction of the project, which are its beginnings at the roots of civil society.

Thus, the democratic project happened to begin with the labour movement, and this movement continued important to it. But what is of analytical importance is that the strategy which evolved for organizing this movement was organic, and not rational, willed, or doctrinaire. This pragmatic and inventive style of organization paid democratic dividends through the strategic alliances that were forged once the labour movement began to advance across the legal-institutional terrain linking civil society to the State; while the opportunism of the Communist Party also favoured further alliances to promote the project. Nevertheless, there are no rules which can guide the construction of such a project, and no way to prescribe for democratic success. On the evidence of the Communist Party's role in making democracy in Spain, not even the democratic actors themselves have to be democratic. The only certainty is that every single democratic project is sustained by several intersecting political strategies; and it follows that the political content of the project is always culturally and politically specific, in that it is defined by the significant strategic choices which have entered its construction. Beyond this, the only constant requirement for people who want to make democracy is faith in themselves, and faith in the future.

Bibliography

Primary sources

ABC
14.5.61 'Retribución del trabajo por cuenta ajena'
7.4.62   'Trabajo fijo en las viñas de Jerez'
8.5.62   'Reunión de representaciones sindicales para regular las condiciones del trabajo'
9.5.62   'Cádiz en la V Feria Internacional del Campo'
12.5.62 'Pleno de la Cámara Oficial Sindical Agraria'
14.12.69 'El Ministro de Trabajo se reune con los presidentes de los consejos de trabajadores'
         'Seis mil quinientos trabajadores gaditanos en paro'
         'El Tribunal Supremo confirma el despido de dos representantes sindicales'
14.1.70 'Paro en factoría de Astilleros de Cádiz'
18.1.70 'Desacuerdo entre las secciones Social y Económica de los viticultores de Cádiz'
         'Pago de salarios a los obreros de los Astilleros de Cádiz'
22.1.70 'El sector agrícola resultó el más afectado or los temporales en Cádiz'
         'Acuerdo empresarios-trabajadores en el "Marco de Jerez"'
25.1.70 'La situación de los viticultores gaditanos'
1.4.76   'Nuevos acuerdos en las viñas de Cádiz'
Alvarez, Santiago
  n.d.   'La retirada, la lucha guerrillera y el cambio de táctica', mimeo
  1972   'Sobre el campo', VIII Congreso del Partido Comunista de España
Baez, José Peñalver
  n.d.   *Un gremio cabeza de lucha de la provincia de Cádiz*
Banco de Bilbao
  1973   *Renta Nacional de España y su distribución provincial*
Bishop of Córdoba
  1953   *Semana social: los problemas sociales del campo andaluz*, XIII Semana Social,
         Córdoba, abril
Boletín Oficial de la Provincia de Cádiz
6.4.63, núm. 81; 27.2.65, núm. 35; 9.5.67, núm. 57; 22.5.69, núm. 116; 24.4.70, núm. 94;
27.4.70, núm. 96; 28.4.70, núm. 97
Cabral Beato, José
  1936   *Defendiendo los sagrados intereses de la Viticultura*, mimeo
Camacho, Marcelino
  1980   *Informe a la reunión de militantes obreros*, Madrid, 17 marzo
Carrillo, Santiago
  1962   'Las "comisiones obreras" y el rol del Partido', *Nuestra Bandera*, núm. 36
  1971   'Tras varios meses de estado de excepción', *Nuestra Bandera*, núm. 67
Catholic Church
  1956   *Declaración colectiva de los Rvdmos. Srs. Metropolitanos españoles en el presente
         momento social*, Fiesta de la Asunción de la Santíssima Virgen, 15 agosto

Cédula de Citación
    Juzgado de Instrucción de Sanlúcar de Barrameda (Nicolás Ruíz Gómez & Eduardo Saborido Jaén)
CNT (Confederación Nacional de Trabajo)
    1936   *Bases de Trabajo Agrícolas*, Jerez de la Frontera
    1936   *Contrato de Trabajo: Federación Patronal Vitícola & Sociedad de Viticultores*, regirá hasta el 31 mayo de 1937
Comisiones Obreras
    1977   *La Unión Sindical de CC.OO. de Andalucía*, 20 fevrero
    1979   *Informe del Secretaría General del Campo*, I Congreso Extraordinario de CC.OO. del Campo de Cádiz, octubre
    1981   *Informe General*, III Congreso del Campo, Federación del Campo de las CC.OO. de Andalucía, Antequera, 30 mayo
    n.d.   *Perspectivas de las Cooperativas Viticulturas del 'Marco' de Jerez*
    n.d.   *Resolución sobre la Reforma Agraria*
Correo de Andalucía
    1.7.81   *Estatuto de Autonomía para Andalucía*
Delegacía Provincial de Trabajo de Cádiz
    1964   *Resolución*, 31 diciembre
    1967   *Resolución*, 12 enero
Diario de Cádiz
    14.12.69   Interview with Manual Romero Pasos (Andrés Alvarez)
    6.2.70   'Desarticulación del partido comunista provincial en Puerto de Santa María'
    29.10.82; 9.5.83; 10.5.83
El País
    10.10.82; 20.2.83; 20.3.83; 8.5.83
Gaceta Sindical
    1980   'Andalucía: lucha de clases y opción nacional', Ano 1, núm. 1, abril
    1981   'II Congreso de la COAN', Ano 2, núm. 13, junio
Gómez, José
    1948   Letter to his wife, La Coruña, 6 September
Gómez, Juan
    1965   'Problemas del desarrollo económico de España', Conferencia pronunciada ante un grupo de trabajadores españoles, mimeo
Gutierrez de Célis, Francisco
    n.d.   *Problemas agrarios y sus posibles soluciones* Puerto de Santa María, ms
Hessler, Manfred et al.
    n.d.   *Pan para hoy – hambre para mañana*, Cádiz, mimeo
INE – Instituto Nacional de Estatística
    1975   *Informe Económico*, Madrid
    1980   *Informe Económico*, Madrid
Jiménez, Jesús Bernabe
    1981   *Estudio sobre el paro* Comisión provincial sindical del PCA Cádiz, marzo
Juzgado de Orden Público
    1967   *Auto de Juez* (Sr. Garralda), 3 enero
    1969   *Acta de Entrada y Registro* (Ramón Gaitero), Jerez, 31 enero
    1970   *Auto*, Sumario núm. 164/70 – Asociación Ilícita, Madrid, 7 marzo
    1971a   *Sentencia de Tribunal de Orden Público*, Sumario núm. (164 de 1970.) Madrid, 31 marzo
    1971b   *Sentencia de Tribunal de Orden Público*, Sumario núm. 93 de 1970, Madrid, 2 abril
Modesto, Juan
    1946   'Experiencias importantes de las acciones guerrilleras en este último período', *Nuestra Bandera* núm. 12, noviembre

Mundo Obrero
1.8.49   'Como crecen y luchan los guerrillas en Andalucía'
6.10.49   'Algunas experiencias de las guerrillas andaluzas'
20.10.49   'El Partido ante el crecimiento de la acción reivindicativa de los trabajadores en el seno de los Sindicatos Verticales'
31.1.54   'Ante las elecciones de enlaces sindicales'
15.2.54   'Como utilizar las llamadas "elecciones sindicales" '
15.3.54   'Para elevar el movimiento de lucha de las masas'
15.4.54
15.4.55   'Carta de un militante sobre la labor de los enlaces sindicales'
15.7.55   'Salario mínimo vital con escala móvil'
15.6.57   'La lucha para la transformación de los sindicatos verticales'
1.8.60   'Los problemas del campo andaluz no se resuelven a golpes de represión'
15.7.61   'El futuro del movimiento sindical español'
15.4.62   'Hasta en su propria guarida'
1.12.62   '¡Uniós todos para que Julián Grimau sea el último español torturado!'
15.2.64   'Por un nuevo impulso de la Oposición Sindical Obrera'
15.8.64   'Los Comunistas y la Oposición Sindical Obrera'
15.8.65   'Sobre la Oposición Sindical y las Comisiones Obreras'
15.8.66   'Por qué se debe votar'
15.5.67   'La lucha contra el paro en el campo'
15.6.67   'La única ley legítima: la libertad sindical'
30.11.67; 15.5.68; 15.6.68
15.7.69   'Para la mayor organización y coordinación del nuevo movimiento obrero'
8.1.70   'La huelga de obreros agrícolas en varios pueblos de Cádiz y Sevilla'
23.1.70   'Jerez: una huelga ejemplar'
6.2.70   'El movimiento campesino en Andalucía se fortalece'
21.2.70   'La represión y la lucha por la amnistia'
             'Las detenciones en Cádiz'
26.6.81; 2.10.81; 1.1.82; 2.4.82
OSE (Organización Sindical Española)
   1947   *Condiciones de trabajo en la viticultura*, Sindicato de la Vid, Cervezas y Bebidas, Jerez de la Frontera
   1950   *Tarifa de destajo para la vendimia*, Sindicato de la Vid, Cervezas y Bebidas, Jerez de la Frontera, 28 agosto
   1951   *Problemas Sociales*, Congreso Regional Agrario de la Organización Sindical Agraria de la OSE, Sevilla
   1963a   *Curso para Trabajadores Agrícolas sobre 'Seguridad e Higiene en el Trabajo'*, Obra Sindical 'Previsión Social', bajo el Patrocinio del Fundo Nacional de Protección al Trabajo, Sanlúcar, junio
   1963b   *Memorandum*, El Delegado Comarcal de la OS, Presidente de la Junta Local de Elecciones Sindicales, septiembre
   1969   *Texto articulado del Convenio Colectivo Sindical de Trabajo en las explotaciones agrícolas, forestales y pecuarias de la provincia de Cádiz*, 8 noviembre
   1974a   *Comisión Deliberadora del Convenio, Jerez de la Frontera*
   1974b   *Pedido al Sr. Presidente de la Hermandad Sindical de Labradores y Ganaderos y Junta de la Mutualidad Agraria de Chipiona (Cádiz)*, noviembre
   1974c   *Al Iltmo. Sr. Director General de Trabajo.* A reply to employers' appeal against compulsory arbitration, from Emilio Fábregas García, Francisco Gutierrez de Célis, José Morales Fernández, Francisco Blanco Amarillo, José Aldana Arniz, Francisco Romero Camacho, mimeo
   1976   *Informe del Letrado Asesor de la Sección Social en la Comisión Deliberadora del Convenio Colectivo Sindical regulador de los trabajos de viñas en el Marco de Jerez*, 23 marzo

PCE (Partido Comunista de Espana)
1960   *Estatutos del Partido Comunista de España*, Aprobados en su VI Congreso
1965a   *Informe de la Comisión Económica*
1965b   'El Verticalismo y las tareas del Partido', Informe del Comite Central, mimeo
1972   'Hacia la libertad', Informe del Comite Central presentado por S. Carrillo. VIII Congreso
1972   *VIII Congreso del Partido Comunista de España*, Empresa Polígrafa '13 de diciembre 1918', Bucarest
1973   *Proyecto de manifiesto-programa del PCE*
1977   'Resumen de la Reunión del Comité Provincial', Jerez, 21 agosto
1979   Informe sobre Organización Interna, Sanlúcar de Barrameda, 17 octubre
n.d.   *Informe General*, I Conferencia Provincial del PCE en Cádiz
n.d.   *El empleo comunitario*, Partido Comunista de Andalucía, Comité Provincial
Poulantzas, Nicos
1979   'La crisis de los partidos', *Le Monde Diplomatique*, septiembre
Romero Ruíz, Antonio
1979   *Informe General*, II Congreso Extraordinario, Federación de CC.OO. del Campo de Andalucía, Montilla, 20 octubre
Saborido, Eduardo
1978   *Informe*, I Congreso de CC.OO. de Andalucía, 19 mayo
1982   *Informe*, presentado en nombre de la comisión ejecutiva al consejo de la COAN, 19 junio
Sánchez, Antonio
n.d.   *La legislación vigente en el campo andaluz desde 1940 hasta la introducción de los Convenios Colectivos*, mimeo
1976   Notes from interviews conducted throughout province of Cádiz during 1971 and 1972
Santos López, José María
1976   *Andalucía en la revolución regionalista*, Sevilla, mimeo
SOC (Sindicato de los Obreros del Campo)
1980   *Resoluciones del II Congreso del Sindicato de los Obreros del Campo de Andalucía*, Puebla de Cazalla, 22/23 marzo
Soto, Fernando
n.d.   *Intervención Inicial*, Reunión del Secretariado y cuadros del PCA dirigentes de masas en el sindicato
1979   *Informe General*, Congreso Constituyente del Partido Comunista de Andalucía, Málaga, 14 diciembre
Vargas, Antonio
1978   *Informe General*, I Congreso Regional de CC.OO. del Campo, 15 junio
Villagrán, Juan Campos
1925   *Triunfo sobre un acidente de trabajo en el año 1925*, Trebujena, mimeo
Ya
8.4.56   'Se comprometen a dar a sus obreros agrícolas un salario mínimo de 40 pesetas'
29.4.56 'Unirse y prepararse para defenderse del comunismo'
15.4.56 'Vuelta al trabajo en Pamplona, Barcelona y San Sebastian. No ha habido la menor alteración del orden'
2.5.56   'Estrecha unidad de los trabajadores católicos'
13.4.57 'El arma eficaz contra el comunismo'
27.4.57 'Las hermandades obreras no son confradias ni sindicatos'
28.4.57 'El día 1 de Mayo es para todos los obreros – la Fiesta del Trabajo'
25.5.57 'Población agrícola y migración'
1.4.58   'Mejoras voluntarias a los trabajadores'
13.4.58 'Signo comunista en los paros laborales de Barcelona y Asturias'

16.4.58 'Los convenios colectivos sindicales aprobados'
18.4.58 'Hemos de revisar cada uno de los engranajes del sindicalismo nacional, dice el senor Solis'
11.12.58 'Los organismos del Movimiento y sindicatos no son entidades estatales autónomas'
20.3.62 'Elaboración de un sistema de moral social: la intervención del Estado en el orden económico'
17.4.62 'Salario fijo para unos 7,500 obreros agrícolas de Jerez'
11.5.63 'Plan de migraciones internas cuestionado por la Dirección General de Trabajo'
14.4.66 'El conflicto laboral de Bilbao en vías de solución'
22.4.66 'El partido comunista pro chino español desarticulado'
4.5.66 'No han existido convenios ni pactos: conversaciones entre Organización Sindical y CNT'
24.5.66 'Comienza la I Asamblea Nacional de Trabajadores del Campo'
4.12.66 'Todas las empresas deberán conceder el tiempo necessario para votar: nota de la Delegación Provincial de Trabajo'
7.12.66 'Se dice que en Barcelona se prepara una manifestación clandestina'
11.12.66 'La ordenanza laboral del campo, pendiente de aprobación'
22.12.66 'Hay que revisar la estructura sindical para adecuarla a la Ley Orgánica'
29.1.67 'Paralización del trabajo en varias fábricas de Madrid'
4.4.67 'Secuestro de libro "Comisiones Obreras"'
9.12.67 'Se confirma la validez de los convenios colectivos que estaban terminados'
24.12.69 'Medio millón de trabajadores madrileños en los convenios colectivos'
7.1.70 'Persiste el conflicto laboral de los vinicultores del "Marco de Jerez"'
14.1.70 'Paro en Astilleros de Cádiz, en Sevilla'
18.1.70 'Pérdidas por más de mil millones de pesetas en Cádiz'
25.1.70 'Situación estacionaria en las minas de Asturias: aparecen panfletos subversivos firmados por el partido comunista'
8.2.70 'Desarticulación de una organización clandestina en Cádiz'
9.1.73 'Ni huelgas, ni despido libre, dice el Ministro de Trabajo en Barcelona'
20.4.73 'Emigrantes españoles: hay que preparar la vuelta a casa'
20.5.73 'Diversas organizaciones clandestinas comunistas desarticuladas'
8.6.73 'Fortalecimiento del cauce sindical en el proyecto de ley de convenios colectivos: estudio de la nueva normativa sobre conflictos de trabajo'
29.8.73 'Los 90 obreros despedidos se recluyen en el palacio arzobispal de Sevilla'
1.9.73 'Cien trabajadores continuan su encierro voluntario en la catedral malagueña'
8.5.74 'Objectivos de futuro para el sindicalismo español: preoccupación por el paro'
1.5.75 'Empresa de todos, sindicato único y salario justo, piden los trabajadores en Barcelona'
10.5.75 'Decreto-Ley sobre regulación del derecho a la huelga'

Secondary sources

Alba, V.
1979 *El Partido Comunista en España*, Planeta, Barcelona
Alfaro, F. R.
1970 *Las clases trabajadores en España, 1898–1930*, Taurus, Madrid
Almendros, F., et al.
1978 *El Sindicalismo de Clase en España, 1939–1977*, Península, Barcelona
Alonso, V., et al.
1976 *Crises agrarias y luchas campesinas, 1970–76* Ayuso, Madrid
Althusser, L.
1976 *Essays in self-criticism*, New Left Books, London

1977a   *For Marx*, Verso, London
1977b   *Politics and History: Montesquieu, Rousseau, Hegel and Marx*, New Left Books, London
Alvarez, S.
1967   'El PC de España y el Movimiento Obrero', *Revista Internacional*, May
1977   *El Partido Comunista y el Campo*, Ediciones de la Torre, Madrid
Alvarez de Toledo, I.
1971   *The Strike*, Grove Press, New York
Amodia, J.
1977   *Franco's Political Legacy: From Dictatorship to Facade Democracy*, Allen Lane, London
Amsden, J.
1972   *Collective Bargaining and Class Struggle in Spain*, Weidenfeld & Nicolson, London
Anderson, B.
1983   *Imagined Communities*, Verso/New Left Books, London
Andrade, J.
1979   *Apuntes para la historia del PCE*, Fontamara
Arango, R.
1978   *The Spanish Political System: Franco's Legacy*, Westview Press, Boulder, Colo.
Ariza, J.
1976   *Comisiones Obreras*, Avance, Barcelona
1977   *La Confederación sindical de comisiones obreras*, Avance, Barcelona
Aumente, J.
1979   *La 'cuestion nacional' andaluza y los intereses de clase*, Mañana, Madrid
Ayucar, A. R.
1976   *El Partido Comunista: treinta y siete años de clandestinidad*, San Martín, Madrid
Baklanoff, E.
1978   *The Economic Transformations of Spain and Portugal*, Praeger, New York
Ben Ami, S.
1980   *La revolución desde arriba: España 1936–1979*, Ríopiedras Ediciones, Barcelona
Benton, T.
1984   *The Rise and Fall of Structural Marxism: Althusser and His Influence*, Macmillan, London
Bernal, A. M.
1974   *La propriedad de la tierra y las luchas agrarias andaluzas*, Ariel, Barcelona
Biescas, J. A., and Tuñon de Lara, M.
1980   *España bajo la dictadura franquista (1939–1975)*, Labor, Barcelona
Booth, A.
1982   'Corporatism, capitalism and depression in twentieth century Britain', *British Journal of Sociology* 33(2), June
Brenan, G.
1950   *The Face of Spain*, London
1976   *The Spanish Labyrinth*, Cambridge University Press, London
Bruce, N.
1972   'A new approach to Spanish labour problems', *Iberian Studies* 1(2), autumn
Brustein, W.
1981   'A regional mode of production analysis of political behaviour: the cases of Western and Mediterranean France', *Politics and Society* 10(4)
Calamai, M.
1976   *Storia del movimento operaio spagnolo dal 1960 al 1975*, De Donato, Bari
Calero, A. M.
1973   *Historia del movimiento obrero en Granada*, Tecnos, Madrid
1979   *Movimientos sociales en Andalucía, 1820–1936*, Siglo Veintiuno, Madrid

Cammett, J.
1967   *Antonio Gramsci and the Origins of Italian Communism*, Stanford University Press, Stanford, Calif.
Canadian Committee for a Democratic Spain
1973   *Spain: The Workers' Commissions, 1966–71.*
Candel, F.
1968   *Ser obrero no es ninguna ganga*, Ariel, Barcelona
Carr, R.
1966   *Spain: 1808–1939*, Oxford University Press, London
1982   *Spain: 1808–1975*, Oxford University Press, London
Carr, R., and Fusi, J.P.
1981   *Spain: Dictatorship to Democracy*, Allen & Unwin, London
Carrillo, S.
1965   *¿Despues de Franco, Qué?*, Editions Sociales, Paris
1967   *Nuevos Enfoques a problemas de hoy*, Editions Sociales, Paris
1974   *Hacia el pos-franquismo*, Informe en nombre del Comité Ejecutivo en el Pleno ampliado del Comité Central, abril, Colección EBRO, Paris
1976   *El Partido Comunista de España*, Avance-Mañana, Barcelona
1978   *Eurocommunism and the State*, Lawrence Hill, Westport, Conn.
Carson-Parker, J.
1985   'Spain: new economic vistas', *Euromoney*, January
Casero, F., and Sánchez, G.
1978   *Nuevos surcos en viejas tierras: el resurgir del movimiento jornalero*, Manifiesto, Madrid
n.d.   *¿ Progresar ... es no comer? Alternativa del SOC (SAT) a la actual situación del campo andaluz*, Sevilla
CES (Comité Economique et Social des Communautés Européennes)
1979   'Les relations de la Communauté avec l'Espagne', (M. Evain), Brussels, May
1980   'Conference sur l'élargissement de la communauté européenne', *Extraits*, Brussels, September
1982   *Las organizaciones socio-profesionales de España*
Chao, R.
1975   *Après Franco, l'Espagne*, Stock, Paris
Chinarro, E.
1978   *Libertad de impresión: 'El Correo de Andalucía' – visto desde la trinchera*
Claudín, F.
1978   *Documentos de una divergencia comunista*, El Viejo Topo, Barcelona
1983a   *Santiago Carrillo*, Planeta, Barcelona
1983b   'Entrevista con Fernando Claudín por Fernando Arroyo', *el País*, 20.3.1983
Colletti, L.
1972   *From Rousseau to Lenin*, New Left Books, London
Colomer, E. C.
1965   *Historia del Partido Comunista de España*, Editora Nacional, Madrid
Comin, A. C.
1976   *¿Qué es el sindicalismo?*, La Gaya Ciencia, Barcelona
Cotarelo, R.
1981   'The crisis of political parties in Spain', *European Journal of Political Research 9*
Couffignal, G.
1979   'Les syndicats espagnols et l'élaboration d'un nouveau système politique', *ECPR Workshops*, Brussels
Crouch, C.
1977   *Class Conflict and the Industrial Relations Crisis*, Heinemann, London

de Blaye, E.
    1976   *Franco and the Politics of Spain*, Penguin, Harmondsworth
de la Cierva, R.
    1975   *Historia del Franquismo: orígenes y configuración (1939–1945)*, Planeta, Barcelona
del Campo, S.
    1972   *Análisis de la población de España*, Ariel, Barcelona
de Maetzú, R.
    1957   *El Sentido Reverencial del Dinero*, Editorial Nacional, Madrid
de Miguel, A.
    1977   *La Pirámide Social Española*, Ariel, Madrid
de Tocqueville, A.
    1946   *Democracy in America*, Oxford University Press, London
Díaz, E.
    1974   *Pensamiento Español: 1939–1973*, Cuadernos para el Diálogo, Madrid
Díaz del Moral, J.
    1929   *Historia de la agitaciones campesinas andaluzas*, Alianza, Madrid
Eaton, S.
    1981   *The Forces of Freedom in Spain*, Hoover Press, Stanford, Calif.
Ellwood, S.
    1976   'The working class under the Franco regime', in P. Preston, ed., *Spain in Crisis*
Equipo EIDA
    1977   *Getafe: lucha obrera bajo el franquismo*, Unión Sindical de Madrid de CC.OO. Talleres Gráficos Montana
Equipos de Estudio
    1976   *La clase obrera, protagonista de cambio*, Ediciones Elías Querejeta
ERA (Estudios Rurales Andaluzes)
    1980   *Las Agriculturas Andaluzas*, Servicio de Publicaciones Agrarias, Ministerio de Agricultura
Espejo, A.
    n.d.   *Andalucía: campo de trabajo y represión*, ALJIBE, Granada
(n.a.)
    1980   *Estatuto de los Trabajadores*, Ley 8, 10 mayo
ETUI (European Trade Union Institute)
    1980   *The social and economic effects of the enlargement of the EEC and the implications for trade and labour policy in Western Europe*, September, Brussels
    1982   *Collective Bargaining in Western Europe 1980–81 and Prospects for 1982*, April, Brussels
Fabre, J., and Huertas, J.
    1982   'La fundació de CC.OO. a Barcelona', *L'Avenç*, 52, September, Barcelona
Ferri, L., et al.
    1978   *Las huelgas contra Franco (1939–1956)*, Planeta, Barcelona
Fishman, R. M.
    1982   'The labour movement in Spain: from authoritarianism to democracy', *Comparative Politics* 14(3), April
    1985   'The moderation of the rank and file, the legitimacy of the State and wage restraint in Spain', Paper presented at the Fifth International Conference of Europeanists, Washington D.C., 18–20 October
Foucault, M.
    1977a   *Discipline and Punish: The Birth of the Prison*, Pantheon Books, New York
    1977b   *Language, Counter-Memory, Practice*, ed. D. Bouchard, Cornell University Press, Ithaca, N.Y.

1978   *The History of Sexuality, Vol 1: An Introduction*, Pantheon Books, New York
1980   *Power/Knowledge*, ed. Colin Gordon, Pantheon Books, New York
1984   *The Foucault Reader*, ed. Paul Rabinow, Pantheon Books, New York
Foweraker, J.
1982   'Authoritarianism and accumulation on the pioneer frontier of Brazil', *Journal of Peasant Studies* 10(1), October
1987   'Corporatist Strategies and the Transition to Democracy in Spain', *Comparative Politics* 20(1), October
1987   'The Role of Labor Organizations in the Transition to Democracy in Spain', in R. Clark and M. Haltzel, eds., *Spain in the 1980s: The Democratic Transition and a New International Role*, Ballinger, Cambridge, Mass.
Fraser, R.
1972   *In Hiding: the life of Manuel Cortes*, Allen Lane, London
1973   *Tajos*, Allen Lane, London
1976   'Spain on the brink', *New Left Review* (60), March–April
Frères du Monde
1969   *Luttes ouvrières en Espagne*, Paris
FSM (Federación Sindical Mundial)
1959   *Veinte años de vida y de lucha de los trabajadores españoles bajo la dictadura fascista de General Franco*, Confederación de Trabajadores de America Latina, Mexico D.F.
Gallego, I.
1971   *El Partido de masas que necesitamos*, Informe en nombre del Comité Ejecutivo ante el Pleno ampliado del Comité Central del PCE, (setiembre 1970), Ediciones Sociales, Paris
Ganz, F.
1977   *Ensayo marxista de la historia de España (1934)*, Grijalbo, Barcelona
Gimore, D.
1980   *The People of the Plain: Class and Community in Lower Andalucía*, Columbia University Press, New York
Giner, S.
1968   *Continuity and Change: The Social Stratification of Spain*, Occasional Papers no. 1, School of Contemporary Studies, University of Reading
Giner, S.
1982   'Spain: dictatorship to democracy', University College, London, April
Giner, S., and Sevilla, E.
1980   'From despotism to parliamentarianism: class domination and political order in the Spanish State', in R. Scase, ed., *The State in Western Europe*, Croom Helm, London
1984   'Spain: from corporatism to corporatism', in A. Williams, ed., *Southern Europe Transformed*, Harper & Row, London
Goldthorpe, J.
1984   'The end of convergence: corporatist and dualist tendencies in modern western societies', in J. Goldthorpe, ed., *Order and Conflict in Contemporary Capitalism*, Oxford University Press, London
Gramsci, A.
1973   *Selections from the Prison Notebooks of Antonio Gramsci*, eds. Q. Hoare and G. N. Smith, Lawrence & Wishart, London
Griffith, W., ed.
1980   *The European Left: Italy, France and Spain*, D.C. Heath, Lexington, Mass.
Guinea, J. L.
1978   *Los movimientos obreros y sindicales en España*, Ibérico Europa, Madrid

Gunther, R.
1985   'Democratization and party building: contradictions and conflict facing party elites in the Spanish transition to democracy', Paper presented to the conference *Spain in the 1980s*, West European Program, Wilson Center, Washington D.C., 25–27 September
Harrison, J.
1978   *An Economic History of Modern Spain*, Manchester University Press
Hechter, M., and Levi, M.
1979   'The comparative analysis of ethnoregional movements', *Ethnic and Racial Studies* 2(3), July
Hermet, G.
1974   *The Communists in Spain: Study of an Underground Political Movement*, Saxon House, Farnborough
1977   'Espagne: changement de la societé, modernisation autoritaire et democratie oc-troyée', European Consortium for Political Research Joint Sessions, Berlin, March
HOAC, Comisión Nacional
1977   *PCE en sus documentos: 1920–1977*, Ediciones HOAC, Madrid
Hobsbawm, E.
1959   *Primitive Rebels*, Manchester University Press
Huneeus, C.
1979   'Transition to Democracy in Spain: Unión Centro Democrático as a "consociational party"', European Consortium for Political Research Joint Sessions, Brussels, April
Huntington, S.
1968   *Political Order in Changing Societies*, Yale University Press, London
Ibañez, V. B.
1924   *La Bodega*, Prometeo, Valencia
Ibarruri, D.
1966   *They Shall Not Pass (El Unico Camino)*, International Publishers, New York
Ibarruri, D., et al.
1964   *Historia del Partido Comunist de España*, Editora Política, La Habana
ILO – International Labour Organization
1969   *La situación laboral y sindical en España*, Geneva
Jessop, R.
1979   'Corporatism, parliamentarianism and social democracy', in P. Schmitter and G. Lehmbruch, eds., *Trends Towards Corporatist Intermediation*
1982   *The Capitalist State*, Martin Robertson, London
1983   'Accumulation strategies, State forms and hegemonic projects', *Kapitalstate* (10)
1985   'The State and political strategy', International Political Science Association Conference, Paris, July
Kaplan, T.
1977   *Anarchists of Andalucía, 1868–1903*, Princeton University Press
Kern, R.
1978   *Red Years, Black Years: A Political History of Spanish Anarchism, 1911–1937*, Institute for the Study of Human Issues, Philadelphia
Labour Party Young Socialists
1973   *Spain*, 12th LPYS National Conference, Skegness, April
Laclau, E.
1977   *Politics and Ideology in Marxist Theory*, New Left Books, London
Laclau, E., et al.
1981   *Estado y Política en América Latina*, Siglo Veintiuno, Mexico
Lechner, N.
1977   'La cuestión del Estado en el capitalismo dependiente', *Estudios Sociales Centro-americanos* 6(16)

Lehmbruch, G.
  1979a 'Consociational democracy, class conflict and the new corporatism', in P. Schmitter and G. Lehmbruch, eds., *Trends Towards Corporatist Intermediation*
  1979b 'Liberal corporatism and party government', in P. Schmitter and G. Lehmbruch, eds., ibid.
  1984 'Concertation and the structure of corporatist networks', in J. Goldthorpe, ed., *Order and Conflict*
Lenin, V. I.
  1967 *Lenin on the National and Colonial Questions*, Foreign Language Press, Peking
  1970 *Two Tactics of Social Democracy in the Democratic Revolution*, Foreign Language Press, Peking
  1972 *The State and Revolution*, Progress Publishers, Moscow
Linz, J.
  1964 'An authoritarian regime: Spain', in E. Allardt and Y. Littunen, eds., *Cleavages, Ideologies and Party Systems*, The Academic Bookstore, New York
  1970 'From Falange to Movimiento Organización: the Spanish single party and the Franco regime, 1936–1968', in S. Huntington and C. Moore, eds., *Authoritarian One-Party Systems*, Basic Books, New York
  1973 'Opposition in and under an authoritarian regime: the case of Spain', in R. Dahl, ed., *Regimes and Oppositions*, Yale University Press, New Haven, Conn.
Linz, J., and de Miguel, A.
  1966 *Los empresarios ante el poder público*, Instituto de Estudios Politicos, Madrid
Lister, E.
  1978 *¡Basta!*, Ediciones del Toro, Madrid
Llorens, C.
  1982 *Historia del Partido Comunista de España*, Fernando Torres, Valencia
Lowy, M.
  1976 'Marxists and the national question', *New Left Review* (96), March–April
Macciocchi, M.
  1973 *Letters from Inside the Italian Communist Party to Louis Althusser*, New Left Books, London
Macpherson, C.
  1966 *The Real World of Democracy*, Clarendon Press, Oxford
Maier, C. S.
  1984 'Preconditions for corporatism', in J. Goldthorpe, ed., *Order and Conflict*
Malefakis, E.
  1970 *Agrarian Reform and Peasant Revolution in Spain: Origins of the Civil War*, Yale University Press, New Haven, Conn.
Maravall, J. M.
  1978 *Dictatorship and Political Dissent*, Tavistock, London
  1982 *The Transition to Democracy in Spain*, Croom Helm, London
Martínez, J. M.
  1976 *¿Por qué no fue posible la Falange?*, DOPESA, Barcelona
Martínez Lucio, M.
  1983 *Corporatism and Political Transition*, M.A. dissertation, University of Essex
Martínez-Alier, J.
  1971 *Labourers and Landowners in Southern Spain*, Allen & Unwin, London
  1983 'The old corporatist ideology and the new corporatist reality in Spain', Summer School on Comparative European Politics, European University Institute, Florence
McDonough, P., Lopez Piña, A., and Barnes, S. H.
  1981 'The Spanish public in political transition', *British Journal of Political Science* 11
  1985 'Political Identity in Spain', Fifth International Conference of Europeanists, Washington D.C., October 18

Miguélez, F.
  1976   *La lucha de los mineros asturianos bajo el franquismo*, Laia, Barcelona
  1977   *SEAT. La empresa modelo del régimen*, DOPESA, Barcelona
  1985   'State, unions and social conflict in Spain', European Consortium for Political Research, Joint Sessions, Barcelona, March
Modesto, J.
  1978   *Soy del Quinto Regimiento*, Laia, Barcelona
Moreno, I.
  1972   *Propriedad, clases sociales y hermandades en la Baja Andalucía*, Siglo Veintiuno, Madrid
  n.d.   *Andalucía: subdesarrollo, clases sociales y regionalismo*, Manifiesto, Madrid
  1981   'Rechazo de la dependencia y afirmación de la identidad: las bases del nacionalismo andaluz', *Jornadas de Estudios Socio-Económicos de las Comunidades Autónomas*, vol. 3, Universidad de Sevilla
Morodo, R., et al.
  1979   *Los Partidos Políticos en España*, Labor, Barcelona
Moya, C.
  1975   *El Poder Económico en España, 1939–1970*, Tucar, Madrid
Moyano, E.
  1984   *Corporatismo y Agricultura: asociaciones profesionales y articulación de intereses en la agricultura española*, Instituto de Estudios Agrarios, Pesqueros y Alimentarios, Madrid
Mujal-León, E.
  1979   'The Spanish Left: present realities and future prospects', in W. Griffith ed., *The European Left*
  1983   *Communism and Political Change in Spain*, Indiana University Press, Bloomington
Nicolas, L.
  1972   *A travers les Revolutions espagnoles*, Pierre Belfond, Paris
O'Donnell, G.
  1978   'Reflections on the patterns of change in the Bureaucratic-Authoritarian State', *Latin American Research Review* 13(1)
  1979   'Tensions in the bureaucratic-authoritarian state and the question of democracy', in Collier, D., ed., *The New Authoritarianism in Latin America*, Princeton University Press
Offe, C.
  1983   'Limits of legal regulation', Conference on *Constitutionalism and Democracy*, Oslo, January
Padilla, A.
  1979   *El movimiento comunista español*, Planeta, Barcelona
Pagés, P.
  1978   *Historia del Partido Comunista de España*, Ricou (Hacer), Barcelona
Paine, S.
  1979   'Replacement of the European migrant labour system by investment in the European periphery', in D. Seers et al., eds., *Underdeveloped Europe*, Harvester, Hassocks
Paniagua, J. F.
  1977   *La ordenación del capitalismo avanzado en España*, Anagrama, Barcelona
Panitch, L.
  1979   'The development of corporatism in liberal democracies', in P. Schmitter and G. Lehmbruch, eds., *Trends Towards Corporatist Intermediation*
  1980   'Recent theorizations of corporatism: reflections on a growth industry', *British Journal of Sociology* 31
  1981   'Trade unions and the capitalist State', *New Left Review* 125

Parti Comuniste Français
1962   *Dos Meses de huelgas*, Paris
Payne, S.
1985   'The role of the armed forces in the Spanish transition', *Spain in the 1980s*, Woodrow Wilson International Center for Scholars, Washington D.C., September 25
Pereira-Menaut, A.
1981   'The regional problem in present day Spain', Political Science Association Sixth Annual Meeting, University of Strathclyde, September
Pérez Díaz, V.
1979   *Clase obrera, partidos y sindicatos*, Fundación del Instituto Nacional de Industria, Madrid
1980   *Clase obrera, orden social y conciencia de clase*, Fundación del Instituto Nacional de Industria, Madrid
Pike, F.
1974   'The new corporatism in Franco's Spain and some Latin American perspectives', in F. Pike and T. Stritch, eds., *The New Corporatism: Socio-Political Structures in the Iberian World*, University of Notre Dame Press, Notre Dame, Ind.
Pitt-Rivers, J.
1971   *The People of the Sierra*, University of Chicago Press.
Poulantzas, N.
1976   *The Crisis of the Dictatorships: Portugal, Spain, Greece*, New Left Books, London
Preston, P.
1976   'The anti-Francoist opposition: the long march to unity', in P. Preston, ed., *Spain in Crisis*
Preston, P., ed.
1976   *Spain in Crisis*, Harvester, Hassocks
Prevost, G.
1982   'The Spanish labour movement six years after Franco', 3rd International Conference of Europeanists, Washington D.C., April 29–May 1
Przeworski, A.
1977   'Proletariat into a class: the process of class formation from Karl Kautsky's *The Class Struggle* to recent controversies', *Politics and Society* 7(4)
1979   'Some problems in the study of the transition to democracy', *Working Paper* no. 61, Latin American Program, The Wilson Center, Washington D.C.
1980   'Social democracy as an historical phenomenon', *New Left Review* (122)
PSOE (Secretaría Federal de Formación)
n.d.   *Apunte Histórico*
Regini, M.
1984   'The conditions for political exchange: how concertation emerged and collapsed in Italy and Great Britain', in J. Goldthorpe, ed., *Order and Conflict*
Reig, E.
1984   'Spain's economic problems and policies – prospects before EEC membership', University of Reading Discussion Papers in European and International Social Science Research no. 2, October
Riz, L. de
1977   'Formas de estado y desarrollo del capitalismo en América Latina', *Revista Mexicana de Sociología* 39(2)
1980   'La transformación del estado: bosquejo de una línea de investigación de las sociedades latinoamericanas', ibid.42(1)
Robinson, R.
1985   'Economic interests groups and the State in Spain: a corporatist mirage?', European Consortium for Political Research, Joint Sessions, Barcelona, March

Roca, J.
1983   'Economic analysis and neo-corporatism (with particular reference to post-Franco Spain)', Summer School on Comparative European Politics, European University Institute, Florence
1985   'Los pactos sociales en el Estado español', *Crónica de Información Laboral* no. 32, January–February, Centro de Estudios Sociales, Barcelona
Rodier, J., and Pidal, V.
1975   *Lo que hemos visto...*, Sociedad de Educación Atenas, Madrid
Rodríguez, R.
1977   *¿Quienes son en Málaga? Partido Socialista de Andalucía*, Lafer, Málaga
Romero Maura, J.
1973   'El caciquismo: tentativa de conceptualización', *Revista de Occidente* 43, octubre
Sagarday, J. A.
1976   *La realidad laboral española*, Sociedad de Estudios Laborales, Fundación Universitaria San Pablo
Sánchez, F. L.
1977   *La emigración andaluza: análisis y testimonios*, Ediciones de la Torre, Madrid
Sánchez, J. A.
1977   *Diccionario de la izquierda comunista*, DOPESA, Barcelona
Sánchez, J. J.
1969   *El movimiento obrero y sus orígenes en Andalucía*, ZYX, Madrid
Sartorius, N.
1976   *El Resurgir del Movimiento Obrero*, Laia, Barcelona
Schmitter, P.
1974   'Still the century of corporatism?', *Review of Politics* 36
1985   'Neo-corporatism and the State', Working Paper no. 106, European University Institute
Schmitter, P., and Lehmbruch, G., eds.
1979   *Trends Towards Corporatist Intermediation*, Sage, Beverly Hills, Calif.
Selgas, C. I.
1974   *El Sindicalismo Español*, Doncel, Madrid
Semprún, J.
1980   *Communism in Spain in the Franco Era*, Harvester, Brighton
Sevilla, E.
1976   'The peasantry and the Franco regime', in P. Preston, ed., *Spain in Crisis*
Siguan, M.
1972   *El medio rural en Andalucía oriental*, Ariel, Barcelona
Soto, F.
1976   *A ras de tierra*, Akal, Madrid
Tamames, R.
1977a   *¿Hacia donde vas, España?* Planeta, Barcelona
1977b   *De la República a la era de Franco*, Alianza, Madrid
Texanos, J. F.
1978   *Estructura de clase y conflictos de poder en la España pos-franquista*, Cuadernos para el Diálogo, Madrid
Therborn, G.
1976   *Science, Class and Society*, New Left Books, London
Tobella, J. E.
1982   *El PCE en la clandestinidad (1939–1956)*, Siglo Veintiuno, Madrid
Tusell, X.
1977   *La oposición democrática al franquismo*, Planeta, Barcelona

UGT
   1978   *Memoria*, Comisión Ejecutiva al XXXI Congreso de la Unión General de Trabajadores, Barcelona, 25 mayo
Valles, J. M.
   1979   'Sur l'experience électorale espagnole de l'après Franquisme', European Consortium for Political Research, Joint Sessions, Brussels, April
Varios Autores
   1979   *Aproximación a la historia de Andalucía*, Laia, Barcelona
Vilar, P.
   1971   'The age of Don Quixote', *New Left Review* (68), July–August
Vilar, S.
   1976   *La Oposición a la Dictadura: protagonistas de la España democrática*, Ayma,
           Barcelona
   1977   *La Naturaleza del Franquismo*, Península, Barcelona
   1981   *El Disidente*, Plaza y Janes, Barcelona
Weber, M.
   1959   *Max Weber: Theory of Social and Economic Organization*, ed. Talcott Parsons,
           Free Press, Glencoe, Ill.
Wiarda, H.
   1973   'Towards a framework for the study of political change in the Iberian-Latin tradition: the Corporative Model', *World Politics* 25
   1981   *Corporatism and National Development in Latin America*, Westview Press, Boulder,
           Colo.
Winston, H., and Luelmo, J.
   1978   *Eurocommunismo y Estado*, Akal, Madrid
Witney, F.
   1965   *Labor Policy and Practices in Spain: A Study of Employer-Employee Relations
           Under the Franco Regime*, Praeger, New York
Wright, A.
   1977   *The Spanish Economy 1959–1976*, Macmillan, London
Yglesias, J.
   1977   *The Franco Years*, Bobbs-Merrill, Indianapolis
Yruela, M. P.
   1979   *La conflictividad campesina en la provincia de Córdoba, 1931–1936*, Servicio de
           Publicaciones, Ministerio de Agricultura

Interviews

This story could never have been told without the help of those who made it. To get the story
I met with many of them and carried out 'interviews'. Most of those whom I interviewed are
happy to have their names mentioned here, and I am pleased to do it. For the remaining few
the old habits die hard, and I respect their wish for anonymity. During the months I spent
interviewing I also learned a lot from conversations with a few friends who offered constant
encouragement and criticism, and their names are included. All helped to the very best of their
abilities (I was never refused an interview), and so I mention their names, as I knew them,
without priorities or distinctions:

Paco Casero; Gonzalo Sánchez; Isidoro Moreno; José María de los Santos; Jorge de Santamaría;
Eduardo Saborido; Jaime Montes; Juan Antonio Romero; José Luis Insavsti Catón; Manuel
Alonso Román; Agustín Espejo González; Eduardo Chinarro; Enrique García; Emilio Fábregas; Miguel Campo Varela; Miguel Ruíz Caballero; Fernando Martín Mora; Manuel Verano;
Francisco Gutierrez de Célis; Manolo Romero Pasos; Manuel Ramírez Delgado; Lorenzo
Marchena Villagrán; José Peñalver Baez; Paco Cabral; Nicolás Ruíz Gómez; Juan Flores;

Rafael Ribeiro; Paco Artola; José Aldana Arniz; Ramón Gaitero; Horacio Lara; Manolo Romero Ruíz; Fernando Guilloto Aguilar; Juan Franco Real; Benito Herrera Abelenda; Juan Caballero Robles; Antonio Marín; Pepe de la Rosa Ríos; Rafael Gómez Ojeda; Luis Jaramillo Barrio; José Antonio Jiménez García; Manolo Espinar Galán; Manolo Nuñez; Antonio Alvarez Herrera; Francisco Romero Camacho; Eduardo Sánchez Fernándes; José Mena Ortega; José María García Caballero; Juan Romero Pasos; Fernando Soto; Antonio Mesa; Antonio Zoido; Manuel Benítez Rufo; Federico Iglesias Villar; Antonio Ortega Gil; Antonio Sánchez; Miguel Marroquín Travieso; Paco Sánchez Legrán.

Index

absolute monarchy (of 1875), 62
Acción Sindical de Trabajo (AST), 94
activists, 3
Acuerdo Marco Interconfederal (AMI), 242
Acuerdo Nacional sobre el Empleo (ANE), 243
Administración Institucional de Servicios Socio-Profesionales (AISSP), 223
agrarian reform, 70, 191
Agricultural Associations, *see* Hermandades Agrícolas
agriculture: in Jerez 49; policies, 64; unemployment, 52
Alba, Víctor, 141, 189
Aldana, José, 17, 20, 21, 23, 25, 28, 38, 39, 42, 44, 113, 116, 120, 126, 177, 178, 197, 201
Alianza Sindical Obrera (ASO), 73, 94
Alvarez, José, 204
Alvarez Herrera, Antonio, 16, 17, 20, 21, 24, 25, 26, 35, 37, 39, 43, 45, 59, 100, 104, 105, 106, 119, 123, 124, 125, 140, 158, 159, 160, 162, 163, 164, 165, 166, 167, 168, 175, 177, 180, 181, 182, 190, 193, 196, 197, 200, 204, 209, 255
American base at Rota, *see* Rota
amnesty, 28, 98
Amsden, J., 84, 111, 127
anarchism, 29, 31, 33, 34; ideology of, 34
anarchists, 18, 22, 30, 33, 36, 49, 59, 62, 86, 95
anarcho-syndicalism, 18
Andalucía, 15, 19, 27, 49, 54, 71; cultivation in, 49, 63; democratic opposition in, 125; geography of, 49, 52; western Andalucía, 31
anti-fascist, 32

Anton, Francisco, 140, 143
arbitration, 110
Arébalo Arias, Carlos, 39, 156, 187
Argentina, imports of wheat from, 64
Arias government, 223
Ariza, Julián, 98, 125
army, 80, 232
Arroyo, José, 104
Artola Beuzón, Paco, 15, 16, 18, 20, 21, 22, 23, 24, 25, 39, 40, 42, 43, 104, 125, 155, 156, 158, 159, 160, 161, 162, 163, 164, 165, 177, 181, 204
Asturias, 31, 34, 74, 82, 90, 96, 117, 205, 219; miners of 29, 30, 82, 88, 90, 92, 98, 114–18, 190, 205; repression in, 207; revolt in, 138; state of siege in, 117
autarky, 64, 217; autarkic model, 66, 67
Axis, 65, 130; defeat of 64
Ayucar, A. R., 141, 147, 189, 203

Bahía de Cádiz, 48, 52, 102
Baklanoff, E., 69, 127
balance of payments crisis (1958), 67
Bank of Spain, 63, 64; nationalization of, 64
Barca de la Florida, 39
Barcelona, 20, 25, 33, 71, 93, 99, 110; financial capital of, 63; firms of, 111
Basque Country, 63, 74, 110; autonomy of, 61; Communist Party in, 149; iron of, 63; nationalism in, 215
beet harvest, 55
Belgium, 145
Benítez Rufo, José, *see* Rufo, José Benítez
Bilbao: banks of, 63, 70; heavy engineering in, 114
blacklegs, 51, 120, 127

279

165, 168–70; Eighth Party Congress of, 148, 149, 151, 155, 191; Executive Committee of, 136, 144, 145, 149, 188, 191, 195; formation of, 137; Fourth Party Congress, 137; Fifth Party Congress of, 141, 143; hegemony over working-class movement, 34; link with workers' commissions, 74–76, 184–98; membership of, 134, 137, 138, 166, 174; Ninth Party Congress of, 151; as only political alternative, 5, 19, 33, 134, 190; organization of strikes and demonstrations by, 119, 134, 137, 138, 166, 174; as organizer and coordinator in El Marco de Jerez, 23–8, 36–44, 160, 185, 193, 218; parochialism of, 168; Party elections in El Marco, 167; political influence of, 134, 135; propaganda apparatus of in El Marco, 178, 180, 187; propaganda apparatus of, 134, 181; propaganda commission, 43; provincial committee of, 136, 163, 167; Second Conference of, 148; Secretariat of, 135, 138, 144, 145, 149; Seventh Party Congress of, 147; statutes of, 144; strategies of, 139, 146, 152, 196; support of prisoners' families, 178; switch from republican to monarchist, 152; unity in El Marco, 166; vertical organization of, 149; working within the Vertical Syndicate, 185, 199, 200, 203
communists, 22, 28, 31, 32, 33, 36, 38, 74, 98, 101, 155, 175, 186, 191
Communist Youth, 19, 26, 38, 42, 43, 135, 138, 144, 147, 159, 175, 178; in El Puerto, 176
Conde de los Andes, 50
Confederación de Derechas Autónomas (CEDA), 62, 62n
Confederación Española de Organizaciones Empresariales (CEOE), 224
Confederación Nacional de Trabajo (CNT), 15n, 19, 31, 32, 33, 56, 65, 73, 93, 129, 139, 192, 201, 204, 205, 206
contingent necessity, 261
contingent political process, 8
contract: plant-based, 111, 112; regional in El Marco, 113
Coordinadora de Organizaciones Sindicales (COS), 224
Córdoba, 30, 48
corporatism, 66, 66n, 79, 230, 233, 235; charismatic, 234, 237, 244, 245; corpo-

rate structures, 79 (*see also* Vertical Syndicate); corporatist bureaucracy, 110; as ideal type, 230; as labour–capital relation, 236; neo-corporatist channels, 226, 227, 241, 243, 244; as political strategy, 245; relation to form of State, 230
Cortes: of Cádiz, 63; under Franco, 81, 83, 84
cortijo, 32
Creix, Juan, 180

decentralized bargaining, 238
Decree (of 1962), 172
Decree Law of the New Economic Order, 67, 68
de la Madrid, Miguel, 159
de la Mata, Enrique, 222
de la Platera, Carmen, 40, 158
de la Rosa Ríos, Pepe, 15, 17, 21, 25, 39, 103, 104, 125, 158, 159, 160, 161, 180, 181, 196, 204
de las Flores, Paco, 16, 17, 18, 19, 20, 21, 23, 24, 25, 26, 38, 41, 44, 101, 104, 116, 120, 123, 158, 160, 161, 165, 177, 180, 194, 195, 197, 204
del Campo, S., 70
Delgado Gordillo, Francisco, 160
de Miguel, A., 71, 73, 111
demobilization of workers, 180
democracy, organic, 65, 65n
democratic centralism, 149–50, 151, 166, 167, 170, 260
democratic pact, 245, 259
democratic practice, 252, 259
democratic project, 6, 7, 185, 212, 221, 245, 259
democratic road to socialism, 148
demonstrations, 30, 43
deterministic axis, 249
despotic power, 65
Development Plans: of 1964–7, 69, 73, 83; of 1967–71, 70; of 1973, 70
Diario de Cádiz, 43
Díaz, José, 137, 138
dictatorship, the, 47, 62, 65, 67, 72, 74, 98, 99; opposition to, 101
diputación, 50
discursive practice, 252
Domecq, 52
Domecq de la Riva, José María, 52
Domecq, José Ignacio, 52